A Year Right Here

A Year Right Here

*Adventures with
Food and Family in
the Great Nearby*

Jess Thomson

Illustrations by Hannah Viano

UNIVERSITY OF
WASHINGTON PRESS
Seattle and London

A Year Right Here was supported by the Northwest Writers Fund, which promotes the work of some of the region's most talented nonfiction writers and was established through generous gifts from Linda and Peter Capell, Janet and John Creighton, Michael J. Repass, and other donors.

Printed and bound in the United States of America
Design by Thomas Eykemans
Illustrations by Hannah Viano
Composed in Garamond and Clarendon
21 20 19 18 17   5 4 3 2 1

UNIVERSITY OF WASHINGTON PRESS
www.washington.edu/uwpress

LIBRARY OF CONGRESS CATALOGING-IN-PUBLICATION DATA
Names: Thomson, Jess, author.
Title: A year right here : adventures with food and family in the great nearby /
     Jess Thomson.
Description: Seattle : University of Washington Press, [2017] | Includes
     bibliographical references and index.
Identifiers: LCCN 2016049014 | ISBN 9780295741543 (hardcover : acid-free paper)
Subjects: LCSH: Cooking, American—Pacific Northwest style. | Local foods. |
     Thomson, Jess—Family. | LCGFT: Cookbooks.
Classification: LCC TX715.2.P32 T563 2017 | DDC 641.59795—dc23
LC record available at https://lccn.loc.gov/2016049014

The recipe on page 239 was reprinted with permission from *True Brews*, by Emma Christensen, copyright 2013, published by Ten Speed Press, an imprint of Penguin Random House LLC.

For Jim,
  who drinks life to the lees.

And for Graham,
  who may or may not do the same.

May we always travel, and not travel,
  together, just the way we are.

Contents

Acknowledgments

First and foremost, thank you to my husband, Jim, and our son, Graham, for being constantly game for new adventures, near and far. Your willingness to participate in this book made it possible.

I am eternally grateful for Regan Huff, my indefatigable editor, who in addition to leaping forward with the University of Washington Press's first food book, jumped up to ride her bicycle unknown distances in training for the Gourmet Century, consumed untold calories enjoying fascinating foods in Richmond, British Columbia, and took on an untested-in-this-format writer with knowing editorial skill and a distinct talent for making good things great. To Jenni Ferrari-Adler, my literary agent, who is always there to guide me forward at just the right time. To Hannah Viano, whose graceful drawings and cuttings adorn this book, and to Casey Barber, for consulting on the cover. And to the UW Press, all told, for carrying this book through to publication—Nancy Cortelyou, Diane Sepanski, Thomas Eykemans, and Margaret Sullivan, and the reviewers who helped shape the book.

Thanks to Kathy Gunst, a mentor in all things relating to food and life.

Thanks also to my family and the friends, old and new, who were willing to become characters in a book they couldn't control: Amy and Steve Howe, Allison Howe, Joshua Howe, Anne Prins, Ben Humphrey, Kate Dunlop, Erik Abbott,

Maggie Kemper, Tracy Erbeck, Aaron Erbeck, Eagranie Yuh, Edith Hope Bishop, Jill Lightner, Hannah Viano, Joe Talbert, Meghan Delaney, Tami and Dan Horner, Erica Goldsmith, and Gina Engle. History can be a strong meddler of emotions. This is how I remember things, for better or worse—comments about your temperaments, opinions, and eyebrows are my own truths, but are never meant to be hurtful. (And they're why I love you.) And to all the folks who helped us help Graham throughout this big year, including (but not nearly limited to) Hunter Hendrickson and Austin Marsh: thank you for being part of our family.

To the crowd who dug out our backyard one raw New Year's Day, which felt like just the right beginning: Aaron and Tracy Erbeck, Maggie Kemper and Ryan Rogers, Dan and Lisa Mudgett, Kim and Mike Caughey, Meghan Delaney, and all their associated offspring. I still owe you eggs. To my father, who fixed the wiring. To PopPop for digging, and to Grammy Nan for always helping out, anytime, any place. To Sarah Barthelow, for inviting me to the killing fields, and to Molly Wizenberg, for the cone. And to Frank and Michelle, for inspiring us in the first place.

To Meg Trendler, Allison Keeney, and Samantha Chulick, for introducing me to the Oregon Truffle Festival, and to Leslie Scott and Charles Lefevre, for starting it. And, of course, to Mike and Jim and Dan, for being such great teachers.

To Dan Ayres, for teaching me to dig for razor clams the first time.

To Vif Wine|Coffee, the *cave à manger* that dealt with my overlong presence a few mornings each week as I wrote this book, for forgiving me for not ordering pour-over coffee. Raelyn, you're a lifesaver.

To Ruth and Lori Babcock, owners of Tieton Farm & Creamery, and to Casey Babcock, for taking us in and showing us how the farm works on the busiest of days. And to Aran Goyoaga, for stating the obvious.

To Matt Costello, for sitting down with me to calmly explain how he does his magic every night at the Inn at Langley, on Washington's Whidbey Island.

To Sharon and Craig Campbell, owners of Tieton Cider Works, for showing me their cider-apple orchards in Yakima and Tieton, and sharing their story. I'll tell all that another time.

To Tracy Clark, Laura Kittmer, and Samantha Geer, for helping me navigate the Okanagan's wine country, and to the winemakers who made time for us—most notably, Jay Drysdale, Val Tait, Michael Bartier, Ingo Grady, and Bill Eggert.

To Emma Christensen, Ben Humphrey, and Duncan, for cider inspiration.

To the Jacqueau family, for hosting me and teaching me French, and inviting us to lunch.

To AmazonFresh, for beginning to charge for grocery delivery.

To my early readers and recipe testers: Claire Horner-Devine, Tracy Erbeck, Kathy Gunst, Rebekah Denn, all the Howes, Lindsay Simpson, Lauren Bedford, Maggie Kemper, Kenneth Howe, Eagranie Yuh, and Jim, of course.

And to Elissa Altman, for planting the seed unknowingly.

• • •

It's also important to recognize that, because travel costs add up quickly, I took four of the experiences in the book in conjunction with trips I made to write separate magazine stories. Tourism Tofino and the British Columbia Wine Institute (www.winebc.com) paid for hotel costs in Tofino and Osoyoos, BC, respectively, and the Inn at Langley and the Ace Hotel in Portland, Oregon, paid for my stays in those places, too. The tourism bureau in Eugene, Oregon, covered my trip to the truffle festival. However, I made the decision to write about these places first, and (I like to think) independently of the offers of hosting.

Although all the facts here are as true as I know them to be, this book is not meant to be a factual guide to the Pacific Northwest. It's my own exploration, based on my own experiences.

ACKNOWLEDGMENTS

A Year Right Here

Introduction

STAYING PUT

O NE fall, when my family returned from a three-week stay in Provence, my husband, Jim, and I had hangovers. The sag was less from the forty-two bottles of wine we'd consumed collectively with various visitors over long lunches and drawn-out dinners, and more from the extended excitement of exploring new things. We agreed we'd had the trip of a lifetime. We'd eaten all of Provence! And over the course of that year, as real life reminded us that the same magic mix of time and freedom and savings might not present itself again for years—decades even—we mourned. The downside of taking the trip of a lifetime is that once you've taken it, it's over.

Then, the next fall, an East Coast acquaintance visited Seattle, where we'd lived for almost a decade. She's a writer, like me. We'd met on many occasions, but I hadn't spent much time with her. As she traipsed her way through the Emerald City—through my own neighborhood, even—I watched her thrill unfold on Instagram with the same interest and bewilderment I felt as I watched another friend journey through Morocco simultaneously. It became clear that the Seattle visitor was treating her trip to the Pacific Northwest the same way we'd viewed our time in France; she skipped from market to café to restaurant to farm to glean an identity from our fair region, ending up, more often than not, in her own rented dining room, as we had in France, with food from nearby and a good bottle of wine.

She reinforced the perhaps obvious concept that while Provence is lovely, we live in a pretty magical spot ourselves. That while I skipped with predictable joy at the prospect of picking up fresh lamb from a small butcher across the Atlantic, I blindly ignored the possibility of buying crab off a dock close to home. That while peeking over the fence from Provence into other corners of France felt like having a free ticket to any number of exciting new places, in Seattle, we are within a day's drive of breathtaking forests, mountains, deserts, islands, and the entire Salish Sea, plus a few other pretty nifty cities, such as Portland, Oregon, and Vancouver, British Columbia. That the region surrounding me—the swath of land generically referred to as the Pacific Northwest, emanating out, in my mind, from Seattle and usually identified as the combination of Washington, Oregon, and British Columbia—is, well, right here.

And so it came about that, rather than pining for a full year in Provence, the sabbatical from life popularized in my own imagination with the publication of Peter Mayle's *A Year in Provence,* I began daydreaming about how I'd spend a year in the Pacific Northwest, writ large. I'd learn more about my own corner of the world without gazing over the nearest shoulder on Facebook to see how shiny and fresh the Sardinian anchovies looked in a friend's digitally retouched photo of an antique fishing dory. In a black-speckled scholastic notebook, I began making a list of things I'd like to see. I titled it "The Here List."

I consider myself a master list maker. When I go to the grocery store, for example, I make the list on paper big enough to allow for multiple columns, because I organize the things I need by where they appear in the grocery store, in little boxes with preordained spots on the page—produce in the upper left, deli in the lower right, et cetera. When I travel, I categorize my clothes and toiletries based on where they will be packed. Day to day, my brain functions like one of those old-school train-departure boards—the kind whose letters and numbers rotate clickety-clack each time a new train's departure time and platform is announced. *Feed dog, pack lunch, write invoice, buy gift.* I can't remember ever having been accused of failing to prepare. I get shit done.

And I come by it honestly. Growing up, my mother taught nine or ten aerobics classes a week, and played tennis competitively, and coached ski racing. And, oh, was also a successful lawyer while raising three children. She makes lists also, but she keeps them all in her head, so as outsiders, the rest of us only see the results. Within our immediate family, since she does so many things, and does them all with maximum vigor, we use her full name as an action verb.

Though her near-constant intensity makes my two siblings and me crazy, it is likely her very propensity to defy all challenges that makes me who I am. It's why, when I was diagnosed with lupus, an autoimmune disease, at twenty-four, it occurred to me to choose my occupation wisely—I am a freelance writer because it theoretically allows me to rest when my body tells me to rest—but it hasn't yet occurred to me to take on less work. It's why I can sit in the hospital for a full afternoon every month with an IV in my arm, receiving a type of chemotherapy that helps control my lupus symptoms, and plan all the things I'm going to do when the needle comes out, nausea be damned.

The Here List was an outcropping of the same personality, which was handed down to me from my mother, and handed to her from her mother before that. The list itself became a well-loved, multicolored affair. It traveled around the house enough being updated that it wound up with something sticky in one corner. Many of my dreams had to do with visiting inspiring places that had already taken their turn in the media spotlight—places like the Inn at Langley, a mind-boggling, single-seating restaurant on Washington's Whidbey Island that has kept its novel shine years longer than most restaurants do, but despite its continued success and influence, had long since lost the newish allure a place requires to be written up. I am a food writer by trade, but I write frequently for the kind of stylistically quotidian publications that might not want to publish anything too negative or personal or opinionated, so I wondered whether the book might allow me to delve into the questions I hadn't yet found the opportunity to ask: Why don't we read more about the Canadian Okanagan region's wine? Why does the coffee scene in Seattle annoy me? Is truffle hunting really a thing in Oregon, and would I like doing it? I also fantasized about facing certain food-related challenges I'd considered but hadn't attempted: going razor clamming as a family, to see whether Graham, our five-year-old son, might begin eating shellfish if he had something to do with its catch. Participating in the Gourmet Century, the hundred-kilometer, food-focused bike ride that winds its way through the sometimes-brutal hills outside Portland each July.

Because I am inherently drawn to a good challenge, the al-lure of checking things off The Here List—of doing all manner of fabulous things, from pulling seaweed out of the ocean from a kayak to learning more about our region's herring catch—was almost as sexy as the idea of the outings themselves (but not quite). Jim, who works as an oceanographer and often manages big handfuls of projects at once, introduced me to the concept of the Gantt chart, which opened an entire new realm of listing possibilities I was horrified to realize I'd missed out on for thirty-seven years. (For the uninitiated, a Gantt chart is one that allows its maker to list tasks on a vertical axis and time on a horizontal axis, so the list's items can be kept on a specific schedule.) I translated The Here List to Gantt format, which allowed me to take the region's seasonality into account. What I couldn't find space for on The Here List or in the Gantt chart, though, was how to categorize the difficulties each adventure might present for our son.

Generally, Graham is an excellent traveler. By age five, he could devote himself to coloring books and movies on airplanes, and played independently for hours at a stretch with *Star Wars* characters or Lego bricks. Graham was also vocally proud of his discoveries abroad. In France, he ate snails and steak and salad (the green kind!), none of which he had previously touched (or will now touch) on American soil.

"Let me know if you have any questions about the food in France," he quipped, unprompted, to more than one restaurant server after our big trip across the pond. "Because I've *been* there." His tone left no room to doubt his expertise.

But on his home turf, he's less adventuresome. Like so many kids, at five, he ate mostly white, beige, and brown things (with the notable exception of sushi—avocado rolls only, please). As my reverie grew, I found myself dreaming about finding a way to essentially trick him into treating some of the foods many folks in our region eat every day—meats and vegetables, for example—with the courage and openness and excitement he had shown us in France. I thought perhaps I could save a lot of money showing Graham that the same kind of epicurean adventure we'd had abroad could happen right here. (*He would try snails*, I thought, *but imagine if he learned to eat a plain old American hamburger. Or a taco. Or, God forbid, a sandwich.*)

Graham also has cerebral palsy, a neurological condition that, in a nutshell, prevents his brain and his leg muscles from speaking to each other in the same language. When he was born, we didn't know. Since I have lupus, the doctors had warned us that pregnancy might be difficult for me. But the worry had been emphatically skewed toward early miscarriage, as opposed to premature birth.

Graham came almost seven weeks early. He was tiny but strong compared to the other babies in neonatal intensive care. He was a little NICU hero, really, so no one said anything about oxygen shortages or bacterial infections or adrenal shock or jaundice—all things he or I had experienced during a complicated childbirth process—leading to anything but a normal life, once we were all home and healthy. It never occurred to us that something could be different, so from the start, we traveled. We took him to Spain for a wedding at four months old, when he was small enough that we could use my husband's backpack as a changing table. We took him backcountry skiing. And when we did eventually get his diagnosis, we kept traveling, simply because we always had.

The diagnosis itself came with very little fanfare. Graham started sitting up independently just after ten months old. At nineteen months, when he still showed no signs of mobility and we'd been to a handful of doctors wondering what might be different about our bright, spunky chatterbox, we had an

MRI done on his brain. The results were clear as day when the nurse pulled them up on her computer screen: looking at an image of a cross section of Graham's little head, we saw a very obvious ring of white in the center of the gray matter. Judging by the picture, part of his brain was just missing.

"So typically, the degree of scarring we're seeing here on Graham's brain is a sign of moderate to severe cerebral palsy," the nurse said with an apologetic smile. "But although he shows some of the physical signs we might expect from that, he seems quite typical for his age intellectually. I'm not sure why, but he's very capable for this much scarring." Another smile. Then: nothing. The appointment was over.

She sent us home with a box of apple juice, a tiny envelope of graham crackers packaged the way saltines are at the end of soup bars, and a book on parenting a child with cerebral palsy. There was no referral. No follow-up appointment. Just that mind-boggling news, which, we told ourselves, was more knowledge than we'd previously had. The next week, months after his peers had learned to walk, Graham started crawling.

Before Graham was born, a friend's parents had told us a sticking tale about parenthood. It went like this: Both mother and father had noted that the shimmering morning sun might lead to the season's first too-warm day, and agreed they wanted to get a run in while the air was still cool. They each made haste to dress for exercise, and met on the front porch. Only then, with running shoes tied, did they realize that one of them needed to stay with their sleeping infant son. That day, they bought a jogging stroller.

For us, the story solidified a point: When one has a child, one must decide whether the parents are born into the child's life or the child is born into the parents' lives. What matters is which life takes the lead role. We'd always planned on taking the latter approach. He'd eat what we ate. He'd see what we saw. He'd go where we went. Graham would be a traveler. When we got Graham's diagnosis, we didn't see any reason for this to change. Airports were easy. *You're so lucky he can't walk yet*, said people with wayward toddlers while Graham rested happily in my arms. I always tried to smile.

At the beginning, there was never a question of going. If it was possible, we went, Jim and Graham and me. We had a series of strap-on baby carriers in ever-larger sizes that Graham graduated into as he grew. For a while, he rode in a rugged framed backpack, and then cruised along in a beefy, big-wheeled stroller. Eventually, around age three, he also started using a small walker, which meant that when he had enough energy, he toddled along next to us like the world's tiniest little old man. When he got tired, the walker fit right on top of the stroller's handlebar, like an awkward metal hat. Sometimes he simply rode on Jim's shoulders, becoming absurdly tall, human stacked on human. He towered over us all.

We still travel energetically as a family, but we travel slowly. At five, after three years wheeling the tiny walker, Graham started using little yellow arm crutches to walk, energy permitting, with an awkward but effective gait. He could cover most even surfaces, but we journeyed through the world in a different way. He fell a lot, so we attracted attention. I'd long given up on controlling how people perceived us as we ambled through public spaces. It was entertaining, in a way, to guess how people would react to us, and to Graham's "sticks": parents typically urged their kids not to say anything about Graham out loud and ushered them away, or used us as a teachable moment, pointing out how all people are different. Toddlers walked right up to Graham and pointed at his crutches, jabbing pudgy fingers into his arm (or more often, his bottom) and staring at their parents with excited, questioning looks. Some tried to steal his sticks. Older kids—

ten- or twelve-year-olds—would look at Graham briefly, then look away, having learned to be embarrassed about being fortunate enough to walk. In the United States and Canada, his diagnosis was relatively easy to explain. (He usually talked people through it well on his own, with an ever-increasing sense of pride that made my heart swell. He said "cebral apology" instead of "cerebral palsy" for the longest time.) And in the United States and Canada, accessibility is law, which means that almost everywhere we went, the world accommodated us with generosity and grace and a smile. And, most practically, with a handicap ramp.

Rural France, on the other hand, has an on-and-off relationship with accessibility laws. When we went there, Graham could still fit in a stroller, and was happy as anything to be wheeled around at farmers' markets and playgrounds. But as he grew and aged, and began using the yellow sticks to walk, he was no longer content to just sit, and no longer happy being a passenger. We couldn't imagine him having as easy a time abroad as he did nearby. And as much as we yearned for his introduction to new lands and new languages, we also recognized that the world is bumpy, and taking a small person to see things the small person can't physically access independently becomes a little cruel. That same three-week trip in France would now no longer work because he was *more* able.

We'd thought of taking him to Tokyo, but he couldn't walk more than a few blocks at a time with the sticks, and seeing Tokyo via taxi wouldn't be the same. We wanted to continue showing him new things without crushing his ego more than I suspected being the only nonwalking kid in a kindergarten class already did. I knew it wouldn't work to take him on all the adventures on The Here List, but I resolved to include him as much as possible. We'd go huckleberry picking at a spot that didn't require any actual hiking, and focus on activities that didn't really require walking—crabbing and razor clamming, for example. And when my husband was home—Jim typically travels around a hundred days each year for work—we'd all go together.

And so I proposed *A Year Right Here: Adventures with Food and Family in the Great Nearby*, to focus on enjoying the Pacific Northwest's food culture with Graham and Jim, and remember that one doesn't always have to board a plane to find the next frontier. I wanted to discover ways to bring Graham into a world of food that interested him, and to give him a way to identify with the wondrous region we call home on an edible level. Part of me also hoped I could use food to literally lure him to his feet. To entice him to begin exploring more from his full height.

Each of the longer chapters that follow is a story in itself, a snapshot of my year spent looking at the way my sometimes-unusual family life intersects with the food and drink and culture of the Pacific Northwest. Among them, you'll find shorter interludes that trace our progress as a family across the year, as well as a recipe or two tied to each adventure.

In the beginning, it was just a start to a new year, with new, closer-to-home adventures for all of us. The plan was to stick to The Here List, with a few exceptions. The natural problem with committing to spending a year in one place is that, in the twenty-first century, our lives rarely happen in one spot. I knew when I started this adventure, for example, that we would be spending Graham's school spring break at a therapy center in California. Cousins announced weddings. There was a conference in Washington, DC, I planned to attend. And partway through the year, we decided Graham would need leg surgery in New York.

The rest, though: the rest of the year would be spent close to home, I thought.

JANUARY

Months after we moved into our 1924 Craftsman home on Seattle's Phinney Ridge, a cold winter wind blew all the dead leaves off the trees. With delight, we realized that if we climbed up onto the bench built into the side of the back porch, ducking to avoid getting the business end of a dried grapevine in the eye, we could see the Olympic Mountains peaking out in the distance. They're ragged and wild looking, even from a hundred miles' drive away. Over the years, we developed a habit of standing on that bench, as soon as the leaves had come down each year, to gaze at two neighboring peaks whose names I've never known—the ones whose slopes form an *M* together.

One day, years later, a friend joined Jim and me on the porch.

"What's *that*?" she asked excitedly, pointing to a little outbuilding in a yard two houses away.

"What?" we asked. We struggled to make out what might exist beyond the neighbors' pristine garden behind our back fence.

"That," she said, directing our gazes. And as we squinted, we realized that the bland metal object we'd always passed over as perhaps a shed or part of a garage was an intricate backyard studio styled like a Russian Orthodox church. There was an ornate miniature onion dome, built out of sheet metal, not fifty yards from where we stood. We'd just never thought to look so closely at something so close by.

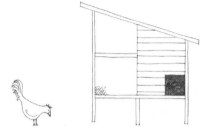

The House That Jack Built

WHEN I chose our cat at the pound on Cape Cod, his name was Hunter. I should have known right then that he'd be the type to strip wild baby rabbits clean of their fur on frigid winter days. That when my husband left for weeks at sea, which was our normal, the cat—renamed Jackson, now called Jack—would take over responsibilities as man of the house and bring me regular meals of live rats, mice, and birds, lest I fear a bout of single parenting would leave me and my child hungry and helpless. Jack has always been a provider. Which is why, when we decided to build a chicken coop, solidifying our identity as true Seattleites by checking a box on the same lifestyle-features list as "commute by bike" and "raise children without toy weapons," we worried first not about who would eat all the eggs, but about who would eat the chickens. And Jack was first on the list of possible offenders.

I wanted chickens because I wanted fresh eggs. Because everyone else in our neighborhood seemed to be getting fresh eggs. Graham wanted chickens because his friend Ely had chickens. And I'd been working less, which meant I was admittedly more project-prone than usual. But I'd also struggled for a time with how I might teach a child with cerebral palsy (who can't easily roam in the garden or pick fruit from trees) how to understand and appreciate where his food comes from. I figured building a coop with a Graham-height egg-retrieval system might bolster his interaction with the outdoors, and in turn perhaps instill in him some interest in other food systems. Theoretically, it would bring about the chicken-and-egg question for a kid who had never really connected the two. I imagined setting both on the table and explaining it all to him.

We almost didn't build the coop at all. In the beginning, Jim was staunchly against the idea. It wasn't that he didn't want chickens. He just felt it was a cop-out. Every third house in Seattle seems to have chickens, and he hates anything that could be qualified as trendy. Jim put up a good fight for getting ducks or a goat instead, which I deflected with arguments about water and space requirements. I won.

We did not take the process of building a chicken coop lightly. Years earlier, Jim had built one for friends up the street, in exchange for a lifetime of occasional egg drop-offs, from which we still benefited. Their coop had a good design; it was clear that every detail, from the human-height door to the cleverly planned storage space that shared the same roof as the hen house, was well thought out. Jim bought me a book called *Free-Range Chicken Gardens*, figuring that any move toward some sort of backyard Hennebunkport estate might require that one of us do some research on how to take care of them. And that the section on predators might teach us how to train a prideful feline not to polish off our poultry.

What I don't think Jim realized when he presented me with Jessi Bloom's book was that it wasn't really about building chicken coops. It was really about redesigning a backyard around plants that chickens like and plants that can withstand the havoc chickens can wreak on greenery—an unintentional step into a long-standing steaming battle over a backyard ignored for the better part of the decade we'd lived in the house. He wanted me to research chickens, but he certainly didn't intend for me to develop a biblical obsession with a book that told me, however indirectly, that chickens wouldn't be happy at our home unless we made some serious changes in the landscaping department.

One December morning, I scanned the yard, eyes burning with the smell of eight years' worth of dog urine on the same forty square feet of poorly drained grass. Those chickens suddenly represented an opportunity to let a small animal stand proxy for my own selfish backyard goals: I'd wanted to put a walkway across our grass to avoid getting our shoes muddy in the winter. *A path to the chicken coop would prevent us from tracking in mud when we collect eggs.* I'd hated our rhododendron bush since it had grown out past its allotted space; it poked me in the eye every time I passed. *This book says rhododendron can be poisonous for chickens.* And, clearly ignoring the smell a chicken coop might introduce, I figured a new plant-heavy garden in the place of our grassy swamp might mitigate the issue of water puddling, thus perhaps improving the backyard's general aroma problem. *Chickens need dry spots so they can take dust baths!* In the span of a few short days, designing the perfect chicken coop blossomed into relandscaping the entire backyard.

It's embarrassing to admit that I knew I was overstepping our project parameters so clearly that I simply planned not to tell Jim what I was doing. (This is not uncommon. I have a nasty but nicely self-serving habit of simply saving all the things Jim doesn't want to do to our house for when he's conveniently hundreds of miles offshore, with little to no opportunity for communication.) I envisioned Seattle's rain-garden program, which offers rebates to homeowners who install rain gardens to prevent water runoff, as manna from heaven, sent to my Safari screen to redesign my backyard for free. I decided I'd do it all on the sly, with taxpayers' money, and we'd have a perfect (and much drier) chicken habitat when Jim returned from his first three-week research trip of the year, in the middle of the Pacific.

Unfortunately, the manna was false. Our property was too small to qualify for the program. Which meant I was left standing next to Colin McCrate, of Seattle Urban Farm Company, in the pouring rain on a Thursday morning just shy of Christmas. His firm is responsible for the rooftop vegetable gardens crowning many Seattle-area restaurant buildings, and he's well known for his informal landscape architecture and the way he makes gardens flow. I'd always admired him for his rugged style and general stewardship practices. (Plus, he's handsome.) So I was standing with one muddy Xtratuf boot crusted in dog poop, listening to him tell me, first, that we probably couldn't count on any city money to help us redesign the backyard, and second, that he had The Perfect Plan for making our ugly space something beautiful, useful, dry, and, most importantly, chicken friendly. No part of my being could say no.

I decided to break the news to Jim. He pointed out that Colin's plan really had nothing to do with Jack, who was theoretically our biggest worry. A nice yard for our chickens wouldn't decrease a cat's appetite. Graham defended the cat.

"Chickens are really big, you know, Daddy," he said with an exasperated sigh. (He tends to have a lot to teach grown-ups.) "Only something really big could eat them, like a raccoon," he explained. He showed me the size of the qualifying predator by patting our ottoman with his hands, and I sent a silent prayer heavenward that our neighborhood raccoons would never outsize our dog.

Jim took a more pragmatic approach. As initially quoted, a formal backyard project would cost about a third of a new roof, which we desperately needed. We started in on the financial round and round of yard versus roof, both of us aware of the fact that, rather than deciding *whether* to spend a big hunk of cash on something, we'd started bickering about *where* we'd spend it. At the breakfast table the next morning, Graham announced that he was a chicken named Fuzzball—the name of one of Ely's chickens—and that his orange juice was really pinecone juice, which apparently chickens love. Then, he asked to draw our new coop.

At that point, Graham's dexterity hadn't quite blossomed into normal kindergartener territory, so we praised any voluntary hand-eye coordination work. He took the wheel.

"Here's our chicken coop," he announced, pointing out a ragged boxlike form with space for chickens and eggs inside. "Here's the fence that keeps the raccoons away. And then here's the door with the door lock that opens and closes." It was all very architecturally sketchy, but it represented an awareness of general chicken safety, which I liked. He seemed to understand that the animals could be both food and pets.

"What's that?" I asked, pointing to what looked like a black sun with pokey rays.

"We made a giant roof with a fence around it to make the raccoons not come in," he explained. His focus on the raccoons wasn't surprising—this was a kid who once lost an entire box of coveted bunny crackers and four packets of hot chocolate to a raccoon family on a camping trip—but I wasn't sure how to break it to him that we had an additional feline concern.

"What about Jackson?" I asked. I thought it might be the wrong time to point out Jack had once downed a pigeon.

"That's what this sign is for," said Graham. The part of the page that read "GOOD CHIcKeNS" was apparently a sign completed by the "cursive" underneath, which reportedly read in full, "Good chickens save the lives of other chickens when they're in trouble, and use their magic powers to heal cracked eggs if cracked eggs happen."

It was a flawless plan: our future chickens were to be protected from the cat's bloody intentions by signage designed by a five-year-old that explained magical powers in imaginary writing for chickens—who, regrettably, can't read.

"Oh," I mused intelligently.

"Our chickens will live," confirmed Graham.

Jim and I exchanged glances. No more words crossed between us, but we both knew we'd be building a chicken coop with all the nearby landscaping accoutrements instead of buying a roof for us humans. Later, I texted him, promising to cut down on costs by dragging friends over to help dig up the yard. Then I e-mailed Colin. We told him we'd be ready for his crew a week after the New Year. Jim went to sea.

• • •

I firmly believe in bribery, and I have no qualms asking people for help. Which is why, on the bright, frozen morning of January 1, eleven adults and eleven children steamed up the windows inside our small living room, munching on applewood-smoked bacon, a huge strata made with a full dozen grocery-store eggs, and a hangover-curing golden beet–juice concoction I was sure would morph us all into better people. The deal was that any who wished could help dig up the sod and the foot of earth beneath it in exchange for a future meal delivery. And future eggs, of course.

As we got started, we began sounding like an overzealous DIYer's version of Chicken Little: PopPop chopped down the rhododendron. Hannah dug out the rhododendron stump. Aaron laid tarps across the front yard for the sod. A big handful of us spent the better part of the day pickaxing through the thin layer of frozen tundra, digging dirt out with shovels, and ferrying it via a rickety borrowed wheelbarrow onto the tarps. My hands, which often ache with the littlest effort as a result of lupus, turned white and tingly. By day's end, we were all walking a little stooped over, but we had done the work Colin estimated would save us $700 in the labor department. We cracked Rainier beers and pretended we'd had the hardest day of our lives. I congratulated friends on earning a lifetime's worth of fresh egg delivery. There was the small matter of the ancient rusting electrical conduit we'd unearthed—something my father would spend the better part of the following week researching and replacing—but we'd dug what we needed to dig.

The next week, Colin's crew took the dirt away to be recycled, engineered little water-channeling drainage paths into the yard, placed culverts and a French drain in the wettest place, and arranged a three-foot-wide swath of flagstones meticulously enough to ensure Graham would be able to walk across them using his little yellow sticks without tripping. We'd decided to put a basic metal-ringed fire pit in the center of the yard, amid the flagstone, so that went in, too. By mid-January, when Jim returned, we were circled around a magazine-worthy fire in folding camp chairs, celebrating the new little patio and coop space with sparklers, marshmallows, and the innovative-but-simple final course that developed after marshmallows, which Graham and his friends started calling "roasted toast."

"So . . . Do the chickens live on the walkway?" asked Jim's sister, a visiting Los Angelena who couldn't see the appeal of raising chickens when buying local eggs at a grocery store four blocks away was a perfectly viable option. We laughed, but she had a point. The chicken coop—the reason we'd started the project—was still just a pile of dirt at the bottom of the porch steps. You can't worry about chickens living or not living when there's no place for them to call home.

Ultimately, we were looking for two things: a coop that could keep the chickens warm in winter and cool in summer, and a refuge where the chickens would be safe from Jack. (To be clear, most people use the term "coop" loosely to refer to the place chickens are kept. Technically, it contains both the run—the spot chickens roam around in within an often mesh-enclosed structure—and the nesting box, which is the warmer, often wood-enclosed area within that structure where they lay their eggs and sometimes sleep.) According to our local Craigslist postings, a lightly used coop was ours for as little as $200. But Jim, who has built our dining table, our beds, and much of our other furniture in a beautifully rustic, bombproof style true to his Maine roots, wanted to build our coop himself. We got plans from our friends Dan and Lisa for a roughly nine-by-four-foot structure, ordered enough wooden materials that they were delivered to our door by a truck with its own detachable forklift, and notified the neighbors that we'd be making noise, and later, hopefully, eggs.

Jim is the kind of person who does everything thoroughly, even if it means being late for dinner. He doesn't build anything lightly. I'd always planned to dive under our bed in the event of an earthquake, rather than wedge myself into a doorframe, because anything he constructs seems ready to withstand some sort of disastrous fallout. I imagined a coop so bulky and tough that when Mount Rainier eventually explodes, everyone in the neighborhood would shout, "Quick! Head to the Thomson coop!" It would be our own personal air-raid shelter, complete with a fresh food source.

But as Jim started on the project, he hewed closely to the plans. Delicate-looking cedar beams supported a clear corrugated-plastic roof. Together, we spent Valentine's Day morning wrapping razor-sharp hardware cloth—you know, the kind of metal mesh whose edges insist on scraping through any exposed human skin—around the framing, and painstakingly sewing it all together with metal wire. Hands numbed by cold, we dug more mesh about a foot into the ground below the coop, so predators like raccoons couldn't attack the chickens from below. It became a hen-hold of wood and wire, a fowl fortress whose tenants could be protected without sacrificing elegance for function. I began to wonder whether I should skip the chickens altogether and turn it into an outdoor office.

As the coop progressed, we addressed the issue of procuring the actual birds. We assumed that there would be attrition among the troops if we followed the typical baby-birds-as-bath-accessories path. It's not that we're so negligent of our animals that we didn't think we could raise our hens from hatchlings in the bathtub. It was that if we put any small wiggly things inside our house, where baby chickens need to be at first, Jackson would figure out a way to eat them. (As Jim worked, Jack had taken to sitting inside the coop's frame and watching, tail twitching.)

We had started looking into getting pullets, young hens who have usually passed the more delicate baby state, when Hannah and Joe, dear friends who lived in the nearby Ballard neighborhood, announced they were moving to the mountains. Their chickens, including Graham's beloved Fuzzball, wouldn't make the trip. And so in the span of a quick phone call, we inherited three two-year-old chickens already proven to be egg layers. And they were already almost as big as cats themselves, which we thought might be a plus.

Over the next few weeks, Jim finished the coop, venturing out weekend after weekend in the pouring rain, veering off plan only to tack a brass beer-bottle opener and Graham's NO RACCOONS sign onto the cedar. Soon after Hannah and Joe had sold their house, we planned for the "girls" to come up to our house in the back of our Subaru. I began to wonder whether I could kill the chickens with the stress of a car ride. Or the stress of a new home. Or, God forbid, the stress of the wrong food, the wrong-temperature water, or the wrong kinds of plants. After all, I had absolutely no experience as a bird handler. But how difficult could a habit so many chicken-dumb Seattleites had adopted really be?

The week the chickens were slated to arrive, I met a Seattle neighbor at a writers' conference in Washington, DC. Sarah lived literally four blocks from me, and she had birds, but before I'd learned her name or shaken her hand, she brandished a strong opinion about chicken ownership.

"Don't get chickens," she ordered flatly. We were sipping through our first drinks at a networking event, not talking at all about writing, and I wondered why, beyond the liquor's effect, she felt so comfortable telling me what to do. And why she was so sure I should change my mind.

"Don't do it," she repeated.

"Why?" I fumbled for a way to tell her that I'd promised to pick up the hens three days later. I futzed with my drink. "The thing is, it's a little late," I added.

"The problem with chickens," she explained, "is that they don't come with a retirement plan." She told me about June, one of her two birds, who had never laid an egg. After much angst, she'd finally decided that, rather than feeding June for another five-plus years, until she died naturally, she needed to kill her to make room in her small coop for another layer. In our increasingly tipsy state, Sarah made me promise to develop a concrete plan, within the following three days, for my chickens' retirement.

She was right; I didn't have a plan. I'd heard of the big farms that basically adopt "used" chickens in the hills outside

Seattle—the city's poultry version of the no-kill animal shelter—but she made me realize that I'd always assumed Jack would eventually do the job for me. That he would be our private form of population control. And as she discussed her precisely laid out chicken-killing plot, I decided that I should probably know how to kill a chicken, in the event my cat didn't—not because I was against the chicken sheltering some find more humane, but because as much as Graham needed to learn to connect chicken and egg, I also needed to connect my flock with my stock. I wanted to know, firsthand, how the chicken that lands on our table each week or so gets slaughtered. So I signed up to help Sarah kill a barren hen who happened to share a name with my eighty-seven-year-old grandmother.

Her idea started with a large orange traffic cone, which was easy enough to steal from a project the city had abandoned in our mutual friend Molly's front yard. The idea, for urbanites not accustomed to killing anything larger than a spider, was to skip some of the emotional and physical anguish of wringing a chicken's neck by trapping it upside down in said cone, with its head sticking out of the hole in the cone's top. (Anyone who's killed a live lobster or fish knows watching the fight isn't always fun. This was meant to reduce anxiety for all involved.) Following the general directions we gleaned from a handful of websites, we trimmed the cone a bit at the top so that, chicken and cone inverted, the beak and head would stick out just enough that Sarah could get a knife to her hen's throat (her chicken, her blade, we decided). Theoretically, without one of us holding a squirming bird, there was less room for failure (or worse, maiming).

So, without much fanfare, we chased June around Sarah's backyard to catch her, stuffed her into the cone, balanced the cone over Sarah's yard-waste bin, did her in, bled her, scalded her, plucked her, and gutted her. Sarah turned June into chicken stock, half of which she delivered to my porch in a quart-size mason jar the next day, labeled "June's Stock." And although it was unusual—after killing and dressing her, we were holding a thing that for all intents and purposes *looked* like a store-bought bird but *felt* like a still-warm, oddly feather-less animal—the process of taking June from breathing to not breathing didn't feel all that cruel or barbaric or inhumane. It felt practical, especially from an eating standpoint. And in the moment of death, as June's life drained into the coffee grounds and weeds in the bottom of the green bin, I knew it might be easier to kill my own chickens myself, quickly, than it would be to watch Jack do it too slowly. It was good to know I'd be able to help him finish the job, if it came to that. I put the used, bloody traffic cone under our back porch.

At dusk a few days later, we brought our chickens home. I tried not to imagine them upside down in traffic cones. Gra-ham decided we'd keep their original names, which were cour-tesy of Ely—the two black ones, both Australorp breeds, were Suki and Tokyo, and the orange one, the Buff Orpington, was our old friend Fuzzball. As the sun went down, Jim, Graham, and I shut them in the coop and sat on the back stairs to watch them settle in. Jack sat nearby, trembling. He was clearly terri-fied. Fuzzball leapt up onto the roost and immediately fell off, which seemed to make the cat feel better. (Chickens don't land on their feet like cats.)

"I just want them to make it through the night," I breathed to the boys. We discussed whether we should keep the cat trapped indoors for the night, or let nature take its course and trust that Jack wouldn't figure out how to get inside the coop.

"We've done all we can," said Jim morosely. We were a res-cue team at a mining accident, mourning what we knew might be a severe loss of life.

But they didn't die. In fact, they all laid eggs the very next day, and almost daily after that. And Jack kept his distance. He continued his weekly rampages—mice, sparrows, rats, you name it—but he never showed any interest in killing a single chicken. *Maybe he's getting old*, we mused. But we didn't complain. He kept his distance from the coop, pausing occasionally to watch the chickens but never stalking them. It was as if the process of watching Jim wrap mesh and pound nails had informed Jack that he wasn't allowed to touch the birds. He became their security guard.

Our dog, Bromley, on the other hand, was a complete pain in the ass. She grew jealous that the girls got our scraps. When the chickens learned to peck at the back door's full-length windows as a means of begging for Graham's sandwich crusts when I made his lunch in the morning, Bromley started lunging into the yard to eat their poop out of their coop. She whined at the back door when we let the chickens out, imploring us to let her follow them around as they dropped. She began drooling when she heard them cluck. It was a disgusting habit, to say the least, but she never showed interest in doing any bodily harm to the hens. And though it made me gag, she did keep the patio clean of excrement.

Now we all have our roles: I've become the hen wife, happy to creep out into the yard each morning and evening to give the girls a little time outside their coop and a handful of scratch, which falls from our porch above them like an edible bombing raid. Jim has fallen in love with them, despite his best intentions to grumble about unofficially joining the Seattle chicken-owning club—in part, I think, because Graham seems to adore them so much. (The boys are the doters.) Together, we've learned to pick up the chickens properly and that they like broccoli but not strawberry tops, kale but not kale ribs. We've learned that letting five small children parade the chickens in circles on the porch in an effort to train them to lay eggs on command actually causes the birds to stop laying for a few days. We've learned that in the late morning if we let them out into the "paddock"—Jim gated off a previously untouched part of the yard so they could roam freely without the dog's close-range sniffing—they'll deposit all their eggs in a little clutch in the lavender. We've learned that when Graham goes out onto the porch to call them, he barks "Girls!" in a way that makes us sing that old Beastie Boys song of the same name for the rest of the day. We have become bona fide chicken owners, all of us—even Bromley and Jack.

Looking back, I think we did the thing right. The chickens are still alive, for one. Graham has learned to identify which eggs come from which animals, and has created a complicated matrix of random *if*/*then* causality statements that guides whether or not the sunny yolks on his breakfast plate will turn out runny when we cut into them. ("If you give me Suki's egg, it's going to be runny again. Give that one to Dad, and give me Fuzzball's, because it won't be runny.") He may not understand that the cook controls the yolk, but he understands that chickens provide what we eat for breakfast, and for me, that is the perfect outcome. Now, instead of liking chickens and liking eggs, separately, he likes eggs that come from chickens (and from our chickens in particular); he's made the connection. And we've internalized why so many people have the birds in the first place: because they're naturally social and sweet and funny, and because they really aren't all that smelly, and because the eggs, whether they're from the runny-egg kind of chicken or not, make a most brilliantly colored lemon bar. And that if you build them the right kind of house, they'll make your house feel more like home. Even if, some day, you have to dig out the traffic cone.

New Year's Juice

Early on the morning of January 1, our house held a cacophony of loud children and a huddle of adults with varying degrees of hangover. I made this sunny-looking juice as a healing potion of sorts. Depending on how much ginger you add—and the amount is really up to you, depending on your taste preference—the brew can be anywhere from pleasantly gingery to downright spicy. Adjust the ingredient amounts according to your taste (and post-revelry intestinal fortitude).

I leave all the skins and peels on my vegetables when I make juice; however, I typically trim off any parts that can harbor actual chunks of dirt. Here, that means I just trim the tops off the beets and carrots.

MAKES ABOUT 1 QUART JUICE
SPECIAL EQUIPMENT: JUICING MACHINE

> 2 pounds yellow beets, trimmed and cut into chunks
> 1 pound carrots, trimmed and cut into chunks
> 1 large tart apple
> 2 thumb-size knobs ginger
> Thumb-size knob turmeric
> 1 large lemon

» Run all the ingredients through a juicer, stir to blend them, and drink immediately.

Lemon Soufflé Bars

Dan and Lisa, friends a ways down the road who put in their fair share of digging when we were redoing our backyard, have a possibly illegal abundance of their own hens that lay the most gorgeous eggs of every shade. Each Mother's Day, they use the eggs to make lemon meringue pie—my absolute favorite. The year we got our chickens, Dan arrived on the front porch on Mother's Day, totally unexpectedly, with a perfectly peaky pie for me.

The problem with lemon meringue pie, of course, is that it doesn't last all that long, and the topping is best if it's made just before you serve it. Not long after Dan dropped off the pie, I decided to make lemon bars using my own eggs, altering the traditional lemon curd section by whirling the egg whites right in with the yolks, for a fluffier texture that puffs in the oven and winds up tasting like a cross between a lemon bar and lemon meringue pie. For me, it's a much easier way to satisfy the same craving—easy peasy lemon squeezy, as the five-year-old set says. Bonus: the bars also last longer.

Because a lemon's size and juice content can vary widely, measure your own zest and juice. By my count, this recipe requires five juicy medium-size lemons, but you may need more or less.

Start making the bars at least four hours before you plan to serve them, because they need to cool before you can cut them. It's even better if you can refrigerate them overnight before serving.

MAKES: 16 LEMON BARS
SPECIAL EQUIPMENT: 8-BY-8-INCH BAKING PAN

For the crust
1 cup (2 sticks) unsalted butter, cold, each stick
cut into 8 pieces, plus more for greasing the pan

1½ cups all-purpose flour

½ cup sugar

¼ teaspoon kosher salt

⅓ cup cold buttermilk

For the curd

8 large eggs

2 cups sugar

¾ cup freshly squeezed lemon juice

½ cup (1 stick) unsalted butter, at room temperature,
    cut into 8 pieces

» Preheat the oven to 350 degrees F. Grease the baking pan with butter and set it aside.

» To make the crust: In the work bowl of a food processor, pulse the flour, sugar, and salt together a few times to blend. Scatter the pieces of cold butter into the flour, then pulse about 15 times in 1-second bursts, until the butter is roughly pea-size. With the machine running, add the buttermilk through the feed tube, and process for just a few seconds, until the dough begins to gather on the sides of the work bowl.

» Press the dough into an even layer across the bottom of the pan. (The dough will be sticky.) Bake the crust for 20 to 25 minutes, until it's just beginning to brown at the edges.

» While the crust bakes, clean the food processor bowl, then make the lemon curd: In the work bowl, whirl the eggs and sugar together until they're smooth and pale yellow, about 20 seconds. Transfer the mixture to a medium saucepan, and stir in the lemon juice. Place the pan over medium heat, plop in the butter pieces, and cook, stirring occasionally with a rubber spatula, until the white foam subsides and the butter pieces have melted. Once the butter has melted, stir more frequently, switching to a whisk if the curd at the bottom of the pan begins to cook more quickly than the top (which it probably will). After about 5 minutes, the curd will thicken significantly all at once, and begin to bubble. When it does, remove the pan from the heat and whisk out any lumps. Pour the curd into the hot crust as soon as it comes out of the oven.

» Bake the bars for 30 minutes, or until the lemon filling is just barely beginning to brown at the edges. (It should be puffy and still wiggly, and might crack a bit, but it should wiggle all as one piece.) Let the bars cool completely, or refrigerate overnight if possible, then cut into 16 squares and serve.

The Rarest
Breed

TRUFFLES are the fruiting bodies of a specific fungus. They are technically tubers, most typically found just above the root systems of trees—most commonly oak and hazelnut trees in Europe, and Douglas fir trees in the Pacific Northwest. They look, quite honestly, like clumps of dirt, but for whatever chemical reason, they taste overwhelmingly delicious to enough humans that across the globe they are considered a culinary delicacy. People typically describe truffles' aroma as ranging from earthy, garlicky, mushroomy, and herbal to pungent and wet-sockish. Whether you are entranced by their smell, like I am, or believe they smell like burned balloons, like my brother does, may depend on your DNA, your exposure level, or the type of truffle you smell. (In general, white truffles smell and taste stronger than black ones, but European truffles aren't necessarily more strongly flavored than their respective North American counterparts, as once thought.)

Although truffles have been foraged for sale at Pacific Northwest markets since the 1980s, it wasn't until 2010 that, after much work by truffle enthusiasts, the Oregon white truffle, *Tuber oregonense*, was officially named as such. That same truffle season, according to the organizers of the annual Oregon Truffle Festival, the Oregon industry had professionally trained truffle dogs working for a living for the first time. Since then, the festival has evolved into a more extended celebration of the increasingly respected Oregon truffle and the dogs that find them.

I'd always wanted to go, and then was invited as part of a media contingent on a trip hosted by the festival's organizers and Oregon's tourism board. It was clear from the get-go that it wouldn't be a trip for Graham, since any forest foraging would likely require walking along uneven ground in dark places, which simply wouldn't work for him. So I invited Jim, thinking we might have a sort of romantic getaway in Eugene, Oregon, learning about something new together.

"No thanks," he said immediately. "What about mushroom hunting? I'm sure we could just find someone who knows a spot that's closer."

In general, my husband dislikes anything a lot of other people like. For years, he refused to set foot in a Starbucks café. He won't wait in line for brunch. Because truffles are generally popular and expensive, he was convinced the whole thing would be oversubscribed and, by extension, unworthy of our time. But beyond his general disgruntlement about popular foods, his curmudgeonly approach was probably more attributed to our own dog, who only ever used her nose to annoy humans, as far as we could tell. A friend dubbed Bromley's walks "sniffabouts," because she had trouble heading in any one single direction, preferring instead a leash-stretching zigzag hunt to identify the scent of every dog that had peed on a given sidewalk since 1987. I think Jim imagined the truffle excursion as an extended practice in the same dog tolerance we'd doled out for more than a decade with Bromley. Over twelve years, she'd convinced us that either dogs were useless or that she was, in fact, a seventy-five-pound Siamese cat.

Because I generally find truffles delicious, because I harbored a secret hope that truffling might be a way to channel

my dog's difficult nose, and because the festival made me wonder whether my completely unfounded bias against American
truffles was perhaps worth reconsidering, I went, alone.

Which is how, one chilly January day, between the spells
of rain blanketing the brilliantly green wine-growing region
southwest of Eugene, I met Massimo, a truffle-hunting dog.
Depending on which source you consult, *massimo*, in Italian,
means "biggest," or "greatest," or, more literally, "maximum."
But because Massimo was a lagotto Romagnolo (which means
"lake dog from Romagna"), a small- to medium-size hunting
breed used for the last couple of hundred years to hunt truffles
in Italy, being a giant at birth translated to a three-year-old
male canine who weighed only about forty-five pounds. (Since
I have a very large dog, he seemed tiny to me. His owner,
Mike, simply called him "Mass," which rhymed with "boss,"
but I got the feeling Mike might be insulted if I called his dog
diminutive in any way.) With Massimo's eyes hidden almost
completely behind his tightly curled gray-and-white mop and
his constantly wagging tail, I found his intelligence hard to
take seriously. But he was at heart, like all lagotti (the plural of
lagotto), a work dog, and good at what he does.

The dogs-beat-humans-at-truffle-hunting theory goes like
this: to find truffles, humans comb through the topsoil under
trees, more or less at random. When a human finds a truffle,
she takes it out of the ground and smells it with her pathetic
human nose to decide whether it's ripe. If it's ripe, she's lucky.
But it might be half-ripe, or almost ripe. If it's not ripe at all,
she drops it on the ground, but it will not continue to grow
and ripen. She takes the half-ripe or almost-ripe truffle home
and passes it off as ripe. Not surprisingly, the truffles she finds
aren't dependably fragrant or flavorful.

When a dog finds a truffle, most typically pointing it out by
pawing at the ground just above it (some bark; others actually

dig), he finds it precisely because it's ripe. Because he has a very good dog nose, he can be trained to point out only ripe truffles. So dogs not only increase the quality of the truffles found but also limit the damage humans do to the forest floor in their hunt. And theoretically, since fewer truffles are plucked and their lives thus ended by humans, using dogs means more specimens stay in the ground for future harvest. So dogs make the truffle hunt more efficient and effective in almost every way.

Perhaps obviously, not all truffle dogs are created equal. Lagotti Romagnoli, widely considered to be the best breed for this particular hunt, usually cost eight or nine thousand dollars at birth, and training them requires the use of additional truffles, or at least truffle oil, which is expensive, too. But since Oregon truffles can sell for fifty dollars per *ounce* at food markets in season, truffle-dog owners can make good money. From an economic perspective, if you're not a Tesla-driving hobbyist and want to make some actual money, buying a lagotto Romagnolo could be like investing in a cuddly metal detector that shits gold.

But like any useful thing, owning a lagotto requires learning how to use it properly, and there are a debatable number of good alternative breeds. Which is why, for a few weekends each winter, the Oregon Truffle Festival serves as the nation's de facto training ground for truffle dogs of all shapes and sizes.

I'd arrived in Eugene the previous day under a gray silk sheet of sky. The festival itself—a gathering of truffle hunters and producers, enthusiasts and cooks, and, yes, truffle dogs and their owners—was in its eleventh year. That morning, before I'd met Massimo, it had become clear to me that while I enjoyed truffles, I had nothing close to the obsession other attendees felt. I am a dedicated fan of truffled popcorn and truffled aioli at restaurants, but I don't tend to cook with truffles in my own

home. Over breakfast, people swooned over truffled hot chocolate, downed plate after plate of truffled eggs. Men gathered in
clumps in the lobby of a bland Hilton, comparing past truffle
hunts the way some talk about the size of the fish that got away.
(Rather than two outstretched arms measuring tip-to-tail fish
length, the truffle storyteller often proffers a fist, to indicate the
truffle's size.) Egos ebbed and flooded visibly, like a tide.

Then, a dog barked. Having my own loud hound at home,
I immediately presumed the voice could belong to any one of
the wagging beasts nearby. But in the truffle-hunting community, where the relatively quiet lagotto Romagnolo is the gold
standard, the arrival of a barker is the canine equivalent of a
bum showing up at your wedding reception. The room froze.
The room turned. The dog owner blushed.

The actual offender, who might have been hired as the
stunt double for the dog who does Target ads if it weren't for
one big brown spot on his back, was wearing an unfashionable
blue rain jacket. *Inside.* (How embarrassing.) While his owner
scrambled to quiet him, the two lagotto trainers I happened
to be chatting with held an emergency conference. Clearly,
the loud dog was anathema to the cause. And, worse, his handler was using the wrong leash. The trainers decided they'd
put their two lagotti on one lead, thereby freeing up one of
their more appropriate leashes—how it was more appropriate,
I couldn't tell—for use on the barker. The swap was made, and
one trainer disappeared with the criminal canine. The two lagotti looked up at me, smiled politely, and wagged.

"So where did you get your dogs?" I asked the remaining
trainer, pretending nothing had happened.

"Well, I'm a breeder also," she explained, patting the brown
dog at our feet affectionately. "This one is due in a month."

"Oh!" I gushed, nodding. "That's wonderful." The woman
looked at me expectantly, like I should take proper notice of

something in particular about her dog. I saw that the mother-to-be seemed to be stretching her back legs behind her, the way all the animals do on the dog shows on television. I was impressed, but I wasn't sure whether it was perhaps expected of such a specimen. (Would it be like congratulating a human on chewing with her mouth closed?) Asking why the hairs around the pup's mouth were stained brown, which is what my child might have asked, didn't seem smart.

"She . . . She looks quite comfortable for a girl due in a month," I stammered.

"Yes," oozed the trainer proudly, patting down her frizzy ginger-blonde hair. "Well, she does carry well. Five puppies inside, and eight last time." She leaned in conspiratorially. "The only thing," she admitted, looking sideways for passersby, "is that she has *allergies*." She spoke this last word like a person might say "herpes" or "Zika" at a family reunion—softly, with an embarrassed, astonished tone. I nodded again.

"They seem to be getting better," she continued gravely, eyes wide. "It might be because of the pregnancy hormones, but we just can't know. I mean, can you imagine? Being itchy all the time? Itching is terrible. Have you ever itched? Can you imagine what this dog must be going through?"

I assured her that, yes, I had in fact been the victim of itchiness before, and that, no, I couldn't imagine anything worse, but that I also didn't need to examine the skin behind the dog's ear, which was apparently inflamed. Her dedication to and concern for the animal was clear, and overwhelming. I thanked her for letting me meet the dog and wondered whether my own dog was a pain in the ass simply because she knew, deep down, that she didn't luck out with the right kind of human.

While the Oregon truffle industry (whose value ranges from $0.5 to $2.5 million per year, depending on who you ask) has branded Eugene, its locus, as a food town, it has also bequeathed to the Pacific Northwest a breed of human I had never before encountered: the truffle-dog owner. In a few short hours at the festival, I learned to differentiate the dog people from the food people. While the dog people inevitably like truffles, their focus is on the dogs. They walk around looking down. They dress like they're going hunting, or for a very wet hike. And in general, they want to make sure you're worthy before you pet their dog. The food people look at you before they look toward your knees for a wag, and they talk about truffles.

Like the woman before him, Jim Sanford seemed like a dog person. Sanford, the generally accepted truffle-dog training master—if not in the world, then at least in the United States—is a tall, kind, self-confident man who hails from Tennessee. He looks like someone who probably flew planes in the navy, but I'd heard he'd fallen into truffling after two decades training elephants. His late dog Tom was a truffle-finding celebrity, sniffing out two hundred pounds of truffles per year in his prime. Sanford sat petting Dante, the large gray lagotto Romagnolo who belonged to the festival's organizers. (Most lagotti seem to have Italian names.)

I started by asking him how he came to train elephants. He leveled me with his steady gaze, somehow managing to look me directly in the eye despite his great height.

"How could you not?" he asked.

"Well . . ." I hesitated. "How *did* you?"

"I stood toe-to-toe with an elephant, and I decided I wanted to train them," he said, like it was the most natural career choice a twentysomething could make.

Although it took Sanford a good decade to find the right mentor, it was essentially that straightforward. And over the course of a life that led him from elephants to the prestigious Blackberry Farm, a luxury resort in Tennessee where he initially led the horseback-riding program, he became the truffle-dog whisperer.

The morning of the truffle hunt, a rotating roster of worshippers stopped to visit Sanford, all seeming to seek a nod of approval or some outwardly visible sign that their dog might also one day be a successful truffle hunter: The owner of Sammy, a sweet ten-year-old golden retriever, claimed without a hint of irony that her old dog was ready to learn new tricks. A coonhound-beagle mix's husky-voiced owner swore her boy had quite a nose on him. A man in what looked like head-to-toe fishing gear toted a fat black Lab that seemed completely disinterested in everything.

On it went. The humans all seemed just a little off—but whether it was because they were essentially a cast repeat from the Christopher Guest movie *Best in Show*, or because they were all crazies looking to strike it rich by finding truffles, or because I was being overly judgmental, I wasn't sure. But they all had dogs that could theoretically smell well. And so, knowing that I'd have the chance to travel to a top-secret location to paw through the dirt in the company of a well-trained lagotto, I said good-bye to Sanford and boarded a tour bus.

"Let's go, kid," Sanford said to Dante, heading in the opposite direction.

On the bus, I remembered that my media minder, Meg, had had last-minute advice for me.

"It's dark in the forest, Jess. *Really* dark. So if you get lost, remember that you should always head downhill. If you hit the fence, follow it down the hill," she'd told me.

In the forest, next to a farm in western Lane County, I realized she was right. The twenty-five-year-old Douglas firs Mike led our large group into—just next to a retired Christmas-tree farm—formed a tall canopy that, even as the morning's petulant weather cleared, acted like a darkening umbrella over the needle-strewn forest floor. We all crowded around Mike and Massimo with our metal truffle rakes—four pointy metal prongs at the end of a yard-long stick—and listened as he gave us the rules.

"Massimo is here to work," he started. "So please don't talk to him, and don't try to pet him or anything. Give him space." He took Massimo off his leash, and the dog bounded toward the forest through tall, wet grass, clearly eager to begin.

"Don't forget to replace the duff after you dig," Mike added, an order he'd go on to repeat several times, referring to the fragile top layer of pine needles and soil we would all inevitably remove in our search for the truffles, which almost always lie within the top four inches of earth. (Dan Luoma, our group's "scientific advisor" and the only person I've ever met who has a PhD in truffles, had told us on the bus that truffles are really just mushrooms that have lost their stems and want to hide underground because they're embarrassed about it.)

It seemed easy for Mike to lead off calmly, but since we'd seen the previous tour group leave the same young forest with what they'd claimed were four *pounds* of Oregon white truffles, we were all wondering how many could be left, and whether we'd need to throw shoulders each time Massimo signaled he'd found a truffle, if we wanted a chance to actually dig. A few more independent-minded participants strayed off into the forest to give it a go without the dog. I stumbled through the grasses, thankful that I didn't need to mind Graham's balance when I couldn't keep my own.

What ensued was essentially an Easter egg hunt for adults. We all knew there was theoretically enough for everyone, but there was a palpable air of competitiveness, and the half of us holding the heavy, sharp rakes were basically armed, albeit in an accidental *Edward Scissorhands* sort of way. But we wouldn't know where the eggs were until the dog told us, and under the canopy, it was quite dark.

Massimo got to work, sniffing along the soft earth. He was quick to find the first truffle, and gave his signal, pawing at the duff and then looking up at Mike expectantly before prancing back to him. Mike rewarded him with a treat, pointed to someone who had been tailing him closely, and told her to dig there. Mass headed off again as we all crowded around to see what the lucky digger might find. I decided my best bet was to hang back and follow the dog until the novelty had worn off, so that perhaps I'd get to dig on my own, instead of with a crowd of onlookers.

Massimo was on fire. Sniff, paw, glance, prance, munch. Sniff, paw, glance, prance, munch.

"Bravo, bravo," Mike told Massimo each time he stomped at the ground above a truffle, handing him a crunchy bite out of a many-pocketed fluorescent orange vest. Mike seemed to have acquired an Italian accent for the congratulating.

"What kind of treats do you give him?" I asked.

"Just kibble now," said Mike. "He was getting too fat."

Eventually, my turn came. Massimo signaled. I ambled over, training my eye exactly on the small indentation his paw made in the duff. I sank to my knees. I dug, first with the rake to remove the top layer, and then with my gloves in the dirt. I came up with what I thought was a truffle, beaming. I ripped off my gloves, desperate to touch the truffle with my bare hands even though I couldn't really feel them, but when I pinched the little clod between my cold, bloodless fingers, it disintegrated.

Tuber oregonense is not quite white, as its English name suggests. On the outside, it's a muddy red. Inside, the color is slightly more brownish or as light as tan, and almost always marbled with white streaks and dots and swirls, so that once it's cut open, the truffle looks like a slice of salami, or a cross section of *coppa* or well-marbled beef. The thing Mike left out when we started—or that I may have missed—was that there's this obnoxious other type of tuber in the forest called a false truffle. It emits a smell remarkably similar to a ripe Oregon white truffle, and like all dogs, Massimo signals it as a true truffle. When you rake where the dog tells you to, you find a little white clump that looks like truffle but simply crumbles into pieces under light pressure. My truffle, alas, was not a truffle. I had trouble not being disappointed in Massimo. *How could he?* I thought.

As we roamed deeper and deeper into the forest, some of us started to wonder whether there was a strategy for when to elbow the others out of the way to dig. Was Massimo pawing differently for real truffles than he did for the false truffles? Was he in fact signaling at times when Mike didn't seem to think, or perhaps wasn't noticing, that he was signaling? Mike got swarmed with hunters wanting to know if what they'd found was a true truffle or a false one. Massimo roamed. Suddenly, we were all truffle-dog experts, reading Massimo's tail twitches and head turns like tea leaves, shouting through the firs when we noticed something interesting. If the truffles could hear us, they'd have surely fled.

Twice more, I jumped on Massimo's signal. Twice more, I found false truffles. I was really bad at all of it—at the looking, the digging, and the identifying. I was disappointed. As I got tired and a little restless, my imagination spun off into the dark. It wandered to a time, long ago, when generations of trufflers might have depended for their livelihood on the very skill I couldn't seem to grasp. I gave up entirely and simply roamed along the duff, feeling grateful I wasn't born into an Italian truffle-hunting family.

It wasn't all that different from growing up me in my own family, I thought. I never felt like I was born the right breed.

THE RAREST BREED

I was a mediocre athlete in a family that, in my mind, valued fitness above all else—the weakling in a group of able-bodied heroes. I came from a whole family of Australian shepherds, a breed that needs to run at least forty miles a day before they can sit still. So even though I grew up doing many of the same things as what someone once termed my "fast family" did—I also taught aerobics when I was in high school, and although I was never a skiing star, I could certainly outski all my non-racing friends—I never felt competent, because my family was always so far ahead. A few paces away, I watched a Lab in training find nothing, and I walked over to give him an understanding little pat.

Down the hill a ways, my assigned field-trip partner, a lovely woman from Portland named Allison, found one Oregon white truffle. We were sharing a bag that I'd been the one holding, and she seemed hesitant to trust her little prize to someone else's safekeeping.

A whistle blew from up the hill. After just a little under an hour, our hunt was over. Massimo needed a break.

Walking back to the bus under weak sunshine, there was an air of deflated satisfaction; almost everyone had a truffle, but as a group, our haul had come nowhere close to what the previous foragers had reported. Allison, who was for the moment my best friend, sent me back to Seattle with her truffle. It seemed small to me—it was the size of the top segment of my thumb, and about the same shape—but the smell was right, earthy and sharp. Back at the hotel, I wrapped it in toilet paper and snuck it into my suitcase, with plans to clean it and then store it, as directed, in a glass jar filled with rice in my refrigerator. (The rice would absorb the flavor, I was told.)

That night, there was what the festival calls its Grand Truffle Dinner, which consisted of six truffle-inflected courses prepared by regional star chefs, paired with Oregon wines. The first course was lovely; down came a foie gras parfait infused with Oregon black truffle, garnished with fluttering bonito flakes and a shower of burnt onion dust. As far as I could tell, it was the best truffle I'd ever tasted. Then there was Alaskan king crab poached in Oregon white truffle butter, which is possibly the only way to make plain crab taste even better. I couldn't see any reason I'd choose a French truffle over an Oregonian one when they tasted this good. But by the third course, it all became too much: there was eggplant and white truffle rillettes, then black truffle– and hen-stuffed cabbage, then truffle-studded pork shoulder *crépinette*, each of which became progressively tiresome as my palate got, in a word, bored. By the last course, a truffled sticky-toffee pudding that actually made my stomach turn, the truffle inflection became an infection. I was done with truffles, possibly forever. By the time I checked out of the hotel, I was turned off by all of it— by the dogs and their over-obsessive owners, by the interest in truffles that by then felt to me like desperation, by the taste of the truffles themselves.

Looking back, I know I thought I was going to come away with a crush on a truffle dog and a head filled with ideas of finding my own truffles in Douglas fir forests closer to home. What I landed with instead was a complete disinterest in eating more of them and a strong belief (if I hadn't felt it before) that despite loving dogs in general, I will never, ever be a dog-show person.

When I got home, I showed Graham the truffle. He shrugged.

"Do you want to smell it?" I asked.

"Not really," he said.

"Neither do I," I said. "It used to smell good to me, but it doesn't anymore."

"You know what smells good?" Graham asked. "Chicken."

THE RAREST BREED

Truffled Ricotta Toasts

The Oregon Truffle Festival was, for me, a bacchanalia gone wrong. When I got home, I squirreled away my truffle in a jar of rice, as directed, and forgot it in the back of my refrigerator. For weeks, I couldn't think about it at all.

But predictably, when my friend Lauren mentioned she was serving ricotta toasts with truffle oil for a dinner party, it sounded delicious. I made my own, but when I opened the jar, hoping to put shavings of ripe truffle on top, I saw that it had spoiled, and I had to throw it away. I served the toasts with just truffle oil and enjoyed every bite.

Most good truffle oils are a mixture of extra-virgin olive oil and truffle oil. Before you buy one, read the label to make sure there are no artificial flavorings or mysterious ingredients you can't pronounce. Also, the salt is just as important as the truffle oil in this simple recipe. Find good flaky sea salt. And if you happen to have a healthy Oregon white truffle waiting for you in the refrigerator, shave a paper-thin slice over the top of each toast. (Just don't overdo it.)

**MAKES ABOUT 16 TOASTS, DEPENDING
ON THE SIZE OF YOUR BAGUETTE**

> Half a baguette, cut into ½-inch-thick slices, toasted
> 1 pint soft, full-fat ricotta cheese
> White or black truffle oil, for drizzling, to taste
> Flaky sea salt and freshly ground black pepper, to taste

» Arrange the baguette slices in one layer on a big platter. Smear a tablespoon of the ricotta on each little toast, then drizzle them all with truffle oil. Shower with salt and pepper, and serve.

FEBRUARY

As a toddler, Graham didn't play kitchen, the way some kids do. There was no well-worn tea set, and no interest in seeing what Mom might be doing over the stove. No messy attempt to make toast next to me, smearing butter on the counter like other kids did. At first, I thought it was just because he wasn't physically able to stand next to me, but as he grew, I decided that he simply saw it as my place. He wasn't compelled to participate. I didn't think food would ever be play for him, the way it is for me.

But one day, after a full day of kindergarten in February, Graham took out a small whiteboard and wrote us a menu in off-kilter capitals. It was an odd list, rife with the kind of misspellings the parents of young children find charming once they succeed in translating what each word means:

LAMMONS

Q CAMBERS

COFE

PARES

BRED AND BOTTER

CAREITS

CHIKIN

I was tickled by his perception of the word *cucumber*, but most thrilled that chicken had, in the month after putting hens

47

in the house in the back, become part of his lexicon. I set my sights on convincing him to eat more broadly by showing him various places where his food comes from. Which meant, for the moment, that I'd need to ignore the things on The Here List that appealed most to me as an eater, and focus on what I thought might appeal to him. I rewrote the Gantt chart, this time on craft paper from a big brown roll, and prepared to spend a little more energy traveling with Graham.

I wouldn't consider Graham a high-maintenance kid the way some kids are high maintenance. He doesn't touch things he shouldn't, or tear things apart, or incessantly ask inane questions. But because getting from point A to point B isn't usually easy, we always have to think ahead when we go somewhere. Which is why, when we decided to go razor clamming—trying to capitalize on Graham's love of digging in the sand—we packed a stack of foot-wide hearts cut out of an old pink yoga mat. The hearts were my friend Tracy's ingenious plan; Tracy is a phenom of kindness, and she's forever coming up with sweet ways to make Graham's life easier. She figured that if Graham had a waterproof platform for digging on his knees, he'd be good for hours. In theory, we'd find enough razor clams to eat for dinner. And in theory, he might actually try them.

Digging Deep

I AM not particularly fond of the ocean. To the casual observer, this may seem strange: I live in Seattle with my husband, whose job as an oceanographer brought us here, and our child, a sea-loving sprite who will take any opportunity to dig or splash, physical ability notwithstanding. But whether it's genetic (my father can get seasick looking at an ocean) or practical (I grew up in the desert of Boise, Idaho), the sea has never seduced me.

First of all, it's salty, which is gross. Lupus has given me the kind of delicate, ornery skin that turns red when the wind blows or the sun comes out or someone sneezes too loudly. Entering salt water has the equivalent effect of pouring nitric acid all over my body; the salt enters each pore and begins a miniature burning process that makes me feel physically invaded by scabies, or lice, or any other number of villainous crawling things that make one feel that one's skin will never be the same. Never, in all my years swimming in lakes and rivers, has freshwater been so offensive. Salt makes my hair stringy, and my feet sticky, and my eyes stingy.

Second, the ocean usually comes with sand. Ever since I bodyboarded in Santa Monica at age eleven, and wound up scrubbing my face against the sand at the bottom of the ocean— scrubbing so the little grains raced up my nose and into my mouth, so I spit out foreign particles for days afterward—I've hated sand, too. It's a constant physical reminder of a lifelong battle with poor coordination. Sand in the wound, if you will. Or scrubbed into the aforementioned sensitive skin.

But it's a double-edged sword, the ocean. I hate how it feels, but I love how it looks. And despite how much I sometimes loathe it—that it nettles me with salt and sand, and that it takes my husband away for weeks or months at a time—it offers something I can't usually find any other way. The ocean gives me delicious things to eat. The ocean gives me razor clams.

Razor clams—*Siliqua patula*, if you go with the Latin name—are the hand-length brown bivalves that call Pacific Northwest shores home. They're a little shy, which is why perhaps you've never seen them; they hide in shiny, oval-shaped shells about a foot down in wet sand below the high-tide mark. You can sometimes find the meat frozen in the odd fishmonger's back walk-in, but ultimately, if you want to taste razor clams, you dig them yourself. Which is why, on cold, rainy winter nights, the Washington coast is littered with groups of clammers coated with sand, salt, and the glow of their pickup trucks' high beams. If you grew up elsewhere, razor clamming, like mushrooming or huckleberry picking, is just an interesting way to find fun food you can't usually get at the grocery store. But the way some natives tell it, it's a Washingtonian rite of passage.

In the past, I've gone razor clamming to find new flavors. Years ago, I went clamming around Thanksgiving, which, although successful, led to a very late, very long night. (The way it typically works, my resident-scientist husband reports, is that in the weeks closest to the winter solstice, the lowest tides happen at night in the Pacific Northwest.) This time around, I wanted to claim my family's identity as Washingtonian. Hoping to include two of Graham's friends, we planned the outing for Valentine's Day weekend, when low tide occurred late in the afternoon, rather than after dark. Why wouldn't he love digging even more if there were other sandy boys involved and a prize to be had at the bottom of each sandy hole? Even better, he'd get a good first dose of a strong regional habit. And I thought perhaps unearthing a new food himself might convince him to try it.

So the day after Valentine's Day, during one of the warmest winters in the state's history, we drove to the Washington coast with Tracy and Aaron and their two boys, and the pink hearts. Heading for the water, I carried Graham's sticks and our clamming gear; Jim carried Graham, because the softer sand made it impossible for him to walk. When we crested the dune separating Highway 105 from the beach at Twin Harbors State Park, which runs right along the Pacific Ocean, another man came at us from the beach, herding a whirling dervish of a child toward the car.

"That kind of a day?" I asked instinctively. I have a terrible habit, when I see people in difficult situations, of pointing it out aloud. The man grimaced.

"It doesn't help that the clams are nonexistent," he threw back. The guy clearly had some experience: he wore what looked like army-issue hip waders, a special mesh clam sack tied to his waist, and the glare of someone who wasn't used to being skunked. Tracy and I exchanged worried glances.

The mood on the beach was grim. Couples wandered solemnly along the spongy strip where the water laps the shore, swinging their aluminum clam guns—big metal tubes with a handle at the top, designed to be pushed into the earth, then pulled up, bringing with them cylinders of sand and the clams they contain all at once inside the tube—but not actually using them. I sauntered onto the beach confidently, explaining to the others how, when a razor clam digs down vertically, it propels itself both by using a triangle-shaped digger foot, on the bottom end, and by spitting water out of its siphon, on the end closest to the surface of the sand. This digging and spitting process sends water right up through the sand, leaving a little dimple—a *show*, in razor clammers' language—at the surface. It's often shaped like an inch-wide doughnut, and sometimes, near the water's edge, you can see the water actively squirting up through a hole in the sand, a sure sign that there's something alive underneath. Theoretically, when you spot a show, you plunge the clam gun into the sand, place your finger over the small hole that creates a vacuum inside the gun's tube, pull up, and paw through the resulting pile of sand to find your clam. But we didn't see a single show. Neither did anyone else, as far as we could tell. No one we met had found even one clam.

The three boys had a grand old time. The yoga mats' heart shape was perfect for the way Graham kneeled. They proved, at first, to be excellent cushions for sand-castle making, and later, as the tide came in and stubborn bodies stayed put, they made little floating islands perfect for ferrying imaginary Ninja Turtles to and from their sand-castle sewer systems. It was a very intricate, well-planned operation, all enrobed in an aura of pink plastic love, but nowhere in that operation were there the shellfish we'd come so far to find. My friends shrugged and cracked open a few beers. I died a little inside, both because I'd led my pals four hours out of our way to the house we'd rented on a beach farther north—we'd run into an accident on the highway and had had to sit for hours—and because now, the creamy razor-clam carbonara I'd planned would have to be made with boring old bacon.

The right way to razor-clam, I've been told, is how I did it the first time. I drove in the freezing rain quite close to the winter solstice with a friend, my dog, and ill-fitting foul-weather gear. We dug for hours, fried clams at a different friend's house, and

53

arrived back home at a leisurely two in the morning. The first time, I'd gone with someone who knew what they were doing. Someone who knew the clam's show, in all its sandy incarnations. Someone who wasn't going to go home without his limit of fifteen clams. So as we drove the dark, windy stretch to the rental house, road weary and hungry, I decided that perhaps the clamming-as-beach-party approach was totally wrong. It wasn't my fault I'd picked the wrong day, but perhaps I'd also picked the wrong demographic to bring with me.

Understand that, in my family, any food-related undertaking requiring both luck and skill has traditionally been achieved successfully by adding a dash of stupidity. I remember my father forever splaying out the contents of his wallet on the kitchen table after swimming in some rushing western river as part of a fishing trip. Every time, my mother would wonder aloud why he hadn't left the wallet in the '84 Volvo's cantankerous glove compartment, and every time, there would be a conversation about risking the wallet in exchange for a few good fish. If the wallet wasn't soaked, there was a speeding ticket, acquired because Tom Petty was singing too loudly. Or a flat tire. Or an injured dog. But those things, not accidentally, happened on the days when there were also fish in the cooler. A near-reckless sense of adventure was always his best asset.

The next day, once the boys had had a good dose of very chilly surfing and Graham's friend had discovered that Graham could "run" a football if he tucked it into the hood of Graham's sweatshirt, I announced I was going back to Twin Harbors to clam on my own. We'd heard someone say they'd had success a bit farther down the beach. I wanted clams, to be sure. But even more, I wanted to hold on to my nascent reputation as an occasional forager. What well-respected food enthusiast would return home without trying again? And what good was The Here List if I couldn't cross things off it?

DIGGING DEEP

In the car, I turned up the Lumineers a little too loudly and retraced our tracks down the same windy road, now shiny in an unusually bright February sun. I intentionally sped through gritty Aberdeen, hometown of the late Kurt Cobain, and back to the same shore, only farther south, past a church whose marquee read, "CLAMMING BOOTS WELCOME AT WORSHIP." (Perhaps that's what Cobain meant when he sang, *Come as you are*.) The two cop cars I passed ignored my attempt to channel my dad, which I thought was a bad sign, so I tried skidding a little too fast for my Outback onto the beach behind a stream of beefy pickups. Alas, the tires held. As I suited up—Xtratuf boots covered with my old ski gear, top to bottom—I tucked my good leather Rapha wallet into my jacket pocket, along with my cell phone, but left the pocket open on purpose.

The positive side of razor clamming alone is that you're alone. Most people with kids will tell you that once you become a parent, there's a unique value in anything you do without a small human clinging to you in some physical or even figurative way. I felt no different; with my husband gone so much, even the littlest slices of time on my own always felt rejuvenating. If you look for it, there's an attractive liberty to closing the car door without watching out for little bodies or wayward toys. To eating your own snack first. To squatting down behind the car to pee in broad daylight, because your husband isn't there to be modest for you, per usual, and your kid doesn't need to pee first. And so with the slam of the trunk, I set off happily toward a much more crowded beach, clam gun and square-sided yellow bucket and dishwashing gloves and all, this time with an extra veneer of freedom reflecting in the sun.

The negative side of going razor clamming alone is that you can't rely on your own crowd to kibitz about where the clams might be, or even pretend you've just discovered the most perfect place to dig. My confident pace slowed as I neared the water's edge and realized I had no clue what I was doing. I watched two women—one with army-green hip waders personalized with pink satin ribbons at thigh level, designed to mimic garters—dig clam after clam with apparent ease. Now, I'd dug for clams before. But the guy I'd clammed with, a burly man named Dan, was experienced. In fact, Dan runs the Washington Department of Fish and Wildlife's entire razor-clam-studying operation. He's like the President of Razor Clamming. So when I assured myself that I could lead a pack of newbies out into the sand to dig, I'd overlooked one small detail that was easy to ignore the day before, when there were no clams: Dan had shown me where to dig every time I'd dug before.

I meandered from show to show (or from what I thought was a show to what I thought was a different show), digging occasionally. Here, it's worth mentioning that "digging" is a bit of a misnomer: it's really a matter of pushing and pulling. The first time I plunged the clam gun into the sand, I expected it to squish through the way Graham's shovel had that same morning—easily—but eight or ten inches in, the granules get significantly more compact. When I decided the gun had gone as far as it was going to go, I pulled up, but the only thing that moved was a small muscle on the left side of my lower back. That moved a lot. I readjusted, panning the crowd to make sure no one had heard my squeak of pain, bent my knees, and copied the twist-and-wiggle motion I'd seen my new peers perform to prize the gun out of the sand. I emptied out the gun's contents, repeated the process until I'd dug down to something that had the texture of Cream of Wheat, and kicked through the resulting sandpile to reveal exactly zero clams. Either my aim was off, or the clam was actually digging faster than me.

After ten or so identical experiences, my self-esteem began to fade. It was suddenly junior high again, and the only thing that separated me from the cheerleading crowd, which was currently wearing puff-painted sweatshirts, hip waders, and mesh bags filled with filthy clams, was a four-inch mollusk. I had the wrong car. I had the wrong clam collector. My clam gun still had the sticker on it from the store, and I wasn't coordinated or strong enough to use it. My ski clothes, which I thought were quite cool, were clearly the threads of a city slicker. Chances were good I was the only one who listened to the Lumineers. The ladies on the beach were still on Def Leppard, and not in an ironic way.

Just as the thought of giving up occurred to me, I noticed a group of guys standing shin-deep in the surf, scanning the sand for shows every time the tide rushed out. I thought again of my father, figuring that perhaps if the water topped my foul-weather boots, something good would happen. I quickly discovered that the advantage of standing at or below the waterline is twofold. First, because the water washes the sand clean with each tidal breath, you can imagine no one else before you has ever thought to dig in that particular place, and that an entire city of clams lies directly beneath your feet. Second, it's where the jerks ignoring the rule that you must take every clam you dig, regardless of what your clam gun might do to one if you dig just a little off-center of the clam's path, throw their mangled clams. And so, with a squeal of delight, I found my first clam—not by digging it up, but by rescuing it, squirming in its razor-clam version of pain, from where it was half-lodged in the sand in plain view. I marched it up to my bucket, plunked it into the bottom, and turned back to the beach. *Ain't no thang.*

My luck improved. Fifteen minutes later, still standing at the water's edge, I glanced in just the right spot as a three-inch-high fountain of water squirted out of the sand. I pushed. I pulled. The clam came out. *Plunk*. I didn't care that the clam had essentially slapped me in the face to announce its location. I didn't care that I'd taken a clam that would taste like PTSD. I had two clams. I scanned some more.

Razor clamming is different from other forms of foraging in that when it's busy, you almost always stand within easy speaking distance of other clammers. There's not a lot of back and forth, but there's a quiet camaraderie that rolls down the beach. I suspect that occasionally, folks can get competitive and cranky with each other over who gets to dig a show two people spot at once, but shockingly, no one seemed intimidated by my presence. As the sun started setting, people began dragging full mesh bags through the surf to clean their clams, then traipsing back to their trucks. Over the course of an hour or so, a few of those people peered into my bucket.

"How's it going today?"

It was a skinny old guy in army-green chest waders. We'd been wandering close to each other for about half an hour.

"I'm pretty terrible at this," I answered. It was a stock answer I'd used playing sports growing up. Before I knew I was probably always tired because I had lupus.

"I noticed," he said, somehow kindly. "I've got my limit, so now I'm looking for you."

"Thanks," I said, unsure of what else to say. I'd become a charity case.

And the second I said that, I spotted a new gurgle in the sand, plunged my clam gun in, and pulled out a fat clam. It was two swift, easy motions, just like in the videos online. The man smiled, and walked off down the beach. *Plunk.* I resisted the urge to chase him down, prostrate myself before him on the sand, and beg for digging lessons.

I bet that if I'd gotten my feet really wet, or clammed until midnight, or turned my jacket a little sideways so my wallet could fall into the ocean, I'd have reached my fifteen-clam limit. If I'd been stronger, maybe, I might have been able to dig as fast as the clams. But in the end, after about ninety minutes of digging, it was just those three plunks. I bounced back down the dunes in my station wagon, past the bullet-pocked beach driving regulations sign, through the depressed towns that filter-feed off passing tourists like myself.

"Three clams," I texted my husband from Aberdeen. "Please take the pork roast out of fridge, oven to 400, cut onions." We'd be tasting clams, but we wouldn't be having clams for dinner.

When I got back to the beach house, the boys gave me a hero's welcome. They didn't know that I'd dug clams for one meager serving instead of eight, or that I'd been an idiot singing country music on the way home, or that I'd be much better at preparing razor clams than I was at actually finding them. They watched the still-live creatures suck their leathery siphons back into their homes as I rinsed them with clean water, and touched their brindled shells with awe.

I put the clams in a big glass bowl, filled the bowl with boiling water the way Dan had showed me, and watched as the clam's shells popped off the meat. I cut out their stomachs with scissors—my friend Jill calls razor clams the "boneless, skinless chicken breasts of the seafood world" because you essentially cut out the parts that could add any sort of unseemly texture—and snipped them into segments based on thickness. I rolled them in sandy cornmeal, then fried them up in butter, adding the thickest pieces to the pan first, and served them with salt, hot and crisp, as the pork roast sizzled next to onions, apples, and potatoes in the oven. The grown-ups oohed and aahed in appreciation of the clams. The children refused to try them.

Simple Pan-Fried Razor Clams

For me, razor clams taste good because they're all the things I hate–salt and sand and coordination and timing and practice–packaged up in a few sweet bites. They're also much easier to cook than they are to dig.

Before cooking razor clams, you need to relieve them of any shellish parts that remind the eater of the sea, and then you can cook them like thin strips of chicken. If you can find them whole, ask your fishmonger how to open them. (Better yet, have him or her do it for you.) If you're buying the clams frozen, thaw them completely, and blot them dry with paper towels. You'll likely see two types of meat: the thinner part that lives under the shell, and the digger, which looks like a hunk of pure muscle. Cook these two parts separately, because while the thin body sections will curl up like bacon and cook quickly, the digger (the part that eats more like a chicken tender) will take a few moments longer.

If you'd like to clean your own clams (this recipe cooks up an average daily catch), the Washington Department of Fish and Wildlife has a great online tutorial at http://wdfw.wa.gov.

Note: Regular yellow cornmeal works best for this recipe.

MAKES: 4 SERVINGS

> 1 pound razor-clam meat (from about a dozen clams)
> Kosher salt and freshly ground black pepper, to taste
> ½ cup (1 stick) unsalted butter, divided
> 1 cup cornmeal
> Lemons, for serving
> Crunchy sea salt, for serving

» Season the razor clams with salt and pepper. Melt 2 tablespoons of the butter in a large skillet over medium-high heat.

When the butter has melted, dredge a few of the razor clams in the cornmeal, and cook them for about 1 to 2 minutes per side, or until the clams are deep golden brown and have curled up a bit, similar to how bacon looks as it cooks (in the case of the body parts) or slightly golden and firmer (in the case of the diggers, which will take longer). Transfer the clams to a paper towel–lined plate to drain and repeat with the remaining ingredients, adding more butter as necessary. Serve the clams right away, with a squeeze of lemon and a little shower of sea salt.

Pork Roast with Apples, Onions, and Dijon-Cider Pan Sauce

When our razor-clamming experience didn't pan out with as much edible loot as we'd anticipated, I served my fallback menu: a simple pork roast, designed with the limitations of a rental kitchen in mind. Cooked entirely on one rimmed sheet pan, this roast, paired with brown-tipped onions and soft baked apples, gets its kick from a simple pan sauce you make on the stove top while the pork rests. Although the thyme and rosemary called for below are what I use most frequently, any mixture of hearty herbs would be lovely—you might add sage, oregano, or marjoram to the mix.

Graham didn't eat a single bite.

MAKES: 6 SERVINGS

SPECIAL EQUIPMENT: INSTANT-READ THERMOMETER

1 (roughly 2-pound) boneless pork roast

4 tablespoons extra-virgin olive oil, divided

Kosher salt and freshly ground black pepper, to taste

1 tablespoon chopped fresh thyme

1 tablespoon chopped fresh rosemary

2 medium onions, peeled and quartered

2 large tart apples, quartered and cored

1 pint dry hard cider

½ cup heavy cream

¼ cup Dijon mustard

» Preheat the oven to 400 degrees F.

» Place the pork on a large rimmed baking sheet, rub it on all sides with 1 tablespoon of the olive oil, and season it on all sides with salt and pepper. Scatter the thyme and rosemary in an even layer over the pork.

» In a medium mixing bowl, toss the onion quarters with 2 tablespoons of the olive oil, and season them with salt and pepper. Dump the onions onto the baking sheet, piling them around the pork on all sides. In the same bowl, mix the apple quarters with the remaining tablespoon of oil, season them with salt and pepper, and set them aside.

» Roast the pork and onions for 20 minutes. Turn the onions, rotate the pan, add the apples to the pan with the onions, and roast for another 20 minutes, or until the onions are browned, the apples are soft, and the pork reads 140 degrees F on an instant-read thermometer when measured right in the center of the roast. Transfer the pork to a serving platter, scoop the onions and apples alongside it, and cover the lot with aluminum foil to keep warm.

» Place the baking sheet directly on the stove top, straddled over 2 burners on medium heat. Add the cider to the pan and cook at a hard simmer, stirring to scrape any brown bits off the bottom of the pan, for 5 minutes, or until the cider has reduced by about half. Add the cream and mustard and whisk together all the ingredients until blended. Cook, whisking occasionally and carefully rotating the hot pan as necessary, until the mixture has thickened to the consistency of thin gravy, about 3 minutes.

» Serve the pork and accoutrements with a bowl of sauce on the side, or slice the pork separately, lay it out on top of the apples and onions, and bathe it in the sauce.

MARCH

About six months after we got married, right after I'd finished culinary school, Jim and I moved to La Jolla, California, with a group of scientists doing fieldwork off the big research pier at Scripps Institution of Oceanography. I was the group's cook, responsible for lunches and dinners five or six days a week. A few months into the gig, my body started behaving strangely. First it was just my hands, which went white with cold multiple times each day, even in the stubborn California sun. Then my limbs started going numb and tingly at night. I was tired, always so tired. My brain felt foggy. All at once, my body began to hurt—first my wrists and elbows, which made it hard to hold a knife at all, and then my hips and knees and ankles. Tying shoelaces and opening doors and carrying grocery bags all became hugely uncomfortable tasks.

One warm December morning, when I was sitting at the counter in our rental house drinking coffee, I dropped the cup. I was staring at it when it happened. My wrist just collapsed sideways on its own, like it had lost all the bones. Coffee oozed between the cracks in the white Mexican tile.

That morning, I decided I needed to see a doctor. After rounds and rounds of testing—for cancer, Lyme disease, mononucleosis, and a whole host of other scary-sounding maladies—it was determined, months later, that I had lupus. I started a handful of oral medications that brought it under control most of the time, and learned over the years to increase

them and manage my lifestyle more carefully in the spring
and fall, when I tended to flare. We moved to Seattle, in part,
because the weather here, despite the reputation for incessant
rain, is relatively even-tempered.

Although lupus hadn't affected my kidneys before pregnancy,
it was clear one March day, when I was pregnant with Graham,
that the combination of lupus and pregnancy wasn't going so
well, primarily because my kidneys couldn't handle the extra
stress. And so toward the end of March, I checked into Seattle's
Swedish Hospital for an indeterminate period of bed rest. On
April 1, it snowed—a notable event any time of year in Seattle—
and my water broke, eight weeks prematurely. My husband and
I hunkered down in the antenatal unit together, doing what we
could to keep that baby inside as long as possible. About a week
later, a spontaneous *E. coli* infection sent me into labor. As my
contractions became intense, I spiked a raging fever, and because
lupus medications often disrupt the body's ability to regulate
the adrenaline involved with great efforts, I went into adrenal
shock. My heart and breathing rates skyrocketed. I peed and
heaved and writhed. At a very odd time, our doula announced
she had to teach a yoga class and simply left. Eventually, a lucky
combination of time and drugs and doctoring steered us in the
right direction, and Graham was born in an operating room.
He was stout for a kid released seven weeks early, but plagued by
the same infection, and jaundice, and breathing difficulties the
doctors assured us were minor.

"He's a good eater," said a nurse named Marta the next
week, hesitant to make any promises about Graham learning
to eat through anything but a tube, but willing to encourage
the idea that very few children born seven weeks prematurely
were what the neonatal doctors called "interesting" cases. We
began to worship Marta. We were relieved that Graham didn't
seem interesting.

But still, we worried. Common practice dictated we refrain from touching or holding him outside certain prescribed hours so that his little baby brain could focus on digesting and growing, rather than on us.

"He's a good eater," said Jim, over and over, nodding each time Marta commended Graham on his robust-for-a-preemie appetite. We watched my pumped breast milk, yellowed by thick colostrum, disappear into his body through a tiny tube in his nose.

"He'll be fine," I agreed.

You've Got to Be Kidding

EIGHTEEN miles northwest of Yakima, a place so perpetually sunny that it bills itself as "The Palm Springs of Washington," is the tiny, windswept apple town of Tieton. It's no more than a blink on the map, and that's only if you're looking for it. Framed by orchards, fruit-packing plants, and farmland, the center of town, frequented mostly by the Mexican immigrants who make Washington's fruit industry viable, is eerily quiet at night. A few hours after dusk one Friday, the glow of a rectangular sign—really a decades-old Mug root beer advertisement, subtitled by the name of the corner café, Bootlegger's Cove—was the only proof of life.

Inside the café, a small man was holding court. Lori and Ruth Babcock, the couple who own Tieton Farm & Creamery, were laughing appropriately as our five-year-old son quizzed the table at top volume on who likes what vegetable or fruit best and whether it's really appropriate for a restaurant to serve breakfast for dinner.

"I like lots of things . . . I like chicken and bread and butter and noodles with butter and apples and blueberries and yellow chicken on a stick and cucumbers with dip and carrots and hummus," reported Graham. He was old enough to have a real conversation but not yet socially aware enough to take breaths at the right time so other people could participate.

And he didn't realize how clearly his list identified him as a typical picky kid.

"But eggs and sausages *at night?*" he asked. His voice escalated into a squeal. "You've got to be kidding me," he hooted, clearly happy that his favorite meal of the day was on the menu. For the evening, bouncing between the proprietress's wide smile and Lori and Ruth's attentions and the curious glances of the few fellow diners Bootlegger's had trapped, Graham was the tiny town's celebrity.

Lori and Ruth had been introduced to Graham years earlier in an unusual way. Lori had been in the audience once while I read a story on how my husband and I had had to fight for the right to give Graham my unadulterated breast milk during his month at the neonatal intensive care unit. The nurses had wanted to give him hormone-laced milk, which was meant to replace my (copious) breast milk until Graham reached a certain weight. As a new mom, I'd been horrified that, instead of having my four-pound-something newborn grow *right*, the doctors only seemed to want him to grow *big*. In the essay, I compared him to feedlot veal, but the nurses' theory wasn't that different from how large modern poultry conglomerates fatten chickens, either. Lori, whose wife Ruth takes great care in raising their milking goats and sheep in the healthiest, most natural way, had instantly likened him to her lambs.

It wasn't odd. I never thought, *Hey, this stranger is comparing my child to a farm animal.* I just thought she understood me. And so, right then, Graham became one of Lori and Ruth's little lambs—one that was born weak and small, but somehow, through deliberate care and perhaps mother's milk, ended up making it.

As Graham had grown bigger and stronger, the couple had watched him from afar. When Lori made cheese deliveries to Seattle, she dropped off paper bags of soft, tangy Bianca—

their version of a plain goat-cheese *bouton*, often made with a combination of goat and sheep milk—for Graham, as if she wanted to make sure that, no matter how his tastes changed, he'd always like goat cheese. We passed by their farmers' market stand occasionally in Yakima, and over time, as our son aged out of all the foods we were proud of him for eating so young and into an era of pale consumables, goat cheese remained a reliable constant. So when we noticed that Graham had more readily bought into eating whole chicken parts once he'd met real chickens, we decided a trip to Lori and Ruth's place might not only teach him where his beloved Bianca comes from but also introduce him to other kinds of animals he might one day eat—cows, pigs, sheep, and ducks, to start.

Lori understood the challenge. "Meatballs," she suggested emphatically, once Graham had ordered his breakfast sausage for dinner. "I bet you could get him to eat meatballs."

The next morning was clear and cool on the bluff just outside Tieton, where the creamery, its owners, and its animals call twenty-one acres home. When we arrived, just before eight, Ruth was already buzzing around, feeding goats and watering cattle, setting ducks free from their coop, and trying to determine how many sheep had given birth the night before. It was lambing and kidding season, and for the second year in a row, Ruth was running a very busy maternity ward without a barn.

If there's one thing every farmer predictably reports, it's that farming is never predictable. Ruth and Lori are no exception. The previous February, a cantankerous ewe had decided to abandon one of her two lambs. In an effort to force the relationship, Ruth put the mother sheep, then called Number 15, into a private pen in the barn with both the loved daughter and the hated son. It was made of wooden pallets and straw, with a heat lamp to keep the babies warm tied in multiple directions from the top of the pen. It would have been the ultimate cozy nursery for bonding, if the sheep hadn't panicked and, in an attempt to get away from the baby she didn't like, piled straw up high enough to reach the lamp, setting fire to the straw, herself, the pen, and ultimately about half the barn.

"It was awful," remembers Ruth. "She was black. All her wool burned black after the fire. But that wool protected her."

In the days after the blaze, with almost all of the breeding flock still pregnant, the Babcocks struggled to scrape together enough money to replace what they'd lost. Although the ewe (since named Phoenix) survived, badly burned, they'd lost the male lamb and a crop of baby ducks and chickens, as well as plenty of expensive hay and tools, like the ear tagger they'd need for each newborn animal. Goat-and-sheep-milk cheese is a high-end farm product, but it still doesn't make farmers rich, and the Babcocks had just poured all their resources into a new milking parlor. Ruth put the small checks that flowed in from the community toward lumber and feed, and over the course of the birthing and milking season, the farm sprang back to life under the twin powers of will and necessity, with only the barn's skeleton intact.

When we got out of the car that blindingly bright morning, the first thing we saw was the bank of simple wooden kidding pens Ruth had built after the fire as emergency housing for new moms. (They still haven't rebuilt the barn.) Crude but cozy, each little stall was just big enough to house and shelter a mama goat, her young, and her feed. I tried to tell Graham that he'd had his own little stall as a baby, but he didn't see the kidding pens. He didn't see the mama goats, with their defensive, alien eyes, or their bleating babies. He didn't see the two black kids, whose mom was ill, and who, as a result, were so weak they hadn't learned to walk yet. He didn't see any correlation between himself and Minuet, the baby whose legs clearly weren't working properly. All Graham saw were the chickens beyond—lots and lots and lots of chickens. He jumped out of the car as fast as his legs would let him and half stumbled, half skipped, as wayward and tottering on his arm crutches as those uncoordinated baby goats were on their wobbly legs, toward the rainbow collection of chickens just beyond the pens.

On a farm, the first priority is keeping the animals secure. We caught Graham before he ran full bore into the electric fence that keeps the chickens safe from wandering predators and watched him watch the animals, fascinated by both their abundance—there must have been thirty birds—and their variety. But as soon as I tried to start talking about how they might taste different if they looked different, Graham spotted the cows. (Good-bye, teachable moment.) And so we wandered across the bumpy grass and sat, with Graham on my lap, on half a bale of hay that poked through my jeans, and watched the cows watch us watching them. Ruth explained to Graham how the cows come in different breeds, the same way dogs do, and how different breeds have different personalities and give different amounts of milk. Graham's eyes bulged at the size of their nursing Jersey's udder, and at the concept that, instead of coming from the store, the Babcocks' milk comes from an animal in a field a short walk from their front door. Normally, unless they make big noises from behind a fence at a zoo, he's not too keen on live animals in general (perhaps because we have a cranky dog that's never given him a reason to love pets). He's only now beginning to pet our friendly-when-indoors cat. So I was surprised that as we settled onto our perch in front of these bovine beasts, Graham didn't seem scared. He took in everything Ruth had to say, as if it were totally normal for him to hang out with cows in Seattle. As if he, like so many city dwellers in the Pacific Northwest, was developing a new-to-most-Americans sense of respect for where his food comes from.

YOU'VE GOT TO BE KIDDING

When Graham had taken in as much cow as he could, we followed Ruth to the baby chicks. He dropped to his knees and instantly asked Casey, Ruth's daughter, to help him hold one of the fluffy peeping bodies. Soon, he'd named a few—there were Yellowfluff, Snowy, and Fuzzy, to start. Just as I began to fear Graham might fully crush a baby bird in his excitement, Ruth announced it was time to milk.

The milking parlor at Tieton Farm & Creamery has come a long way. Until recently, they milked in an adapted truck— literally an old delivery truck fitted with milking equipment, which left just enough space to milk two goats or sheep at a time. In their new, more traditional parlor that had room for nine gals at once, Ruth had barely begun milking for the season, and some of the sheep were less than content to have their teats cleaned and tugged. They seemed to know that each morning, when they were milked, they were giving Ruth some of the nourishment that could have gone to their lambs and kids. (I wished there was a way to tell them that at most dairies the babies don't get much milk at all after the colostrum clears in the first ten days, but here, Ruth bucks many industrial traditions. She gives the babies their mothers' afternoon and evening milk until they're eight weeks old.) Graham giggled as Ruth struggled to arrange each ewe's head near the appropriate grain bucket as they came in, and laughed right out loud when Black Pearl, a notoriously difficult goat, went into a kicking rampage as Ruth attached the milking machine to her udder. Melissa, a deep-throated sheep named for Melissa Etheridge, gave us a good talking-to.

As the animals settled in, we grew quiet, and Graham began to nod his head to the monotonous beat of the milking machine. He was clearly enjoying himself, dancing even, as Ruth went into the less kid-friendly details of their cheese-making process, like how they always mix the day's goat and sheep milks in their cheeses, so every day's cheese tastes a little different, and how rather than relying on breeds known for producing the most milk, they go for the types of animals that produce the best, richest milk. Graham liked learning that, in the parlor, you can tell sheep from goats from behind: goat tails go up and sheep tails go down. He liked it even more that we could talk about butts here without being reprimanded. "There's a goat butt!" he shrieked, instinctively preparing for a reproving look.

"Why do you have to feed the animals so much hay?" he asked when Ruth told him how much more they like the grain in their buckets in the milking parlor than they do hay. He also wanted to know why they only have bottom teeth. Ruth explained that grain is a little bit like candy for goats, but that grass and the things they forage for on the farm are more nutritious for them. (In March, since the grass hadn't started growing yet, they were eating hay instead.) And that since they have four stomachs, goats and sheep don't have to chew things quite as well as we do before swallowing them, so one set of teeth is enough.

When all the new moms had been milked, we moved out to watch them greet their babies. It was a bleating, baaing madhouse, with animals clamoring frantically toward their moms' voices, and Graham loved the show. He made no connection between his role as a child and the lambs' and kids' roles; it was just a show. And like any show, when it ended, we left. One minute we were pretending to be dairy farmers and laughing at baby ewes; the next minute we were looping back toward Yakima on Highway 12 with a cooler full of cheese.

For the first few days after our visit, I was ready for Graham to take a completely different approach to eating meat. I thought perhaps he'd either avoid the meat he'd been eating before (mostly sausages, bacon, and chicken) or he'd dive in wholeheartedly with all meat. There were slight changes in his eating habits—Graham ate a Dick's Drive-In cheeseburger when we lied and told him the center was made of sausage, and thus hamburgers entered his lexicon of edibles—but the visit was clearly not the life changer I'd hoped for. Over the next few months, when we were eating, I tried to reconnect Graham to the farm.

"This is like the cheese Lori and Ruth make from their sheep milk," I'd proclaim over a block of Manchego (despite the lack of true taste similarity).

"I like Jarlsberg better," Graham would say flatly.

A few days later, when I complained to my friend Aran about Graham's pickiness, and his insistence that his foods not mix, she challenged me. There's a difference between teaching a kid about where food comes from and teaching him to like what you like, she argued. She wasn't sure dragging a kid somewhere to learn about cows, presuming that might help him eat a cow rather than allowing his tastes to change naturally and spontaneously, was the right approach for a parent to take.

"I mean, what's wrong with him eating simply?" she asked. "You told me yourself that you were picky as a kid."

"I don't want to cook simply," I said.

"So maybe this is about you, not Graham," Aran countered. I couldn't say she was wrong.

A Mom's Meatballs

Over the course of the weeks after our visit to the farm, I tested a litany of meatball recipes, hoping that the combined spirits of the animals Graham had visited and the sausages he so prized eating for breakfast could someday come together as an additional dinner-table option for all of us. I played with the size to which I chopped the ingredients, and how I cooked them, and of course how I served them—plain, and with tomato sauce, and with noodles. It became a sort of plague for Graham, I think. But I was determined that my sausage- and suddenly hamburger-loving kid was going to learn to eat a goddamned meatball. It became, for a time, my holy grail of motherhood.

If I could tell you a lovely family story of how eating meatballs came to be, in my mind, the postmark of a kid's move away from pickiness, I would. But I can't. I don't come from meatballs. I come from roast beef and Yorkshire pudding at holidays and, otherwise, from plain chicken and steamed broccoli forgotten in the microwave—if we weren't eating on the road. I come from a mom who *could* have cooked meatballs, if it had occurred to her. But I remember wondering, as a child, why that song about the meatball that rolled away when someone sneezed was significant, because who ate meatballs, anyway?

My husband, however, grew up with meatballs every other week. His mother's version, which relied on oats for thickening instead of the more traditional bread crumbs, is something he remembers vividly.

Eventually, starting on a night when I strategically paired a meal of meatballs with no bits of visible flavoring in them with a hungry child and one of his more food-adventuresome friends, he ate them. He *loved* them. And because they were rich with a mixture of beef, lamb, and pork; laced with fennel seed, garlic, and plenty of herbs; and lightened with pulverized oats, so did we.

YOU'VE GOT TO BE KIDDING

Use grass-fed meats, if you can find them. (These are also delicious made with ground turkey.) I added the powdered kombu, a kind of seaweed, because it's rich in the minerals normally offered by the kinds of dark, leafy greens Graham still doesn't eat, and no one notices it's there. Take it or leave it.

Serve these little kid-size meatballs warm, as they are, or serve them stirred into hot tomato sauce and draped over cooked pasta (topped, inevitably, with a flurry of Parmesan cheese).

MAKES: 70 (1½-INCH) MEATBALLS

> 2 tablespoons extra-virgin olive oil,
>   plus more for baking the meatballs
> 1 large (¾-pound) leek, white and light-green parts only,
>   rinsed thoroughly and very finely chopped
> 3 large cloves garlic, finely chopped
> 2 tablespoons finely chopped fresh parsley
> 1 tablespoon finely chopped fresh tarragon
> 1 tablespoon finely chopped fresh thyme
> 1 teaspoon fennel seeds, finely chopped
> ½ teaspoon dried oregano
> 1 cup dry red wine
> ¼ cup tomato paste
> 1 cup rolled oats
> 1 pound ground beef (approximately 15 percent fat)
> ½ pound ground lamb
> ½ pound ground pork
> 2½ teaspoons kosher salt (or to taste)
> Freshly ground black pepper, to taste
> 1 cup freshly grated Parmesan cheese (optional)
> ½ teaspoon kombu powder (optional)

» Heat a large skillet over medium-low heat. When the pan is hot, swirl in the oil, then add the leeks. Sauté for 5 minutes, or until the leeks begin to soften, then add the garlic, parsley, tarragon, thyme, fennel, and oregano. Cook for another 5 minutes, stirring occasionally, until all the ingredients are soft and beginning to brown. Stir in the wine and tomato paste, and cook for a few more minutes at a hard simmer, stirring, until the mixture doesn't come back together when you draw a spoon through it. Set the pan aside to cool for a few minutes.

» Preheat the oven to 450 degrees F. Line a rimmed baking sheet with aluminum foil, smear it with a light coat of olive oil, and set it aside.

» In the work bowl of a food processor, whirl the oats until they're chopped fine enough that the mixture looks sandy. Transfer them to a large mixing bowl and add the beef, lamb, and pork; the warm leek mixture; and the salt, pepper, Parmesan, and kombu powder. Mix thoroughly—you can use a spoon if you'd like, but I find the only way to make sure the ingredients are totally blended is to use my hands.

» Form the meat mixture into 1½-inch balls. (An overflowing 1-inch ice-cream scoop—the old-fashioned kind with the lever that boots the ice cream out when you push it—works great here.) Arrange the meatballs on the prepared baking sheet so they're not touching, and bake for 15 to 20 minutes, until they're well browned and cooked through. Serve hot.

» Note: You can use the same mixture to make larger meatballs, if you prefer. Just cook them longer—20 to 25 minutes for 2-inch meatballs, 25 to 30 minutes for 2½-inch meatballs, et cetera.

YOU'VE GOT TO BE KIDDING

APRIL

I met Jim in the first week of college, before classes had even started. I heard his voice first, low and certain. He was outside my fourth-floor dorm room, knocking on the door beside mine to say hello to a different girl. They'd been hiking the day before, and she'd broken her ankle, and along with a few other guys, he'd carried her out of the forest. She had a crush on him, and on his wild, curly blond hair, and on his inimitable kindness, so I couldn't have one myself. But I did. And by Halloween of freshman year, we were inseparable.

For twenty years, Jim has been my rock. But when he goes to sea, I often feel like I'm the one sinking. After our trip to Tieton, Jim was gone half of March, bouncing between coasts for meetings and over waves for his research in between. I had no control over when he left or where he went or whether he'd be safe wherever he was, and as a result, I felt no control over the time I had to spend on myself and my own work.

Jim's parents, who live just up the road from us and are always happy to help, often took Graham for whole chunks of weekend days, and helped me shuttle him to activities and all his various therapies. But emotionally, the person who helped me carry it all when Jim wasn't home was often Maggie, a friend I met through Graham's preschool, whose younger daughter, Hazel, will always be Graham's first real crush. Maggie always seemed to be there, listening to my gripes or helping me decide how to handle an issue with my writing. Maggie understands how I can sandwich a meeting with a book editor between "Oil change" and "New tigers arrive at the zoo!" on my calendar. She understands what it is to be equal parts mom and wife and writer, in that order. But that month, she and her husband had decided to move to San Francisco. We were devastated.

One weekend before their departure, when Jim had returned, Maggie and I arranged to take a trip together up to Whidbey Island, to the swish Inn at Langley, whose gorgeous rooms overlook Saratoga Passage, which separates Whidbey from the mainland. We'd be too early for the yearly orca-whale migration, but we'd have an evening at the inn's restaurant without any familial responsibilities. *Our last hurrah*, we called it wistfully, like lovers destined to opposite poles of the planet. And so we boarded a ferry in the car, agreed not to be in a rush for at least twenty-four hours, and checked into a giant hotel room with sweeping views of the water. We had a full hour to relax before dinner. Instantly, Maggie noticed how terrible I am at doing nothing.

"Jess, do you know what I do sometimes?" Maggie asked. "I drop the girls off at school, and then I go home and stare at the wall. Literally—I just stare. Because sometimes that's what you need to do. It's okay to need that, you know. To need to not think about your kid or anything else in your life." And without further comment, she went out on the porch and just sat, looking at the water. I sank into the couch and tried to copy her until it was time to leave for dinner.

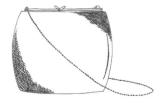

Spoon-Fed

COUPES of pink champagne in hand, we surveyed the operation at the inn's restaurant. Matt Costello, the chef, looked like a young wizard caught in the awkward stage before he begins to really age. He'd grown his graying beard out to top-button length in the years since I'd seen him last, and when we arrived, it was the beard I saw first in the kitchen beyond the hulking stone fireplace—first the beard, gliding silently around the stove below the chef's intense eyes as he put the finishing touches on his dinner preparations. Then the strange spherical glass terrariums hanging from the room's large steel chandelier. There were no strong food smells.

It was my second time dining at the Inn at Langley, where in the decade or so since he'd taken over the hotel as innkeeper and chef, The Great Costello, as I thought of him, had turned a twenty-four-seat restaurant into a mecca for diners looking to taste whatever it is he feels like plating. The inn is not where you go for tender local lamb, or for spot prawns and smelt in the spring, or for perfectly cooked artichoke custard or rose-flavored taffy. You will eat all these things, certainly. You just can't choose when or how. The dinner—one seating that starts promptly at 7:00 p.m., three or four nights a week, depending on the season—is self-selected by the kind of eater who can check all tendencies toward a type A personality at the door and hand all control, including the responsibility for having fun, to someone else for the night. It is for the eater who prefers the culinary equivalent of riding a roller coaster blindfolded to choosing predictable items from a menu.

Our calisthenics began with choosing how much wine. I brought my food-curious friend because I wanted her to taste what I consider to be an edible encapsulation of the Pacific Northwest before she moved. It was my going-away present to her. In the spirit of modesty, under the influence of the restaurant's handsome sommelier, we perused the menu's "featherweight" option, which promised, we thought hilariously, "a pared down pairing for those who still wish to enjoy the connection between food and wine." To be clear, its three pours included neither the two glasses of champagne we'd already enjoyed, nor the old-fashioned, the mojito, or the mysterious "gin and tonic experiment" listed later in the menu. As moms tethered to the habit of constantly explaining household menu items to dubious, picky kids, Maggie and I were wholly enamored with the not choosing, and the wine step jaded us. She wondered aloud what would happen if we simply refused to choose.

"I am a featherweight, though," I reminded Maggie.

"I know you are, but what am I?" she shot back. We ordered the trio.

That night, as every night, Costello helmed the coaster's controls. And from the moment we were seated, the wizard made it clear that he intended to surprise us all with magic we would never really understand.

The room grew silent as the chef breached the invisible line we all intrinsically assume lies between an open kitchen and a dining room. The Great Costello had come tableside to welcome us to our evening. Maggie began fidgeting with her empty champagne glass. Costello showed an unusual ease walking among us; more than in other restaurants, this room seemed to be the chef's, not ours. In an instant, he morphed us from customers accustomed to always being right into children welcomed along for the ride. We were so thrilled to be tall enough.

"Before I was here, I was never allowed out of the kitchen," said Costello mischievously, pacing along the communal table that seats a third of the night's customers. Our places had been assigned before we arrived—Maggie and I were at a table for two next to the fireplace, as if someone knew we needed time together—and we agreed that the chef's admission seemed akin to that of a killer just recently released. I saw newbies glancing around nervously to see whether their position in the room meant anything specific or dangerous. Sounding less lethal, Costello explained how he believes that when a chef introduces himself and his ingredients to his customers, a finer, more enjoyable dining experience follows. (He explained later that his job, as he sees it, is to bring us joy and whimsy and culinary bells and whistles, in all the right proportions. Our job, as customers, is to have some fun.)

Costello motioned to the maple boards poised next to each of our champagne glasses, which would be the stages for our first course of snacks, a foursome of edible curiosities. The night's menu looked like a series of haiku printed on a long strip of paper. The first course was a list:

eggs, potato chip and caviar
mojito stick
pinenut ravioli
an old fashioned

He explained the list matter-of-factly. The first was a duck egg with a crumble of potato chips and osetra caviar. The second was a sugarcane stick soaked in rum with a bit of mint, which we were to pick up and suck on, but not chew. The ravioli was straightforward, he said; the wrapper was edible paper. And the last was actually a lightly candied kumquat filled with a jelly made of bourbon and bitters, topped with a dehydrated cherry. We were to pick up the fruit by the small ceramic pedestal it sat on, rather than picking up the kumquat directly, because the fruit was fragile and sticky.

And just as quickly as he'd appeared, Costello was back in the kitchen, and we were left to wonder why we had teensy spoons and why the wine guy was so magnetic and modelish and whether this, the first of twelve courses, would exhaust us mentally before we had even really started dinner.

When the course landed, it defied imagination—at least, the combined imaginations of Maggie and me, two people who are essentially creative for a living. The egg was really an airy whipped duck egg served in a double-layered glass teacup over that perfect pinch of salt-and-pepper potato chips you usually have to eat with your fingers from the bottom of the bag. The servers instructed us to use the tiny silver spoon to mix the egg with the chips and osetra at the bottom, so each bite was like egg-flavored air, crunchy and poppy and salty and melting all at the same time. The mojito came in a miniature square wooden ice bucket, and we sucked on it exactly as described, but next in the lineup was the old-fashioned, not the pine-nut ravioli that the menu promised would be third. I bit my tongue to avoid asking the perky waitress whether the bites were intentionally placed in a different order than they were on the menu, because every decision seemed so important.

The ravioli—really a thin triangular smear of pine-nut butter flavored with lemon-infused olive oil and enrobed in a transparent potato-starch wrapper—exploded in my mouth, a loose peanut-butterish ooze with unmistakable pinenut flavor. The wrapper dissolved instantly. Three bites in, my mind was already reeling: Was there that much rum in the sugarcane? Could there possibly be potato-chip dust under my fingernails?

What variety of healthy things could I convince my child to eat if I learned to puree and wrap them into clear, candy-like packages? Do I even have a child?

When we tipped the little white pedestals toward our mouths as instructed, the candied kumquats melted against our teeth. Maggie and I both puckered with surprise; there really was alcohol involved. We had somehow just done an old-fashioned shot by eating a small orange, and we laughed out loud. If that had been Costello's idea of a before-dinner drink, this clearly would not be a boring night. Or a sober one.

The spoons set out for the next dish appeared to be jumbo-size Baskin-Robbins ice cream–tasting spoons, made of mother-of-pearl instead of pink plastic. The same pink, apparently, had been put into the kind of dainty glass compote bowl typically reserved for desserts, but it was in liquid form. Costello told us the fluid was lightly sweetened rhubarb juice, garnished with primrose petals; a small flotilla of white, unripe almonds; and a scoop of fresh, house-made, farm-style cheese. The server directed us to get a bit of juice and a bit of cheese and a few floating things into each spoonful, but no one told us whether the sauvignon blanc that had just been poured was meant for this course or perhaps the next. (We had already, on only the second haiku, become sheep, waiting for signals from the servers before doing or eating anything. It was gastronomical Simon Says.) But between the cucumber flavor of the immature almonds, the rhubarb juice's tartness, and the rich cheese mounded into the bowl's central indentation, we were most definitely in savory territory. The wine worked perfectly. Maggie moaned a little too loudly. But gears were changing fast, and no one was listening to us.

"Okay, here come the utensils," Maggie said, as two very typical silver spoons landed on our maple boards, which we had come to know as the utensil staging grounds. There was nothing special about these spoons, but because each utensil seemed so intrinsically connected to the dish that followed, we started a guessing game. The next course, "artichoke, Dungeness crab, chicken skin and buckwheat," would, we predicted playfully, be a bowl made of crisp chicken skin, piled with a crab and artichoke and buckwheat salad that we would eat with the regular spoon.

We were wrong, obviously. A small, deep Japanese-style ceramic pot with a matching lid landed in front of each of us. Inside, we were told, was a thin layer of the chef's version of *chawanmushi*, an egg custard flavored with artichoke, topped with the meat of two whole crab claws, a slice of artichoke heart, and a mirepoix of sorts—a mix of buckwheat, diced crisped chicken skin, and small pieces of more artichoke heart. On top, there was a single branch of *kinome*, technically the young bud of the *sansho* peppercorn plant, whose lemony leaves cause a bit of numbness on the tongue. We were to put the lids on the maple blocks as soon as we took them off the crocks, pick the individual leaves off the *kinome* branches, scatter the leaves over the dish, and dig in. Only, there were so many directions that when I finished picking the sesame seed–size leaves off their itty-bitty stem, I couldn't remember whether there was something special I was supposed to do with the stem itself, and I was momentarily paralyzed. Like we were suddenly playing a board game, and I'd forgotten all the rules. Maggie showed me how one could breezily add the stem itself to the bowl without causing any apparent harm, and, thus relieved of my panic, I dug into a dish that paired strong seafood and poultry flavors seamlessly without overwhelming the silky texture of the delicate *chawanmushi* at the bottom. It was perfect Japanese comfort food with the flavors of spring and sea and citrus (from the *kinome*). But we couldn't for the life of us figure out why we'd gotten the spoon instead of chopsticks, which seemed more appropriate for what was clearly passing as Japanese food. We flagged down the server for an emergency equipment consult.

"We don't want you to have to scrape across the bottom for the *chawanmushi*," she explained. "It's really hard to eat custard with chopsticks."

Fair point. We agreed and released her.

As the alcoholic lubrication set in, our table-setting game got more involved, and Maggie and I began getting competitive about our ideas on what form each dish would take, based on both the utensils set before us and the words on the menu.

"He can't play 'Stump the Diner' all night," she insisted. Maggie won the next haiku, "pretzel roll, caraway butter, and tiny radish." ("We will get a roll with butter," she promised. "And a cute radish on the side." She was right.) But while I began to grant Costello lenience for skipping my preferred Oxford comma on "razor clams, peas, pickled onion and camouflage," neither of us could forgive him for calling out camo as an ingredient.

"That's not a food as far as I know," said Maggie combatively, and I wondered if she might stick her tongue out at him. "He's even adding fake foods. That's *cheating*." This time we did have chopsticks, but I ventured that no one in the room had ever eaten camouflage (whatever it might turn out to be) with chopsticks. Costello was winning the game.

Camouflage turned out to be a combination of various paper-thin crackers, really ragged quarter-size flakes placed carefully over what looked like a pasta dish to obscure it completely. Made with a combination of almost fluorescent grass-green flakes, black flakes darkened with squid ink, and actual flakes of boring old dried seaweed, the colors did have a camouflage effect together. (Neat trick, but I kept thinking of flaked fish food.) Underneath, a tangle of razor clam "noodles" played with pickled onions and peas and preserved lemon, all over a thin bed of pea puree the same eerie, fresh shade I'm familiar with from my computer's Excel logo. The flavors, together, became spring and sea and citrus, again, but in a completely different way. It was a new expression of the same season, and of the same place. It was delicious. And with the chopsticks, it was very, very hard to eat. So it became a course of technique: Chase slippery razor clam and onion tangle. Eat tangle. Grab slippery pea. Roll pea in pea puree, hoping snowball effect will gather more green. Drop pea. Stretch cramping hand. Start again. Maggie got it down early. I'm not terrible with chopsticks, but this dish made me feel completely inept. Or possibly tipsy.

We breathed. The playlist—one that had to that point included Johnny Cash, Lucinda Williams, and Ryan Adams—turned to the Cure, who belted out "Just Like Heaven." *Show me, show me, show me how you do that trick*, crooned the vocalist. We wondered whether and how Costello had choreographed the music, because in front of us, served with simple silver knives, was a biscuit, bacon jam, and a perfectly toasted parsnip marshmallow, speared on a fork that looked a lot like the roasting sticks you buy for camping. We craned our brains to grok how pure parsnip flavor could take the form of a childhood treat, but there it was, sweet and bouncy and pure white inside. How many tricks did he know? We simultaneously decided not to be impressed this time.

"It's too difficult," I announced, trying to spread the marshmallow onto the dense whole wheat biscuit like butter.

"It's too sticky," agreed Maggie.

"I need a spoon," I whined, fighting the runniness of the bacon jam.

"You don't get a spoon," said Maggie, switching momentarily back into mom mode.

But we were falling in love with our dinner despite our best intentions, and, like teenagers, we were simply playing hard to get. The parsnip marshmallow was actually quite lovely, so we hypothesized how one might go about making it. Would you strain pureed parsnip, or leave the fiber in for textural contrast?

Outside, the soft rain turned to sudden pelting hail. It found its way down the big stone chimney and bounced around in the fireplace beside us, somehow appearing to only be bouncing up, not down. By my count, only a few hours after leaving Seattle, we were halfway through dinner. I felt like I was on a different planet, and it was one where I'd lost control of everything, including gravity.

Next, there were hammered silver spoons and straight-sided bowls, and no directions. And as if the chef sensed we were suddenly tired of speed and twirling, dizzy from the ups and downs, he gave us a dish that was more grounded and less precious, and left the roller coaster to someone else. The wine dandy poured an Oregon pinot noir from a winemaker called "Love & Squalor," whose literary namesake he challenged us to guess without using our phones. We were so busy raking our combined American literary knowledge—the wine was named for a 1950 J. D. Salinger short story—that we didn't even have time to guess what "black cod, sunflower, ham and lemon balm" might mean. We peered into our bowls to see delicately seared and roasted black cod atop sunchoke puree, with sunchoke chips, sunflower seeds, dehydrated prosciutto salt, purslane, lemon balm, and baby sunflower petals.

Maggie couldn't help herself. "Good COD, that's delicious," she cooed, pretending poorly that she hadn't been stewing over the pun for a full minute. It was sweet and soft and crunchy and earthy all at once, and with the lemon balm and the baby purslane, we again got sea and spring and citrus. It was the first bowl that felt like a real course rather than a bite, and even through the wine, I realized that thus far, with all these different spoons, perhaps Costello had also been intentionally, and literally, spoon-feeding us. He was giving us Whidbey Island in April in as many forms as he could reasonably fit into a single evening. Only instead of thwopping us over the head with the localness of it all, in the form of a menu that touted producers, *Portlandia*-style, or radius-driven dining, he was letting us discover the island ourselves. It was the culinary equivalent of Montessori learning: Costello "prepared the environment," then let us follow our instincts with the information he gave us.

At least, that's what it seemed like, until the "gin and tonic experiment" landed, complete with small clear spoons that looked like they might have come with a chemistry set. Maggie and I were briefly stumped by how the spoons might be applicable. In front of us were shallow glass petri dishes, each filled about halfway with an agar-set quinine tonic topped with the roe-like insides of a finger lime, ground juniper berry, and a "colony" of hydrated basil seeds that made me feel like I was about to eat something that could cause pregnancy. Across the dish, a server had balanced a plastic pipette filled with Hendrick's gin, which we were directed to squeeze onto the gelatinized tonic. We needed clear instructions: using the spoon, we were to scoop the gin and tonic—effectively a fancy Jell-O shot inspired by eleventh-grade biology class—into our mouths. It felt soft and crunchy and illicit all at once, and the basil seeds got stuck in my teeth.

Just as the wave of liquor cascaded over my shoulders, the lamb course landed. It was awfully pedestrian looking, but also perfect: two rib chops, cooked evenly pink, splayed across a smear of mustard greens, with mustard flowers, fava beans, and baby morel mushrooms. It represented the ultimate plate of spring, served with an appreciated lack of humor and pith.

Costello had received our safe word via ESP, and he responded by slowing the ride. Then, to calm us, the sommelier poured Maggie and me each a splash of a Leonetti merlot—a pairing we didn't order, and a cult wine neither of us had had the pleasure of drinking. It came almost like an apology. Like a liquid hug the staff somehow knew each of us needed if we were to walk out that night with our palates and psyches intact. It reminded me of the French woman I'd lived with for six months in Paris in college, simply because she always cooked exactly what I needed to eat on any given evening, even if I hadn't known I'd needed it.

We sat back, assuming there would be a pause before the three desserts listed. Darkness had shifted the room since our arrival. It seemed smaller. It was moodier. With less to look at outside, the room itself paid homage more obviously to Langley's reputation as an artists' town. On one wall, a foot-square sculpture featured layers of pristine white paper sheathed in some sort of wax that seemed to freeze the pages midflutter; there was a metal armadillo hiding halfway under the fireplace. I wanted to touch everything. The servers began glancing up toward those glass terrariums, now twinkling in the lights of the chandelier, which seemed to have taken on some particular artistic significance.

The significance, it turned out, was that through the small opening in the side of each glass orb, we would eat the plants inside them, dirt and all. The room murmured as Costello and the other servers casually began cutting the strings that suspended the spheres. One by one, they placed our "pre-dessert," called out on the menu as "flavors of Turkish coffee and cream," in front of us, and we all faced a dessert terrarium filled with mysterious puffy green "plants." Costello explained: on the bottom, there was a simple pastry cream, which wasn't really visible, but he assured us we'd taste it. Seeping into and obscuring it, there was "soil," which was really a streusel—the kind you might see on top of a coffee cake—that had been toasted, flavored with coffee, cardamom, fennel, and black pepper, then sifted until fine and piled on top of the pastry cream like dirt (with an appropriately muddy bottom). Sponge cake dyed an earthy green with spinach powder and torn into a ragged shape formed the "plants," which were topped with one perfectly intact apple blossom and a few leaves of sweet cicely, an herb with anise flavor. He asked us to steady the rounded bottom of the terrarium with one hand and use the other to eat, so the dish wouldn't run away with the spoon. It tasted like drinking Turkish coffee (including the dredge at the bottom) in the middle of a wet apple orchard in April. The combined pleasure of the surprise and the sweetness and silliness of eating dirt for dessert left me completely sated; it was the ultimate magic trick. I realized, with a twang of guilt, that I wanted the dinner to end right there. I wanted to get off the ride before someone got sick. But it refused to end.

The penultimate plate turned out to be an adult version of Dippin' Dots ice cream, the overpriced cups of tiny ice-cream pellets sold at ball games. "Strawberry, meringue, yogurt and rose water" appeared as a lumpy line of miniature strawberry sorbet and yogurt spheres, each made by dropping the ingredient in question into liquid nitrogen, which freezes small particles of food on contact. In the center of the line, there was a miniature yogurt panna cotta, about the size and shape of half a Ping-Pong ball, covered with what looked like a big pink contact lens—but which was really gelatinized rose water that melted in the mouth with a faint, pleasant, flowery flavor. Pink English daisies danced across the plate over a smear of crème fraîche. Miniature meringue kisses gave the dish a little crunch and some cuteness. I resisted the urge to pick each separate component up with my fingers. The whole thing tasted like what Barbie might make if she were into molecular gastronomy; it was light and fruity and all kinds of pink.

But we were tired. *Really* tired. (We wondered whether our own children feel this way every time they eat out; no wonder they get cranky.) I could sense a wave of relief swelling between Maggie and me; after eleven courses, the only thing left was "Grandma's handbag," which, as the last round in "Stump the Diner," we had pegged as a beggar's-pouch-style pastry dessert filled with some sort of chocolate explosion, perhaps like chocolate melted into the bottom of someone's purse. But Costello appeared at our table with a giant slate board. "Okay, people," he announced to the room as the board descended in front of us. "Now things get literal."

What he meant was that on the board, exactly as described, lay a real cloth handbag that might have belonged to any of our grandmothers. It was a black snap-top number with a gold chain, embroidered with curlicues and roses and daisies. Its contents spilled out haphazardly onto the slate, evidence of various habits and a long day: rumpled Kleenex, vitamin supplements, random unwrapped gummy candies, a few coins, some unlabeled airline-style liquor bottles, lipstick. The spilling made me feel like I'd done something wrong; I wondered briefly how many times this chef had dumped out his grandmother's purse as a child before the memories of pawing through my own grandma's things started surfacing.

But before I could even suspect that The Great Costello was giving our stomachs a pass in favor of an odd trip down memory lane, he began describing the handbag's eccentricities, all of which were edible, in a bored quotidian tone. (Did he tire of this game also?) The lipstick was rose taffy, like an artisanal Starburst-type candy, molded into pink lipstick form. The tissues were really sheets of flattened white cotton candy. The coins were thin mints—one a milk-chocolate variety

94

infused with clove, one dark chocolate with a thin layer of eucalyptus cream that mimicked the inside of an Andes mint in form, but not flavor. The abandoned candies were guava and jalapeño *pâtes de fruits.* The mysterious vitamins were clear plastic capsules filled with blueberry dust, which we were to ingest by opening the pill containers and dumping the sweet powder onto our tongues, Pixy Stix–style.

Maggie and I goggled at each other. "So we just bite into the lipstick?" she confirmed with her eyebrows raised. She wasn't sure she could be that silly. We each took one. (Grandma carried two of everything, of course.) The lipstick combined the daredevil kicks of eating a grasshopper and taking a shot of Jägermeister and getting into Mom's secret closet, all rolled into one squishy pink bite. The rose was too much. But it was exactly Grandma-flavored, as Maggie pointed out. The airline-bottle shooters contained a refreshing clear greenish juice made with celery, wheatgrass, cucumber, apple, and sauvignon blanc, which, after we tried all the other goodies, turned out to be the ultimate palate cleanser. The distorted reality of the handbag rattled us back into a more adult state. There was an audible sigh of relief. We were finally done. The Pineau des Charentes that had accompanied us through the desserts gave way to (real, liquid) coffee, and we stretched our backs.

"Now, if you don't mind," started the chef. *Where did he come from?* asked Maggie's eyes. We'd just confirmed that the staff had finished cleaning the kitchen. We'd been caught feeling relieved.

"You're not quite finished with the purse," Costello continued. *Panic.*

"Inside the pocket of each one, you'll find photographs of the staff," he informed us, pacing again. "You're welcome to guess who's who, or ask us about them, or ignore them entirely."

We pulled out the hidden sheath of shots—girls in frilly T-shirts, baby boys with their mothers, curls and toothless grins and '70s haircuts. As we perused them, the staff became whole characters again, instead of servers and cooks, and we were reminded, through the photographs, that in the end we are all people with bad #tbt photos enjoying an evening together. That we are all allowed to be children, experimenting and playing and having fun, even if it means being spoon-fed occasionally. Maybe what I liked about eating there, I thought, was that I could never predict what might come next.

Parsnip Marshmallows

If Matt Costello turns parsnip marshmallows into a trick, I've turned them into a reality—a marshmallow that tastes like parsnips, which is an odd savory pleasure. Many rounds of testing before the recipe you see below, I started with the directions for "How to Make Fluffy Marshmallows," from TheKitchn.com.

MAKES: ABOUT 3 DOZEN MARSHMALLOWS
SPECIAL EQUIPMENT: FINE-MESH STRAINER, CANDY
THERMOMETER, AND 8-BY-8-INCH BAKING PAN

  1 pound parsnips (about 4 medium),
     peeled and cut into ½-inch-thick rounds
  1½ cups cold water, divided
  2 (¼-ounce) packages unflavored gelatin
  1 tablespoon canola oil, divided
  1½ cups granulated sugar
  1 cup light corn syrup
  1 teaspoon kosher salt
  1 teaspoon pure vanilla extract
  1½ cups confectioners' sugar
  ½ cup cornstarch

» In a small saucepan, combine the parsnips with 1¼ cups of the water. Bring the liquid to a boil, reduce the heat to low, and simmer the parsnips, covered, until they're completely soft, about 15 minutes. Using an immersion blender, whirl the parsnips with the water until they're completely smooth. (You can also transfer the parsnips and water to a blender or food processor and blend them that way.) Pass the mixture through a fine-mesh strainer. Transfer ½ cup of the strained parsnip puree to a small bowl to cool, and reserve the rest.

» Put the remaining ¼ cup cold water in the work bowl of a stand mixer fitted with the whip attachment. Sprinkle the gelatin on top of the water, stir until it looks like thick applesauce, then stir in the ½ cup cooled parsnip puree. Set the mixture aside.

» Grease the baking pan with about half the canola oil, then use a paper towel to wipe the pan out carefully so that all its inside surfaces are covered with a very thin layer of oil.

» In a medium saucepan, stir 1 cup of the reserved parsnip puree (it will probably be almost all of the remaining parsnip) together with the granulated sugar, corn syrup, salt, and vanilla until blended. Cover the pan, place it over medium-high heat, and cook for 3 to 4 minutes, until the mixture is translucent and syrupy. Uncover the pan, scrape down its sides, clip a candy thermometer onto the side of the pan, and continue to cook until the mixture measures 240 degrees F, approximately 7 to 8 minutes. Once the mixture reaches this temperature, immediately remove the pan from the heat.

» Turn the stand mixer on low speed and, while it's running, slowly pour the parsnip syrup down the side of the bowl into the gelatin mixture. Once you have added all the syrup, increase the speed to high. (At this point, the mixture will be a yellow-tinged liquid.) Continue to whip until the mixture becomes very thick, creamy white, and is only lukewarm (as opposed to hot), approximately 10 minutes.

» Rapidly transfer the marshmallow mixture to the greased pan, scraping as much of it off the whisk and sides of the bowl as possible. (The marshmallow will begin to set up as soon as the mixer stops.) Working quickly, use the remaining oil to grease your fingertips, and gently pat the marshmallow into a roughly even layer. Set the pan aside at room temperature, uncovered, for the marshmallows to firm up, at least 6 hours. (At this point, you can save the marshmallows overnight, covered with plastic wrap.)

» When the marshmallows are firm in the center, cut them: first, in a small bowl, blend together the confectioners' sugar and cornstarch. Dust the top side of the marshmallow patty with about 2 tablespoons of the mixture. Dust a large cutting board with the mixture as well, loosen the edges of the marshmallow patty with a small, flexible knife or an offset spatula, then invert the marshmallow pan onto the board, tapping it gently to release the marshmallow patty from the pan. (You may need to use the knife or spatula to convince the marshmallows to pop out.) Dust the fresh side of marshmallow with another 2 tablespoons of the sugar mixture, using your hands to pat sugar into any sticky parts you see.

» Using a large, sharp knife, cut the marshmallows into about 36 squares. (It helps if you rinse the knife in hot water between cuts.) To prevent sticking, dust all the cut sides of each marshmallow with a little of the sugar mixture, using your hands to pat it into any uneven crevices.

» Store the well-dusted marshmallows in an airtight container at room temperature. (They really taste best the day you cut and dust them.) Eat plain, or melt into hot chocolate.

MAY

The last day of seventh grade, I broke my right collarbone. I'd been weaving my new-to-me Nishiki mountain bike between a series of wooden posts along the path that lines the Boise River, near Boise State University. I stopped weaving and looked back for a friend over my right shoulder, taking one hand off the bike. When I turned to the front, my right hand simply missed the handlebar, and my arm dove straight into the ground, with my full weight on top of it. I heard the snap. Instead of taking me straight to the hospital, where a doctor would inevitably tell me to do nothing, my parents gave me a shot of Grand Marnier and sent me to bed. I was insulted that every decision they made about my care seemed to be predicated on the idea that whatever was wrong with me was probably imagined. (Ditto for the lupus diagnosis: they shrugged over the phone, and told me to take more naps.) But more than anything, after my crash, I was embarrassed. I hadn't been able to handle my new bike. When I did see a doctor, he told me to do nothing, as my parents had predicted, and slowly, over the course of a sad summer, it healed.

Since that first bone break, there's been an ache in my right shoulder before any big storm. It's not exactly painful—twenty-five years give a body enough time to heal—but I still feel the change in atmospheric pressure before a big rain. It's actually quite convenient when we're camping.

As the spring progressed, there weren't many storms. We had an unusually beautiful April. But in my bones, in the same way, I felt the electricity of impending change. I was thrilled by the sense of possibility the trip to Langley had given me. Like I could do something new, and not quite have control. Graham was in a good place, positively in love with his kindergarten teacher and starting to walk independently in short, barely balanced bursts between the small tables at school.

Since I'd signed up for the Gourmet Century, the hundred-kilometer group ride near Portland, and Jim and I had planned a cycling trip in British Columbia's wine country, I started riding a bike again. I knew the training I needed to do would be difficult, and I wasn't really looking forward to it. I was a stringy kid who, despite eye surgery and glasses, still saw double. Before I broke my collarbone, I'd been trying tennis, which the rest of the family loved. It went okay as long as I went for the correct ball. In a family of ski racers, I learned to steer well clear of the gates, because for the longest time, I saw two gates at each turn instead of one. During puberty my vision improved, but I was still pretty uncoordinated, and always exhausted. I flailed in gymnastics, fired up by the floor-routine music but too inflexible for the rest. I limped through college crew, not because I couldn't see well by then, but because it was really hard. As an adult, marathons and triathlons never interested me. I was generally active, but not really fit—not by my own fast family's standards, anyway. Not in a family where going to the gym a couple times a week and being able to run three miles without stopping was completely unremarkable. Although learning I had lupus had justified my having always felt tired and weak, it didn't make me any more athletic.

When Graham was diagnosed with cerebral palsy, I felt like I could identify in my own way with his lack of coordination. But watching my child work so hard every day, oblivious to how much slower he was than his classmates, I started to appreciate how much he *could* do. And how much he bragged about his abilities, actual ability notwithstanding. I wondered whether it was time to stop thinking of myself as the perpetual weakling and just get on the bike.

On Parking-Lot Barbecue

WHEN my sister, Allison, lived in Seattle during college, and Graham was in his first summer, we often took him with us to Harbor City Restaurant in Seattle's International District, to have dim sum for breakfast. There was one server there, an ancient woman, who took to the habit of lifting baby Graham out of his child carrier and taking him away when we arrived. Allison and I would stare at each other, each wondering how a babbling baby had learned to flirt in Cantonese, as he disappeared into the kitchen. We presumed that, at her age, the waitress had either had or been in contact with enough children to remember not to drop him, but in any case, we weren't sure we had a choice. We drank jasmine tea awkwardly until someone remembered we'd come to eat, not share his cheeks. When he started eating solid food, he tried everything there. But when he became a toddler, he stopped.

As I began to give up the idea that I could decide what he'd eat, and as I internalized just how much Jim would be gone in June and July, I started assuming that I'd do any food-based adventures on my own. And what I wanted, as the spring weather reminded me of those first months when Graham had been out of the NICU and roaming Seattle's dim sum kitchens, was dim sum.

Richmond, British Columbia, is where the Pacific Northwest goes to eat really good Asian food. Theories on why Richmond's dim sum, for example, is better than Seattle's or even Vancouver's are varied: Some say that, when swathes of Hongkongers relocated across the Pacific, they brought their talented private chefs with them, and those chefs eventually opened restaurants. Some say it's because Richmond has a large population looking to eat authentic food from China or Hong Kong or Japan or Malaysia, and that the population is wealthy enough to eat out often. Still others point to Vancouver's adventuresome eating habits, and to the nearby city's diverse population. Whether the four hundred or so Asian restaurants that call Richmond home bloomed out of accidental cultural habit—if enough people from Elsewhereistan move to Fargo, then Fargo will naturally develop a clutch of Elswhereistani restaurants—or out of a population's intentional attempt to re-create their homeland on a different continent, is uncertain. But today, its food scene is reputed to be refined, varied, and extensive. And today, when you ask a certain set of Seattleites where they go for good dim sum or Chinese barbecue in Seattle, they'll point north. Which is why, on a sixty-degree day in May, I decided to drive across the border to eat in Richmond for the first time.

When I pulled into the handicapped spot to drop Graham off at school that morning and opened the back door for him, he just sat there, stunned.

"What's wrong?" I asked.

"You're going to Canada for lunch," he confirmed, looking confused. "Why do you have to go to Canada? There's a lot of food in Seattle."

"Because they have one of my favorite foods there," I explained. "And I might also get to taste some new things." Using Graham-friendly vocabulary, I listed off some of the items I'd researched: waffles that have round holes instead of square ones, really yummy soups, and a different kind of barbecued meat.

"Oh," he said, apparently satisfied. Then: "Do they speak English in Canada?"

"In some places," I said, helping him down the step stool he uses to get into and out of the car.

After I'd helped him navigate the coded door and the lockers and the bathroom and his backpack and coat and signing his name—while other kids had begun using lowercase letters, he still wrote in fat, lopsided capitals—he barged into the kindergarten classroom.

"My mom is going to Canada for lunch," he announced. "For . . . What was it, Mom?" he whispered, forgetting the name of the food.

"Dim sum," I explained with a smile. The teacher looked at me like I had three heads. "I'm going with a friend to eat Asian food."

But before I gassed up our aging Subaru, equipped with an appetite and this book's hungry editor, Regan Huff, I didn't stop to ascertain what I might expect from Richmond physically. I'd polled my Chinese Canadian friends about their favorite soups, hoping for a life-changing rendition of my favorite hot-and-sour, and combed the Internet for must-try dishes. I'd heard about Taiwanese beef noodle soup and bubble waffles, but at no point did anyone tell me that Richmond is, to the newcomer's eye, made up uniquely of malls—strip malls, outdoor malls, and enclosed indoor malls, for variety, but almost all malls. Smeared onto the flat farmland that once sprawled between the spiky Coast Mountains and the Pacific, the city's downtown has emerged in the last half century as a web of squat boxes and parking lots, a paved paradise between two of the province's most beautiful natural assets. It probably

ON PARKING-LOT BARBECUE

wasn't what inspired Joni Mitchell's 1970 song "Big Yellow Taxi," but it might as well have been.

Only, there were no taxis to speak of. Driving down No. 3 Road, the city's main retail drag, we waited at stoplights underneath the raised tracks of SkyTrain, metro Vancouver's transit system, next to very, very nice vehicles. In a city of about two hundred thousand residents, the large majority of whom emigrated from Asia (mainly Hong Kong, China, and Taiwan) relatively recently, status symbols—cars chief among them—seemed to carry heavy value. This mass economic exodus of the last quarter of the twentieth century translated visibly, on that day at least, as a procession of Maseratis, Bentleys, and Mercedes-Benzes.

Richmond is not a walking city. Richmond is like Los Angeles, where to get from point A to point B, you usually get in a vehicle. Richmond is where Porsche goes on parade. And since the most reputed restaurants are in or attached to malls, on second stories next to nail salons or immigration consultancies, if you want to eat interesting Asian food all day, you'll inevitably end up in a mall, parking next to cars worth three times yours in value, at the very least. From the moment we'd parked, deciding to walk for the day because we'd been in the car so long, I wondered whether all the food might have the faint taste of gasoline. Maybe Graham had been right to doubt my lunch plans.

The city's landscape thus surveyed, Regan and I found our way first to Empire Seafood Restaurant, where we would be meeting my friend Eagranie (pronounced "ee-GRAW-nee," although my mother is forever calling her "Negroni"). It seemed clear that we should start with dim sum, the midmorning meal the Cantonese originated centuries ago, when teahouses along the Silk Road learned that tea was good for digestion and began offering small snacks as accompaniments. (In Cantonese, *dim sum* is often used interchangeably with *yum cha*, which is the tradition of drinking tea.) Today, dim sum (which translates to "touch the heart") is a regular habit in Hong Kong of nibbling on shrimp dumplings and steamed barbecue pork buns and baked egg tarts over tea and the morning's newspaper. Eagranie, a Vancouver native whose parents emigrated from Hong Kong in the 1970s, had agreed to be our culinary usher. We arrived at Empire Seafood first.

I've had dim sum in jeans many times, but in Richmond, carrying the scuffed nylon Marc by Marc Jacobs purse I scored on eBay rather than a Chanel bag like the person behind me, I felt underdressed and, by extension, incompetent. Just over a hundred miles from home, I felt more foreign than I ever did in Japan (or anywhere else, for that matter). It was as if suddenly, I couldn't trust my taste buds to remember what dim sum should taste like since I was the only person besides Regan at Empire who couldn't speak Mandarin or Cantonese. I developed a case of nervous giggling.

When she arrived, Eagranie laughed with me—not just because I clearly felt less comfortable than my usual self, but because in a room I embarrassingly but honestly admitted I'd perceived as wholly Chinese, she realized she saw faces I didn't. She saw Cantonese origin in certain noses. She saw Hong Kong, too: newer arrivals in pearls and twinsets, and longtime immigrants, like her family, looking more westernized. And on our table set for three, she saw a deep cultural history familiar to her but to which Regan and I were completely oblivious.

I usually decide what I want to eat based on what sounds good to me on a menu, but here, I didn't have taste memories associated with many of the dishes. Sure, I've had *xiao long bao*, soup dumplings served in the bamboo baskets that give them their name, and shrimp and pork dumplings. I know I love egg tarts (who wouldn't?), congee, and turnip cake. But steamed

ON PARKING-LOT BARBECUE

rice rolls with mushrooms? Couldn't even guess which mushrooms were in them. Steamed silky chicken with fish maw? No
idea. Phoenix claws in pepper broth? Never had it, actually. We
pawed our way through the menu slowly, each choosing something familiar and something we'd never had.

Then we started, naturally, with tea. When I go to dim
sum in Seattle, tea is simple: I pour it. Other people pour it.
Someone asks that the pot be refilled. I am totally oblivious
to the concept of doing tea the correct way. In Richmond, as
in much of Asia, the ritual carries much deeper significance.
When tea arrives, the host always pours for others before pouring for himself. Traditionally, each pouree recognizes the generosity of the pourer and thanks them by tapping a finger or
two gently on the table (two fingers if the pouree is married,
one if single)—a custom instigated by the guards of an ancient
emperor. As the story goes, when the emperor took his guards
with him to have tea incognito, to hear what his subjects said
about him when they gossiped anonymously at teahouses, the
guards felt they should still honor their ruler in secret. Because
bowing to the emperor publicly would give away his disguise,
the guards tapped their fingers to show their respect. Today,
it's still done as a sign of both thanks and respect—though, as
Eagranie pointed out, more between guests at a table than between guests and servers. In general, unlike in American-style
restaurants, where the waiter often participates in the table's
conversation and gets thanked for delivering things, a dim
sum server is not often included in the conversation. Rather
than asking a server to refill tea, one sets the empty pot's lid
askew atop the pot. It's a different system; whereas Americans
tend to rely on conversation to indicate wants and needs, the
dim sum experience depends more on physical convention.

But even tradition is malleable. In Richmond, the typical
dim sum setup, where servers push trolleys filled with bamboo

baskets between tables while diners pluck their favorite dishes off the trays, has given way to a more refined experience, where one orders dim sum by marking menu items on a paper order form. Again, although the servers deliver the food, there is little to no interaction between servers and diners. At first, I was sure this had more to do with my lack of Cantonese and Mandarin, but Eagranie, who speaks Cantonese, assured me it was business as usual. As we made our way through more-delicate versions of many of the dim sum specialties I've come to call favorites—delicate shrimp *siu mai*, and a tender *hum bao* made by stuffing fluffy buns with a ginger-studded, pulled-pork filling much less sweet than those I'd had before—I began to realize that the social process of eating out was totally different just two hours from my home.

The difference, suggested Eagranie, might pertain more to political history than to food. Her parents moved to Canada after the Cultural Revolution of the late 1960s and early '70s, as protests and brutality became widespread across China and Hong Kong. Unlike the initial waves of Chinese migrants—gold miners and railroad laborers who came in the mid-1850s and early 1880s, respectively, in search of work and economic opportunity—many families' entrances after Canada's immigration policies loosened in the early 1970s were spurred as much by a desire to leave China as an interest in finding better lives in Canada. In the decades leading up to the 1997 Chinese takeover, many wealthy Hong Kong residents—entire communities that intentionally uprooted themselves together to claim a sort of financial manifest destiny in Canada—left the capitalist-ruled island, fearing that the Communist takeover might squelch their prosperity (or their freedom to spend how they wanted). "For people living in Hong Kong under British rule, the idea of Hong Kong being under Chinese rule had far too many unknowns, and not the kind that many were interested in finding out about," Eagranie said.

From an outsider's perspective, the entire room at Empire Seafood, with their pearls and handbags and keys to nice cars, seemed not to be showing off, but to be celebrating a still-relevant generational success story. Everything from the pillow-like, sound-absorbing ceiling tiles and well-dressed servers to the pretty, branded take-out bags and perfectly presented dim sum dishes made Empire seem like Richmond's way of championing a good group decision. It felt like an edible, experiential Chinese translation of the adage "have your cake and eat it, too."

But because I'm an outsider, Vancouver dim sum didn't taste like childhood or freedom or financial emancipation to me. It tasted like rich, delicate duck wrapped in shredded Chinese pastry that reminded me of Greek *kataifi* desserts. It tasted like spicy beef shank served without either the tripe or the spice implicated in the dish's Chinese name. (I presumed the server changed the order for us, but Eagranie said it's quite atypical for a dim sum spot to customize a dish for Western palates.) It tasted clean and plain, because at Empire, one does not adorn one's dim sum with Chinese mustard or chili sauce or soy the way one might in Seattle. (The dishes should be properly seasoned when they hit the table, said Eagranie.) It left Regan and me wondering two things: first, how we'd fit our three additional planned meals into the remains of the day; and second, whether, despite the relatively low actual cost, all the food in Richmond is tailored to people who are, well, rich.

Our next stop was Rainbow Cafe, a small stall famous for bubble waffles, at the edge of an indoor mall's food court. The cheery, talkative proprietress told us she'd been there for eighteen years, pouring her crepe-like batter over and over into the bastardized waffle maker that churns out her specialty: treats that look like a cross between a Belgian waffle and an oversize, edible version of the Bubble Wrap frequently used for shipping. We watched her pour the batter for our order out of a well-used plastic beer pitcher, the way I'd done recently at a chain motel's breakfast buffet. She slammed the metal device closed, then flipped it over violently—a motion we guessed helps the waffles' bubbles gain their signature steamy, hollow centers. Together, we waited with this little cherub of a woman. She smiled while I counted out my Canadian change with the awkwardness of a child new to holding money, then handed over the waffle. It was folded into a cone like a crepe built to go. We ate it by breaking off bubble after crisp bubble, feeling the hot, sweet dough melt against our tongues.

After a stop at a Japanese candy store and a bubble-tea shop—the tea was so sweet that we wondered whether border agents ever check travelers' glucose levels as they return back to the States—we settled in for a late lunch at Chef Hung. Also nestled into an indoor mall, the restaurant is famous for its Taiwanese beef noodle soup, which pairs thick, slurpable, spaetzle-like noodles with beef whose taste, in an inoffensive but very specific way, reminded me of the burgers my brother and I ordered from Burger King as children.

Regan and I stared around the empty room. The noodles, shaped like long strands of Trident gum, were different from anything either of us had had, all eggy and bouncy between the teeth, and delicious. The tripe in Regan's bowl had the cut's hallmark barnyard flavor, but was appropriately soft and tender. The soup itself was only lightly spiced, and perfectly clean tasting, like the stock was clarified multiple times during its cooking process. We were both thrilled with our orders, but ultimately had a hard time trusting the food to be authentic and enjoyable when we were eating in a mall.

ON PARKING-LOT BARBECUE

Our final stop, before braving Vancouver's evening traffic, was HK B.B.Q. Master, a cave-like one-stop shop for Hong Kong–style barbecue nestled into the corner of a parking garage underneath a massive grocery store on No. 3 Road. At this point, there was no reason we should have been capable of hunger, but as Regan and I queued up to order barbecue pork ribs and roasted pork—the service model conjured up *Seinfeld*'s Soup Nazi—we started salivating. Only, the tables were all either dirty or full, and we had spent a grand total of four hours wandering Richmond's now-rainy roads on foot (an irony that wasn't lost on us), so we weren't ready to wait for a seat. We took heavily burdened containers back to the Subaru, and between snacks on our Japanese candies, elbows bumping, we ate again, mostly in silence, savoring the sweetness of the ribs and the deeply flavorful shoulder meat. I turned the car on to ward off the damp chill, at which point my taillights signaled to all hopeful grocery shoppers that I might soon be backing out of my parking space. There was disgruntled beeping when, one after another, people realized we were staying put.

Somehow—despite the cramped quarters and the full belly and the messy napkins and the beeping—it was this Richmond meal, sticky-sweet and overfilling, that I found most satisfying. And I realized, with a surge of fresh cultural guilt, that perhaps I liked it most because I was eating it where, compared to all the other places I'd eaten that day, I simply felt most comfortable. Because I was so used to chatting with servers and entering restaurants from lovely neighborhood roads and eating without parking-lot views that eating out of a box in my front seat actually felt good, even if the lot smelled a little like gasoline.

Hot-and-Sour Soup with Ginger and Seaweed

This is not traditional Chinese hot-and-sour soup, by any stretch of the imagination. It's more a reflection of my mental state when I got home from Richmond. The next day, feeling simultaneously overwhelmed by our tasting spree and disappointed I hadn't gotten to taste more, I made this stew-like, vegetable-heavy version, which relies on a few more traditionally Japanese ingredients—shiitake mushrooms, slivered ginger, and seaweed—because I have them in my kitchen more frequently than more typically Chinese ingredients, such as bamboo shoots and wood ear mushrooms. It's also much chunkier than traditional hot-and-sour, so the vegetables give bigger bursts of flavor.

This version doesn't have the thickness that some traditionally Chinese places achieve with a good dose of cornstarch, because I don't tend to prefer soups with that thicker consistency. But by all means, if you want something thicker, stir in an additional tablespoon or two of cornstarch.

I also use wakame seaweed—the kind you're probably used to finding at the bottom of a bowl of miso soup—first, because I've always felt hot-and-sour soup deserved something green, and second, because it's good for you. Eat your seaweed.

MAKES: 4 TO 6 SERVINGS

> 1 cup (¾ ounce) dried shiitake mushrooms
> ¼ cup cornstarch
> 3 tablespoons cold water
> 2 tablespoons soy sauce
> 3 teaspoons toasted sesame oil, divided
> 1 teaspoon sugar

1 tablespoon canola oil

3 medium carrots (about ½ pound), peeled (or not) and cut into ¼-inch batons about 1 inch long

8 cups (2 quarts) chicken or vegetable broth

8 ounces firm tofu, cut into ¼-inch batons about 1 inch long

Thumb-size knob ginger, slivered (about 2 tablespoons once cut)

2 teaspoons dried wakame seaweed or similar dried sea-weed (optional)

⅓ cup plus 1 tablespoon white vinegar, plus more to taste

¾ teaspoon freshly ground white pepper, plus more to taste

1 large egg, beaten

» First, soak the mushrooms: Place the shiitake in a medium bowl. Add boiling water to cover, then let the mushrooms re-hydrate for about 30 minutes. (You may need to use something like a can of soup to weight the mushrooms and keep them submerged.) When the mushrooms are soft, trim off the tough stems and cut them into ¼-inch-thick strips.

» Meanwhile, in a small bowl, blend together the cornstarch, water, soy sauce, 2 teaspoons of the sesame oil, and the sugar with a fork until combined, and set it aside.

» Heat a wok or large soup pot over medium heat. When it's hot, add the canola oil and the remaining teaspoon of sesame oil, then the carrots. Cook for about 3 minutes, stirring, then add the mushrooms. Sauté for 3 or 4 minutes more, until the carrots are soft. Add the broth, then the tofu, ginger, and seaweed, and bring to a simmer. Stir the cornstarch mixture, add it to the soup, and bring the soup back to a simmer, stirring occasionally, until it looks a bit thicker and almost glossy, then let it simmer for about 5 more minutes.

» Remove the pan from the heat, stir in the vinegar and pepper, and taste for seasoning—you'll probably want a bit more vinegar and/or pepper, so tinker with it until it's seasoned to your liking. Stir the mixture around in a circle once or twice, creating a very gentle whirlpool. Stop stirring and drizzle the egg into the moving liquid—it will cook upon contact into long, thin strings. Let the soup sit for a minute so the egg can finish cooking, then serve it hot.

JUNE

In the late spring, around the time he turned six, Graham grew officially too big for me to carry comfortably—years and pounds past when most kids get too big to carry—and we realized we either needed to shift our family's focus to making him more comfortable walking on two feet, or invest in a good wheelchair. Although our doctors pointed out that the chair might give Graham a certain new form of independence when it came to mobility, it seemed to us to be a step backward. Toward the end of kindergarten, even though he was still on legs he couldn't fully straighten, he'd started walking more and more—first across the classroom, then, during the last month of school, to the bathroom down the hall. We thought the more independent he could become at six, on his own two legs, the better. And the more fun we'd all have together.

And so we decided to go through with an unconventional surgery on both of Graham's legs, under the knife of a specialist in New Jersey, just outside New York City. The goal was to change his body's musculature so his legs and ankles were no longer permanently (and sometimes painfully) incapable of straightening past about 120 degrees. So he could someday, theoretically, stand still on his own two feet, instead of always needing to hold on to something for balance. We scheduled a date in early August.

It was clear to me, as it would be to any parent, that Graham's health superseded any personal goal not to leave the

Pacific Northwest that year. But with the firm decision to go through with the surgery—a maverick operation that Graham's Seattle doctors found too unproven to actually recommend over the more traditional approach performed at our local children's hospital—came an anxiety that floated to the surface whenever I was with Graham. I was scared of the operation itself, to be sure. (We'd be putting our full trust in a stranger whose talents we'd read about mostly on Facebook.) But more than anything, I was nervous about how our increasingly spunky, independent child would take to having what burgeoning abilities he had stripped away, even temporarily. I didn't know if he could withstand the effort of recovering emotionally. And really, I didn't know if I could, either.

Plus, there was The Here List. At first, there had been an enticing calm to not traveling too far away. There was a certain satisfaction to exploring the *here*. But thus far, few of our combined adventures had really ended the way I'd hoped. I'd learned to hate truffles. I sucked at razor clamming. And Graham still wasn't eating much differently. The Here List started feeling like a misguided bucket list, which is a concept that has always given me hives anyway. And I couldn't square trying to make Graham a "better" eater when my bigger responsibility was clearly to focus on his physical development.

I looked at the time frame on my Gantt chart that started after the scheduled surgery date, which was just after the Gourmet Century:

> *Pick at 2007 huckleberry spot (August–September)*
> *Find someone who hunts mushrooms (September–October)*
> *Go hunting with Josh (October–November)*
> CASINO FOOD? *(When is Jim gone this fall?)*

JUNE

I felt overwhelmed by the goals I'd set out for myself, and frustrated that The Here List both failed to offer very many things I could do with Graham and lacked adventures I could undertake by myself. I suddenly felt like I needed time off from mothering—time alone to think through our decisions and prepare myself for the surgery. The list began to feel less authentic, because it ignored the simple fact that other things in life had suddenly become much more important. I no longer wanted to carry Graham up a mountain to pick huckleberries. Not because I couldn't always carry Graham, but because when I was with him, I couldn't always carry the worry.

So when the time came to explore the Okanagan Valley with just Jim, in the part of British Columbia that borders Eastern Washington, I was excited. It sounded much more fun to ride our bicycles up and down the desert hills of a wine country that we didn't know as well as we've come to know Washington's than it had been to ride on Seattle's busy bike paths. And, because we'd been perseverating on the surgery decision so intensely, it sounded nice to go somewhere without being reminded at every turn, and with every crowd-attracting fall on the pavement, that Graham had big challenges ahead.

The Other Western Wine Country

THE Okanagan wine industry, in British Columbia's Okanagan Valley, didn't just sprout out of the ground in the 1990s. Centuries ago, fur traders kept alcohol ledgers as part of their meeting notes; the region has a well-documented history of enjoying libations. The first attempt to grow grapes in the Okanagan dates to the late 1850s, but it wasn't until the 1930s that the first commercial winery opened. For most of the twentieth century, growers planted both *Vitis labrusca* varietals, or table grapes, and *V. vinifera* varietals, or wine grapes, but there was no real regulation that determined which could be bottled for booze. The result was largely unreliable, frequently unidentifiable jug wine with a few exceptional examples from dependable *vinifera* producers. In the '70s, growers determined thirty-three *vinifera* varietals that grow well in the region (read: a huge variety). In 1988, the General Agreement on Tariffs and Trade (GATT) put pressure on Canadian wineries to grow better wine. After that, across British Columbia, *labrusca* vines were torn out as the province committed to higher-quality vineyards. In 1990, British Columbia established its Vintners Quality Alliance (VQA), a body that sets and monitors the standards for the province's wine. In the decades since, yearly sales of BC VQA wine have boomed, and a large majority of that wine comes from the Okanagan Valley.

But "boom" is relative: winemakers have increased plantings across British Columbia from about two thousand acres in the early '90s to more than ten thousand acres about twenty-five years later. By contrast, the state of California has roughly half a million fruit-bearing acres, depending on who's counting, and France grows about two million acres. According to one winemaker I met, there's a blending tank at Australia's massive Yellow Tail winery (you know, the yellow-labeled bottle with the kangaroo?) that would fit all the wine produced in the Okanagan in one year at one time. So the Okanagan is booming, as a wine region, but it's still not big.

The Okanagan Valley is a full tank of gas from Seattle, northeast as the crow flies. Technically, the valley winds north to south down the province and dribbles into Washington State, where its glacially formed geography continues through the American border town of Oroville and toward the sleepy Washington farm burbs of Tonasket and Orondo. In the United States, the valley is fruit country, known for a few brief weeks in June for Orondo Ruby cherries, and in the late summer, at least locally, for rodeo. As Jim and I drove up the American section of the valley—spelled "Okanogan" in Washington, curiously—we passed rodeo fund-raisers but no sign of wine, save the odd smattering of FedEx and UPS shops that sprouted up immediately next to the border to afford Americans traveling in the Canadian Okanagan a means of shipping wine home legally. Crossing the border felt a little treasonous, like tasting Canada's new agricultural pride might be akin to exposing Washington's dirty little secret—that our fruit state's fruit country doesn't just end at the forty-ninth parallel. We wondered how different the wine was north of the border.

JUNE

Months earlier, at a wine festival in Sun Peaks, British Columbia, I'd listened to a talk by Ingo Grady, the cheerful, bearish director of wine education at Mission Hill Family Estate, one of the oldest and most established Okanagan wineries, about the state of Okanagan wine. "Let's face it," he'd laughed. "In the world wine consciousness, the Okanagan is somewhere between obscure and emerging." He poked fun of the Americans in the crowd for thinking that all the Okanagan has to offer is ice wine.

In Sun Peaks, I'd brought this up with Michael Bartier, a confident, experienced BC winemaker who claims to have made wine for Jesus but still looks quite fit, like a sun-kissed professional cyclist. Bartier just wanted to tell me a story about hockey.

In 1955, the Penticton Vees, an Okanagan community hockey team that was made up mostly of farmers, bootstrapped their way to the Canadian national championship with little more than sharp skates and determination, surprising everyone but themselves. They won, and wound up representing Canada at that year's Ice Hockey World Championships—and soundly beating the country's then archrival in hockey, the USSR, 5 to 0 in the final. It was a riotous upset, after which the players basically went back to their farms and resumed life as usual, knowing that they were the world's best.

I retold the story to Jim as we settled into our room at the Waterfront Beach Resort in Osoyoos. The way Bartier sees it, I explained, his generation of Okanagan winemakers are those Okanagan hockey players of the '50s: None of them have centuries-long winemaking lineage, the way many European winemakers do. They're not government subsidized. In many cases, like Bartier, they've started from scratch with little to no land of their own. But like the hockey players, they're farmers at heart—intrepid stewards of the land, willing to do what it takes to grow the best fruit possible. (In that sense, said Bartier, you could perhaps just call them "Canadians.") And they're trying to make the best wine in the world.

I recounted how, as Bartier told the story, he waved a blindingly white arm cast around—he had flayed open the flesh of his palm the preceding evening on a broken wineglass—lamenting that some winemakers in the long, arid valley probably wouldn't make the proverbial team. Historically, Bartier said, while some Okanagan winemakers have been self-reliant, others have been uncertain pioneers. Some have been helicopter parents, hovering over their grapes with one eye on the vines and one eye on the rest of the globe. As a result, the valley is smattered with foreign accents; part of the initial start-up cost of a winery here for decades seemed to include hiring a foreign winemaker—the Russian coach, in hockey terms—as a means of ensuring success. He seemed to be telling me that while the Okanagan Valley has the capability of morphing from fruit country into a well-defined wine-producing region, it didn't, at that moment, have the gumption to do it without some type of foreign aid.

And so the next day, we set off to find out, from a taste standpoint, whether the Okanagan is essentially an extension of the Washington wine regions two hundred miles south, or more of a transplanting of traditionally European winemaking practices, or a third thing totally new to us. Since we were also theoretically training for a one-hundred-kilometer road-biking ride that would require more persistence than I, for one, had ever mustered, we'd agreed to spend the weekend on two wheels instead of four, tolerance willing.

Ingo Grady was right, as far as I know; few wine lovers in the United States know the Okanagan for much besides ice wine. I'd certainly perceived the region as small and sleepy, perhaps compared to the bustling wine-tasting trails in Woodinville or Walla Walla, Washington. But on our first day of tasting, pedaling north out of Osoyoos on dusty Highway 3A, we saw that the loveliest wine country we'd never heard of was brimming with visitors, traipsing their way toward the region's two-hundred-ish wineries with the same gusto and expertise one normally associates with a place like Napa. We'd planned a mix of larger and smaller wineries, some of which are known for being a little rebellious, and some of which are just plain big. And as we headed north next to a line of traffic, I was thankful that our first day would take us around a winding twenty-five-mile circle on mostly small back roads.

"Wait, we're only a few hours north of Walla Walla," said Jim, digesting the geography. "How could the wine be that different here?"

Conscious that talking too much in the first few miles is frequently my downfall on any bike ride, and not wanting to waste my energy for the pedaling and drinking to come, I started spouting some of Grady's other facts to Jim in short little barks as we rounded the top end of Osoyoos Lake. We wound up in a game of telephone.

"The Syrah here is supposed to taste like cinnamon," I remembered. "But that's farther north. More cabs and hot-weather grapes down here."

"Okay," said Jim from twenty yards ahead. "But Jess, I think you'll be fine. We won't need a cab, we're not going that far." He consulted a regional map while pedaling, and I hated him a little for being so coordinated. "Wait, which part are we in now?"

"Osoyoos," I said. I'd explained to him earlier how British Columbia has five distinctly identified wine-growing regions, now (after many changes) called Geographical Indications (GIs), similar to American Viticultural Areas (AVAs) or France's Appellation d'Origine Contrôlée (AOC) system. The

Okanagan is just one of those GIs—as terrible an acronym as could be concocted in the culinary world—but within the Okanagan, there are subregions that vary enormously. So to the casual observer, the Okanagan appears to encapsulate the growing climates of California, Oregon, and Washington—or all of France, if you want to think of it in European terms—in an area about half the size of Switzerland.

"Southern Switzerland," I reminded him. "Minus the cheese."

"Ahh," he sighed. We turned off the main road and rumbled across a series of rough metal cattle guards, heading toward our first set of wineries on Black Sage Road.

"Grady said the first chard planting, they won the IWSC, in '94," I lobbed up to Jim. "That's a big deal."

"What? Who?" asked Jim. I mumble most days, but it's especially bad on a bike when I'm breathing hard.

"Mission Hill," I responded, realizing I also hadn't given him any context.

"There's a mission here?" Jim asked, confused, pointing at the dilapidated old barn we were passing. He was as annoyed with my inarticulateness on a bike here in the Okanagan as he is at home.

"No, Mission *Hill*," I half yelled.

"This is Mission Hill?" Jim yelled, now incredulous, turning fully around on his bike. We could see rich blue sky through the barn's broken windows. I motioned for him to stop.

"No," I panted, reaching for water. "Sorry. Starting over. Mission Hill is up north. They were probably the first real-deal winery here. Their first big planting of chardonnay won the Avery Trophy. In the '90s, I think. For 'Best Chardonnay.'"

"Better than, like, all the chardonnays in France?" asked Jim, eyebrows raised. He moved his hand around in the air to his right, as if indicating that France took up the entire globe to the east of where our tires rested on the road. "Or best in Canada?"

"In the world," I confirmed. "It's the big prize at the International Wine and Spirits Competition in London. That's when people started noticing this place. They're, like, the Canadian Chateau Saint Michelle," I said, comparing Mission Hill to one of Washington's biggest wineries, realizing that I was myself perhaps one of the reasons the Okanagan always defines itself in terms of other places.

"Huh," he grunted. He's generally unimpressed by awards, but it was clear he hadn't put Canadian wine on a world map any more than I had. "Why are you telling me that now?"

"Just so you don't snub all the Chardonnay before you taste it," I teased.

"Touché," he replied grumpily.

"And so you'll slow the fuck down for a second," I added.

Our first few wineries were an exercise in learning to cycle and taste wine in tandem in the Okanagan Valley, which is so named, like most valleys, because the land rises up quite steeply on each side. Here's a primer: When you arrive at a winery, it's better to drink water before tasting the wine, and to drink Gatorade and eat a snack after you leave, when you don't have any immediately impending need of your palate, because wine and Gatorade or wine and PowerBars are bad bedfellows. It's also smart to wait until your breathing is slow and steady to taste wine, because if, as is the case at Burrowing Owl Estate Winery, the entrance to a tasting room requires significant uphill effort, the physiological requirements of extreme physical exertion make any wine consumed right afterward taste (to me) like sheet metal. It took me three wineries to learn these lessons, before I eventually sat down to a delicious, licorice-tinged glass of viognier at Black Hills Estate Winery, whose tasting room is mercifully built at the same elevation as the road on which it sits. The sauvignon blanc and Sémillon blend we tasted there next—which is made in the Bordeaux style but drinks like a Loire Valley white, an employee told us—was bracingly crisp.

"Rhône varietals do really well down in this part of the valley," he said. I loved it, but I couldn't tell if it tasted like a Loire or like wine made from Loire Valley grapes grown by a Canadian. It seemed a little brighter than most Loire whites, but I didn't trust myself enough to say so.

By the time we reached Michael Bartier's new place, a low-slung concrete building about twelve miles from our home base, I'd had enough cycling to stop talking but not enough wine to start again. Bartier, who for years had made wine for other vintners, had recently opened his own winery and tasting room on the west-facing slopes of Osoyoos, where his own first vines had been planted years earlier in anticipation of the day he'd have his own label. Learning that we were going to be cycling there, he'd volunteered to give us a tour as a rest stop, even though there wouldn't be wines to taste yet. When we arrived, he took a break from doling out instructions to the workmen to talk bikes with Jim, absently rubbing his newly repaired hand. Back and forth they went, dishing the way only two guys with instant cycling man-crushes can about brakes and shifting components and carbon fiber. After what I thought might be a polite period of time, I interrupted.

"So Michael," I started innocently, tilting my head side-ways toward the next room. "What goes in the tanks?" In the winemaking room beside us, what looked like two super-size wooden wine barrels took up the space usually occupied by metal crushing vats. "You making wine yet? Or you got a min-iature ice rink in there for the Penticton Vees?" I asked. I liked that I felt I could spar with Bartier a little, even though I didn't really know him. The Okanagan is a friendly kind of place.

Bartier turned very serious very quickly. Bikes were fun; hockey and wine were business. He began explaining how a lot of Okanagan vintners are embracing their grapes' distinctive identities, and that they're also pushing away from some long-standing old-world winemaking practices. For his fruit, he said, that means focusing his efforts on leaving the winemaking to the grapes themselves. Okanagan fruit is generally lively, clean, and bright, he explained. Oaking the wines the same way winemakers might in, say, France, is what he called a brainless choice. "Why spend the money to cover a natural flavor so unique to this area?" he asked. Instead, he ages his wine in a combination of oak and concrete tanks. The oak ones I'd pointed to hold four thousand liters of wine, compared to the 225 liters of a typical oak aging barrel, so the oak only imparts a fraction of its hallmark flavors in the aging process—to clean, bright, lively effect. He is essentially retooling a very traditional part of the winemaking process so that the character of the grapes is more apparent in the final product. We got back on our bikes invigorated with the sense that we'd discovered a winemaker who doesn't follow the rules.

Descending one side of the valley, pumping across the highway that snakes up its center, and climbing up the other slope, we found our next stop, Fairview Cellars. From the moment we met him, it was clear owner Bill Eggert is proud of what his grapes can do. ("It's red, and it's good," he said of his own cabernet franc as we tasted through his reds. "Certainly better than a kick in the ass with a frozen mukluk.") Eggert is a burly, jovial Canadian with obvious Irish roots, unabashed in his opinion that wines should taste good before they taste like specific other things. He wanted our reactions, not our tasting notes.

"Our strength in the Okanagan is in our diversity," reported Eggert, kicking into educational mode, insisting that because each rise and fall of the land produces a grape with a different flavor, it's hard to generalize the Okanagan. He started by championing the region's ability to grow completely different wines in a relatively small physical area by holding up a bottle of that cabernet franc. "In a lot of places, cab franc just doesn't ripen," he explained. "Here in the Okanagan, it does, and because the region is so dry—most of the valley doesn't even have a water table—the grape doesn't face the rot problems it suffers from in Bordeaux." In the Okanagan, he said, cab franc grapes stay on the vine much longer, which means the grape moves beyond its traditional vegetal flavors and you wind up with a wine that has, say, chocolate, cherry, coffee, and brandy flavors (all flavors typically reserved for other, more robust varietals). But all of his bottles might taste different from the wine across the valley because of how different the terroir is there. And in any case, he just wanted to know whether we liked it. We nodded vigorously.

Then, seeing that we were listening, Eggert got political. In the Okanagan, *terroir* is a loaded term, he said; whether British Columbia's wine appellations, or GIs (such as "Okanagan Valley") should be further segmented into smaller subappellations ("sub-GIs") and labeled as such is a topic of hot debate. At the moment, one subregion, the Golden Mile Bench on the west side of Osoyoos Lake, where Eggert's land lies, was the only approved sub-GI. Eggert said that knowing a wine is from the Golden Mile Bench allows drinkers to connect the bottle to the place, which strengthens the Okanagan's identity because it captures its diversity. We realized, as we cruised back down the hill, that we'd hit on something: that while all the Okanagan winemakers we'd met by that point seemed very proud of their region, they didn't all seem to agree on what their region should look like from the outside. And that perhaps one of the reasons we don't hear as much about Okanagan wine in the

States is because the Okanagan's wine industry simply hasn't been around long enough to come to a labeling consensus.

Next, we found the long, steep road to Tinhorn Creek Vineyards, one of the South Okanagan's biggest wineries, whose high, princely perch over the verdant valley just south of Oliver, BC, gives it an air of exaggerated grandiosity. It's the kind of place that seems designed to attract tourists, complete with an amphitheater for concerts and a glass-walled, Mediterranean-inspired restaurant called Miradoro, which is known for pizza and pasta. *This is the kind of place that wants the whole world at its doorstep*, I thought.

Only, I wasn't sure I could get there. The road seemed heinously steep, and only wide enough to barely accommodate a car, much less a car and a cyclist who couldn't seem to keep her bike going straight.

"I'm sorry, Jess, but if I go any more slowly I'll fall over," said Jim. After years of competitive rowing, running, and cycling, Jim has what our friend Alex calls "legacy fitness," the impressive aerobic base former collegiate athletes get to rely on for the rest of their lives to do things they may not actually be training for. He blamed it on the gearing of his fancy road bike. "Is it okay if I just meet you at the top?"

I pursed my lips together. I was so slow. I'd been training, for Chrissake. When we'd gone to California for Graham's therapy, I'd even taken a SoulCycle class, where a woman dominating the front row had apparently just given birth. "Laura Marshall just had TWINS!" the instructor had hollered, to which the class responded with a series of impressed whoops. Her efforts had not helped me feel less exhausted or more fit. The instructor's voice thundered on forever. Maybe we should consider being more like Ms. New Mother, she had suggested—stronger, even, since the rest of us hadn't just given birth. "Raise. Your. Standards," the waifish leader had repeated to the beat of hammering pedals. I think I was supposed to be impressed, or possibly motivated. I just wanted to buy Laura Marshall a doughnut. But still, I'd finished the class.

Until that point, Jim had been patient with me, somehow seeming to coast uphill next to me while I huffed and puffed. Now he was telling me it wasn't physically possible for him to go as slowly as I needed to go. As he danced off toward the top, I began mentally berating myself for being unable to keep even a normal slow pace, heaving myself quite ungracefully off and on my bike as necessary to stand with it in the roadside brush when cars needed to pass. Slowly, I limped my way to the top. The only legacy I was accumulating was a series of scratches on my left leg.

"It's so *mainstream*," I whined to Jim in the big parking lot at the top. "Look at the buses. It'll be bland noodles and bad Caesar salad."

"Jess," he said calmly. "We need to eat. This was our plan. And you need to be in the shade, you're getting sunburned."

I hadn't realized how hungry I was. The food was delicious; I downed three pieces of shattery cornmeal-crusted fried chicken. The wines were unremarkable, but I didn't care. Now that I was fueled and rested (and definitely more than pink), the road on the hill's opposite flank seemed absurdly steep even going down, and I forgave myself for being so exhausted on the way up. I was feeling positive about tasting a bit more wine and still surviving our remaining eight miles.

Our next stop was at Road 13 Vineyards, whose tasting room sits along the same high ridge in a literal stone castle whose turrets look like the tip of a chess set's rook. The winery is named for the road it sits on—starting near the town of Oliver, the roads are named in ascending numerical order, from Road 1 to Road 22 if you're driving north to south—and branded with an antique tractor and the tagline "It's all about the dirt." That, the tasting-room employee told us with an air of embarrassed secrecy, is a load of marketing bullshit. Only, it's not. It simply can't be. The Syrah we tasted, cofermented with about 10 percent Viognier, had a distinct sesame-oil aroma on the nose—a smell I was very familiar with from cooking but had never thought to associate with any wine in any way. In my mouth, there was none of the peppery business that typically turns me off with the varietal. It tasted smoky and meaty, almost bloody. It was Syrah, but a Syrah unlike any I'd tasted, and I said so. The guy, clearly a new employee, went to great lengths to explain the winemaker's references to French Syrah style, and described in minute detail the medium toast of the French oak that held the wine for eighteen months. At no point did he mention that perhaps the Syrah was good— and different from anything I'd had—because it was made in the Okanagan, where the landscape (and maybe the dirt) is nothing like France's or Australia's, or even Washington's. It was almost like he was ashamed to admit the grapes were grown in the Okanagan. The hockey-player confidence Bartier had talked about was completely missing.

Over the course of the afternoon, we visited three more wineries, two of which also seemed embarrassed to call themselves Okanagan at heart. "Here, we do a play on northern Italian whites and Tuscan reds," announced a man at LaStella Wines, in Osoyoos, when we sat down on the terra-cotta-tiled porch of its Tuscan-style villa-slash-tasting room. The winery does a solid job with grapes that, obviously, have also been grown in Italy for many years—pinot grigio, Sangiovese, merlot, chardonnay. (The same owners have a separate French label that sells what they call "French-style wines made with Okanagan grapes.") Strangely, neither winery makes what it calls Okanagan wine—or calls it out as such, the way, in my experience, Washington winemakers typically talk about

Washington wine when they talk about their own products.
We wondered whether the practice of refusing to take credit for
what, in the end, is simply good wine from grapes grown well
might be the young industry's stubborn self-consciousness,
or whether it may be that the newer winemakers are simply
Canadian, and too polite for their own good.

Around five, I waved the proverbial white flag, and we
wound our way back to the hotel, where we drank yet more
wine out of plastic cups in the lakeside hot tub, then took
the time to jot down the bottles we wanted to pick up at the
provincial liquor store the next day. We spent the evening discussing our excursion, finally feeling our cumulative consumption tally take effect. We didn't debate whether the wine was
good—we had certainly loved almost everything we'd tasted,
once we'd figured out when not to drink Gatorade—but rather
whether the mix of prideful and embarrassed winemakers was
typical of the region, and whether and how that might change
in the years to come. Just before eight the next morning, one
of us nursing sore legs, we drove north with the bikes on the
car to the Naramata Bench area, where the west-facing slopes
south of the town of Kelowna gaze over long, narrow Okanagan Lake, which keeps the region's weather quite moderate
(and ultimately suitable for grape growing).

While the previous day's ride had been a series of climbs up
and out of one main valley road near Oliver, BC, we planned
to ride the second day along the undulating hills of windy
Naramata Road, along the lake's eastern shore, with only two
main stops: first at Bench 1775, a winery under the guidance of
a spunky, no-nonsense woman I'd met in Sun Peaks, and then
at Bella Sparkling Wines, whose pink bubbly I'd also fallen
hard for at the wine festival.

Val Tait welcomed us to Bench 1775 with a plate of salami
and a spot in the shade on her tasting room's sprawling porch.

(In the dry Okanagan, where the pavement shimmers with heat in the summer, most wineries take their shade situation seriously.) Val is an opinionated person who stands strong in her boots, so I assumed, correctly, that she'd have thoughts on why so many of the folks we'd met the day before seemed shy about their own (very good) wines.

"So many Okanagan winemakers are apologetic about their wines, not because they're bad, but because the winemakers themselves are just not that confident yet," she reasoned. Val, who is unabashedly Canadian, said she's found a distinct Okanagan identity in her wine because she's learned to pick grapes at exactly the right time, based on what she knows about *her* grapes on *her* land on the Naramata Bench, not based on what she knows about what different varietals do in other parts of the world. "We want to respect French winemaking style, sure, but ultimately, the terroir of this place comes first, eh?" The Okanagan's success, she seemed to intimate, will depend on winemakers' ability to commit to their own region.

Perhaps no small winemaker has committed to showcasing the Okanagan more than Jay Drysdale, a roundish, cheerful homesteader who makes sparkling wine exclusively. His winery, Bella, makes every bottle using chardonnay grapes grown in different places all across the valley. As such, he has a unique ability to demonstrate how much climate and soil variations within the Okanagan GI can change the grapes, and in turn the bubbly he produces.

"It's the enological equivalent of cooking the same steak from six cows fed six different kinds of feed," I told Jim as we perused the menu in the tasting room—really more of a little box tacked onto the side of Drysdale's house and painted a deep Pepto-Bismol pink inside, where one can taste *blanc de blancs* from the valley's east or west side near the town of Oliver, from up north near Kamloops, or from Keremeos, one valley to the west of Oliver. As it turned out, his sparkling chardonnay from Oliver's east side was leaner than that from the west, and both had far less minerality than the sparkling chardonnay from Kamloops, farther north, made from grapes grown on a hillside literally between a concrete plant and a limestone quarry. But, notably, every sparkling wine we tasted had an intense acidity that you'd never find in Champagne or prosecco or cava; tasting through his different wines highlighted how they compare to sparkling wines from other places.

"So why are you doing it this way?" I asked Drysdale. "Why not blend all the grapes together? Or why not make some still wines with some of the grapes?"

He smiled gently, and took on what seemed to be the same patient voice he'd been using to call the pigs he'd been feeding when we'd arrived. I was clearly not the first to ask.

"More than anything, I want to find BC's voice," said Drysdale. "I want people to say, 'Oh my God, *this* is BC.' I want us to stop chasing Champagne and cava." And, like Bill Eggert an hour's drive down the valley, he explained how he thinks being allowed to label bottles with sub-GIs that differentiate, say, his Oliver bubbly from his Kamloops bubbly will help teach wine drinkers how different Canadian wines taste when they're sourced from different areas.

"Personally, I don't think subappellations would dilute the Okanagan wine industry as a whole, but make it stronger," he said, telling us in undertones how some of the bigger wineries feel threatened by possible labeling changes. He also pointed out that sub-GI labeling may help give Canadian winemakers a louder voice on the world stage.

"Does that mean putting sub-GIs on a label will allow me to buy your bubbly in Seattle?" I asked bluntly.

"Don't bet on it," Drysdale laughed.

On the final stretch back to the car, we decided that whether the Okanagan becomes popular worldwide boils down to whether Americans (and other powerful buyers) will ever be ready to make the Okanagan itself a brand name, the way, say, France's Champagne region has been for centuries. We fantasized how visitors like ourselves might slowly contribute word-of-mouth popularity to the region.

"But seriously, can you imagine a Seattleite spending fifty dollars for a bottle of Bella sparkling wine, like she might for a bottle of Veuve Clicquot?" Jim asked.

I couldn't. Not at first.

But maybe she would, I mused, drinking a last glass of rosé in my bike shorts at the Vanilla Pod, an elegant restaurant attached to the tasting room at Poplar Grove Winery. Maybe one day a Veuve Clicquot lover would come to the Okanagan and visit the big guns such as Tinhorn Creek in a tour bus, or experience wineries like the elegant Mission Hill, with its sprawling hilltop estate (complete with a Marc Chagall tapestry and cultish three-digit bottles), and pause to look at the sculptures, like we had on our third (bike-free) day there. And on the next visit, she'd branch out. And maybe she would catch the same crush we did when we met small, quirky, kind vintners like Bartier and Eggert, and feel the same pull from the deep green of the Okanagan's cultivated valleys and the cracking grays of its highest cliffs, and understand that because no place looks quite like the Okanagan, no place can make wine that's quite the same either—not quite as bright, or quite as clean, or quite as different, north to south. And maybe each of those times, she'd cross the border back into the United States, like we did, with a couple of cases of wine to save in her nonexistent wine cellar, to share with friends.

And suppose one day she remembered, like we did, having had the unavoidable and enchanting sense that she was watching something become the world's best in real time. Maybe then she'd ask Whole Foods to import Bella specifically, and by then, Jay Drysdale would be exporting. Maybe then, we thought, she'd buy it, and start spending more on Okanagan wine, because she'd be betting on the enological equivalent of a hockey team that had already won a few times. And then—and perhaps only then—the Okanagan winemakers who didn't seem to believe in the land they stood on might graduate out of their pubescent self-consciousness and onto the podium as a real team.

Corn-Fried Chicken

It's a rare body that can absorb foods like pizza and fried chicken in the middle of a long bicycle ride, but happily my husband and I both carry the eating-while-exercising gene. It is Jim alone, though, who can seriously drink wine and ride at the same time. Partway through our bike ride-cum-wine-tasting adventure, we stopped at Miradoro, the restaurant at Tinhorn Creek Vineyards, off Road 7, near Oliver, British Columbia. It's a magnificently modern cantilevered box whose windows give diners a stunning view of the southern part of the Okanagan wine region. It might have been the preceding effort or the wine-tasting flight, but the fried chicken I ordered there—juicy and tender on the inside, crisp and corn-flavored on the outside, and crumbling all over, with just the perfect hit of heat—seemed, at the time, a gift from heaven. This is my version, whose crunch and flavor I like just as much when I'm not drunk and exhausted.

I fry at home by filling a heavy, high-sided pot about halfway with oil (which is three quarts of oil, for my pan) so that the chicken is fully submerged as it cooks. I like this approach for a few reasons: first, it makes less of a mess than if I use my cast-iron skillet; second, avoiding turning my chicken means this rather delicate crust stays intact and prettier; third, it allows me to fry in more oil, which means the oil temperature changes less when I add the chicken. Obviously, if you have a deep fryer, use it here.

I cook my chicken in three batches. The first is still warm when the last is finished, but for good measure, you could let the cooked chicken pieces hang out in a two-hundred-degree oven while you finish the rest.

I prefer the variation a whole chicken provides, but you could just as easily use ten of the same cut here—or purchase two each of legs, thighs, wings, and bone-in breasts, which I usually cut in half before frying.

Note: You can let the oil cool after you use it, strain it, and reuse it four or five times before discarding it, as long as it never gets so hot it smokes.

MAKES: 10 PIECES FRIED CHICKEN
SPECIAL EQUIPMENT: INSTANT-READ THERMOMETER
OR DIGITAL DEEP FRYER

1 (4- to 5-pound) whole chicken,
   wing tips removed, cut into 10 pieces
1 quart buttermilk
Canola oil, for frying
4 cups corn flour
   (you want fine corn flour or masa harina,
   not cornstarch or cornmeal), divided
4 tablespoons all-purpose flour, divided
   (omit it for gluten-free chicken)
4 teaspoons kosher salt, divided
2 teaspoons *piment d'espelette*,
   or 1 teaspoon cayenne pepper (or to taste)
1 teaspoon garlic powder
2 large eggs
1 cup whole milk

» In a large bowl, combine the chicken pieces and buttermilk, turning the pieces to coat them evenly. Cover the bowl with plastic wrap and refrigerate for at least 8 hours, or up to 24 hours.

» About 2 hours before you're ready to eat, remove the chicken from the fridge and transfer the pieces to a wire rack set over a baking sheet, using your hands to wipe most of the buttermilk off the chicken as you transfer each piece. Let the chicken sit over the rack for about an hour, to come to room temperature and let any excess buttermilk drip off. (Frying room-temperature chicken helps prevent the oil temperature from dropping radically when you begin frying.)

» When the chicken is no longer chilled, fill a large, heavy pot with about 3 inches of canola oil and place it on the stove over medium-high heat. Attach a thermometer to the pan so the tip is in the center of the oil and it's easy to read without touching the pan, then heat the oil to 330 degrees F, adjusting the burner's temperature as needed. (If you have a deep fryer, heat it to 330 degrees F.)

» While the oil heats, prepare the chicken coatings: First, arrange 3 medium bowls on a clean work surface. In the first, whisk together 2 cups of the corn flour, 2 tablespoons of the all-purpose flour, 2 teaspoons of the salt, the *piment d'espelette*, and the garlic powder. In the second bowl, whisk together the eggs and the milk. In the third bowl, blend the remaining 2 cups corn flour, 2 tablespoons all-purpose flour, and 2 teaspoons salt.

» Next, coat the chicken: Line a baking sheet with parchment paper. Working with one piece of chicken at a time, dip the meat first into the flour mixture, taking care to coat all sides. Shake off any excess flour, then dunk the chicken into the egg and milk mixture, again submerging it on all sides. Let any excess milk drip back into the bowl, then dredge the chicken in the cornmeal, again taking care to get it into the cracks and crevices. Give it a little shake and transfer the chicken to the prepared sheet. Repeat with the remaining pieces, rubbing your fingertips clean in one of the dry mixtures as necessary to remove built-up batter. (The chunks that form will actually make the chicken coating stick better.)

» When the oil has come up to 330 degrees F, carefully add the dark-meat pieces (legs and thighs) to the oil. Fry for 6 to

8 minutes, depending on the size of your chicken, or until the chicken's crust is deep golden brown and the meat is cooked through. (You can cut into a leg if you're nervous about the temperature inside, or carefully check, using a meat thermometer, that the temperature has come up to 165 degrees F in the meat next to the bone.) Transfer the chicken to a paper towel-lined plate to drain, and let the oil come back up to 330 degrees. Repeat with the breast pieces, which will take 5 or 6 minutes, and then the wings, which usually take 7 to 9 minutes.

» Eat the chicken hot, holding the pieces with paper towels.

JULY

My younger brother, Josh—"Uncle Josh" to Graham, which means that to his great consternation we now call him "UJ" for short, while my sister, Allison, gets the comparatively adorable "Auntie Al"—is a kind and reasonable person. Over the years, in a cross between devotion to our father's family's hunting history and a preoccupation with eating interesting things, he's become a hunter.

"It's really quite straightforward," he once joked. "You're just looking for the second-stupidest animal in the forest."

But in earnest, he approaches hunting in what seems to me to be a very rational way; he's appropriately wary of ammunition and happy to come home empty-handed. Hunting, Josh likes to say, is really just an expensive armed walk in the woods, unless it becomes something more. It's hard and only occasionally lucky. As I was making The Here List, I told him I wanted to go.

When we met in Portland in July, the warm night before the Gourmet Century, during which he planned to take Graham to a movie and generally spoil him rotten, we'd discussed a hunting trip together. Fresh off my trip to the Okanagan, I was up for another big adventure and feeling positive about my athletic prowess.

"What's up in October?" he asked. "Do you want to go into the woods with guns and hope a deer runs into us?" He addressed the advantages of hunting for something like elk or deer, which he'd done often enough, versus going for ducks or grouse, which he'd done fewer times, but which was typically a more successful way for beginners to get into hunting. And he reminded me that it would require a *lot* of walking.

"Sure," I agreed. "As long as you're safe and by extension can teach me to be safe. I don't care what flavor animal. I just want to try killing my own dinner." I'd done some research on Washington deer country and what I'd need to do to prepare.

"Just to be clear: I'm not very good at hunting," he said. "You should probably take a hunter's ed course."

"Wear orange, don't shoot people?" I quipped uneasily, both of us keenly aware of how frequently gun violence plagues America.

We set a date in October. I assumed that, by then, Graham would have recovered from the August surgery.

The Gourmet Century

I'M told some who register for the Gourmet Century, the hundred-kilometer ride Jim and I had signed up to do together, are intimidated by the variety and quantity of food the organizers expect one to consume along the way. The preevent e-mail, which I received a week or so before the ride, read like an ode to all of *Portlandia*, and it didn't even include the dinner plan:

> At mile 19, you will have the chance to refill water and snack on a selection of small morning offerings.
>
> Lunch will take place in the field at Sun Gold Farm, 33 miles into the ride. Rick Gencarelli of Lardo and Grassa will be putting a delectable spin on his farm-fresh approach to lunch. After collecting their meals riders will have the opportunity to relax while they enjoy their picnic-style lunch before taking on the next leg of the ride.
>
> 56 miles in, riders will find themselves at Chris King's barn for an afternoon serving of delicious charcuterie and small sandwiches by Chris Carriker of

23 Hoyt. Salt and Straw ice cream will be on location to cool everyone off, and there will be a barista to give you a quick caffeine fix.

A wave of satisfaction flooded over me when I read that e-mail. *Finally, someone understands how I want to exercise.* I imagined cyclists stopping halfway up hills, extracting chocolate from pockets—locally made chocolate, naturally—and discussing bean origin. I might forget about how much my ass hurt from my bike seat, I thought, if I had chocolate to think about instead.

As the spring rolled along, I'd begun riding my bicycle two and three days a week in preparation for the event—something I'd never done before. My siblings had both ridden bikes across the country, my father had been a longtime runner, and my mother had run multiple marathons after turning fifty. I'd had no interest, and even less confidence, in that kind of effort. But none of the things my fast family participated in—things I'd always felt guilty for not doing—had been paired with a day-long eating schedule, complete with mobile espresso machines and fancy Portland chefs. For the first time, I felt fully engaged in an athletic endeavor of my own accord, and devoted to a training schedule. I was *interested.*

I rode at my own leisurely pace, but still, I was moving, often next to Tracy, my friend and unofficial cycling coach. Though she was a competitive cyclist, she treated me with the same care and gentleness she showed Graham. I became Tracy's Padawan, following her around to learn things I thought I already knew: how to yell at offensive vehicle drivers, how to open a packet of energy gel blocks while pedaling, how to relieve numb or cramping hands. When I bought the wrong new bike seat (which, I learned the hard way, is referred to only and always as a "saddle"), she sent me to a special physical therapist who specializes in bike fitting and injuries. (It's not a place that makes a person who's now broken both collarbones falling off a bicycle feel comfortable about deciding to ride *more*.) I bought a very white, very hard saddle—an experience that required a very awkward young man to propose that perhaps I needed a different seat because my pelvis and its associated parts had widened since childbirth—and wrapped my handlebars in white tape to match, because that's what you're supposed to do. Tracy encouraged me the whole time.

When June hit, I'd survived a twenty-eight-mile ride (with! hills!) behind Tracy. Then I rode thirty-seven miles with my husband in the rain without screaming at him or myself. I'd scorched my face riding through the Okanagan Valley, but I'd survived it and felt more or less okay afterward—a milestone for me, because often, getting sunburned causes a lupus flare that leaves me stiff and sore for weeks. And once I'd passed what I considered the halfway point—the point at which I'd ridden half the distance required on Gourmet Century day, July 18—I started talking a big game. I told everyone who would listen that I was training for a Big Ride, and that it was going to be Type 2 Fun, at least, and that my goal was to finish without crying. (If you're not aware of the classifications, they're easy: Type 1 Fun applies to an activity that is fun both in reality and retrospect. Type 2 Fun may require suffering in the moment, but is enjoyable when you look back on it. Type 3 Fun—the type that, truth be told, I associate with most outdoor recreation—describes an experience that is neither fun in the present nor when you think about in the the past. It may be interesting to other people, though.)

"Wait," said a friend when I told her about it. "I don't get it. Are you eating, or riding, or both?"

Her confusion was understandable; when I explained the Gourmet Century, I usually got flustered and hopscotched between my reservations about the riding and my excitement about the eating. I'd been training for both, focusing on eating while training to make sure my body was up for the combination. But stomaching anything halfway through a workout has never been my issue; surviving the workout itself is another story. I started attending a spinning class more regularly. The instructor, Tommy, always seemed to look at me when, after big pretend hills on our stationary bikes, he'd bellow, "This is *not* a *working recovery period*. This is still the *work* part."

My friend Sarah and I hyphenated a hilly forty-miler with brunch and lemon-drop shots (her idea) at mile twenty-five. Two weeks before the event, I rode fifty-two miles, complete with stops for bacon-cheddar-avocado breakfast sandwiches and copious quantities of caffeine. I'd learned that I could keep a decent tempo on a decent hill if I sang Anna Kendrick's "Cups" song from *Pitch Perfect* a gazillion times in a row under my breath. (Try it. It's annoying, but it works.) I followed a friend up Norway Hill, across Lake Washington from Seattle, humming that song under my breath.

But in that same e-mail, one thing got me: instead of sixty-two miles, which is the technical equivalent of a hundred kilometers (and the distance I'd trained for), the e-mail reminded riders that we'd be going sixty-eight miles. And in the days before the event, the six-mile differential started to intimidate me. Suddenly I couldn't imagine my legs lasting that long. How could I garner the strength for sixty-eight, when fifty-two felt like a thousand million miles already?

I started planning the little things. Having lupus means that, in a pinch, my adrenal glands don't work quite the same as other people's. (That's why I went into adrenal shock during childbirth.) Hard exercise can also cause my immune system to go into overdrive, so I usually feel pretty terrible after large efforts, and I wanted to minimize the post-ride joint pain and fatigue, insomuch as one can with a sixty-eight-mile ride plan. I figured I should be able to recognize the physical signs of serious trouble if I worked too hard. Still, the rational part of my brain knew that deciding to do the Gourmet Century might just be stupid. I planned out my medication dosage properly, so I was giving my system the support I needed (in the form of an oral steroid) without actually doping.

The day before the ride, Graham and I picked up my husband from his most recent work trip to Alaska. We drove to Portland and checked into the Ace Hotel, a bespoke spot downtown. The next morning, their breakfast nook—really a converted guest room on the creaky second floor—supplied me with enough smoked trout and buttered rye to last me until our real burrito breakfast at Chris King's factory. Chris King, the talented machinist who makes very shiny, very expensive bicycle components whose true mechanical advantages I very much fail to understand, is the brains behind the Gourmet Century. Each year for this ride, his factory essentially puts on a big breakfast, waits a few hours, then throws a giant dinner party.

Shortly after dawn, Graham ambled off to explore Portland with my brother. I worried about them both—about whether Graham would have the stamina to survive the science-museum-movie-ice-cream-dinner-party-playdate day that Josh had planned, and whether Josh would have the stamina to talk about *Star Wars* for twelve hours. I waved to both of them as they drove off, hoping my brother had figured out how to use the car seat properly.

When we wheeled our bikes up to the factory under already-relentless sun, one of Stumptown Coffee's mobile espresso machines was revved and purring, with one of Portland's lithe, flannel-clad-hipster types beginning to sweat at its helm. Lines already snaked out of the espresso zone, and out of the registration room and the clothing-check room and the rest-room. For a brief moment—before my friend Tracy arrived and before I'd had a beautiful heart-kissed latte—I wondered who, besides my husband, would notice if I just snuck around the back and disappeared. The pro-looking guy with the polka-dot bike kit wouldn't notice. The lumbersexual latte dude wouldn't notice. Chris King certainly wouldn't notice.

But my mother would notice. She'd done half the ride the day before with Uncle Josh, either to help "prepare me" for it or to prove to me that she could do it faster and better, depending on your point of view. And on the day of the ride, despite all the prepping and training and bike primping, it was her presence a few miles away that I suddenly realized might be my biggest battle.

The truth is, the ride brought up much more than an ath-letic challenge. Embarking on a daylong endeavor meant I'd be riding for six (or more) hours, in theory. It meant I'd be sitting on the same saddle, pedaling in the same shoes, clench-ing with the same gloves for six hours. And it meant that for each of those hours, I'd be riding in relative silence with my own brain and my own memories, my own ghouls and ghosties—which, as any long-distance athlete will tell you, are the heaviest things to carry on any long journey.

For as long as I can remember, I've done athletic things first and foremost for my parents. I was under the impression, from a very early age, that because being outdoors and being active were crucially important to them, my parents might only love me if I followed suit, and did the things they loved doing well. Because I always felt slow and weak and annoy-ing to wait for, I conditioned myself to believe that if I was breathing hard, I probably wasn't going fast enough or work-ing hard enough, even if I was indeed going fast or working hard. I trained myself for athletic failure. Even as an adult, and even with a lupus diagnosis that likely explains much of my "weakness" as a teenager and young adult, feeling slow has translated to feeling intimidated in athletic situations. And although I've labored over the years to shake the deeply engrained (and likely incorrect) belief that one earns less love if one flails athletically, I'd be lying if I told you that every time I lace up athletic shoes—every single time—I don't push aside a preemptive assumption that I will do terribly at whatever I'm about to undertake. It's a heavy, swinging door I can only open with all of my body's weight, and it always swings closed again.

A week before the race, as I was telling my mother I might not be up for the new yoga class she wanted to try a few days after the Gourmet Century, she conveniently pointed out that I'd never seriously trained for a long-format athletic event before in my life. And so as I hopped onto the bike to begin the six-hour ride, that devil on my back—along with my mom's texted opinions about the ride—came right along with me. I reminded myself one last time that my goal was simply not to cry. I started sweating before we left.

At first, morale was high. "We're going to have a super ride together," said Tracy's husband, Aaron, a Wisconsin-born cyclist with a megawatt smile who seemed to think I'd be fine. "And you're lookin' good." Like Tracy, Aaron had been a dependably positive presence during my training. The week before the ride, he'd given me a nifty pair of cycling socks to match the orange jersey Tracy had gifted me the month before. And he was right. We all looked good.

Our little pack meandered out on "Dirty 30," as cyclists commonly call Portland's in-town Highway 30, a train-track-side stretch of industrial zone that divides downtown from the crest of hills in the city's gorgeous Forest Park. We passed a barely moving train.

"See?" Aaron said, sensing my nervousness. "We're faster than a speeding bullet."

It's one thing to go for a long bike ride with friends. But embarking on a ride with people whose lives revolve around cycling—who have, for literally decades, been tackling long distances with ease and regularity—is scary. And as soon as we'd hit the first steep ramp toward the hot two-mile climb up into Forest Park, a couple of things became clear: first, that their idea of taking things slowly would not accommodate my own relatively leisurely pace for very long; and second, that the day's weather projection of ninety-four degrees Fahrenheit would be far too low.

"The first hill is really intimidating," my mother had told me. As if I hadn't read the ride profile online, and hadn't heard it from others, and needed to be intimidated further. As if my brother's direction to stop and pick blackberries halfway up hadn't suggested I might need a break five miles in. But as I crested the top of that first hill, not yet ten miles into the ride, I realized she'd been right. I seriously doubted my ability to finish. Jim rode with me every inch of the way, winding back and forth across the road, urging me up the steepest parts zig by zag when I didn't have the strength to go straight up it on my side of the double yellow. He played LCD Soundsystem and Daft Punk at the top of his ancient iPhone's effort, whispering whatever words of encouragement he thought might land him on the correct side of the faint line between helpful and maddening. He picked blackberries for me (while riding, naturally, because he was still hardly breathing), and passed them directly into my mouth. At the top, our friends cheered. I felt like I might be done for the day, but I knew the first pit stop was just a few miles ahead. And as much as I hated that the group had waited (and waited) for me, I also knew they were determined to help me finish that day. It felt so good to ride with people who had no connection to my decades of athletic self-doubt. I opened my first energy gel and chugged some water.

After a hilltop stop for those "small morning offerings," which turned out to be vegan peanut butter–chocolate ice-cream bombes—"Yeah, you're supposed to digest that while riding, but fear not, there's a downhill ahead!" said the guy doling out the cups—our little troupe cruised along Skyline Boulevard, riding the ridge that separated us from Portland, to the east, and the sprawling green farmland in the valley deep to our west. A sharp right turn led us down the same elevation we'd just come up, and then some—five fast miles down a newly paved winding road. I tucked in behind Aaron's wheel, thankful for years of ski racing that had trained me, even be-grudgingly, to feel comfortable going fast down hills. The as-phalt, which was at this point still nicely shaded and quite clean, didn't seem dangerous. My speedometer hit twenty-five miles per hour. Then thirty. At thirty-eight, the road began to level out. Aaron glanced back—presumably to see how far behind I'd fallen—and he did a double take. Tracy sidled up beside us easily.

"You didn't tell us you're a downhiller, Jess!" she screamed, presumably shocked by my daredevilish descent.

"I'm *not* a downhiller," I objected. "I'm just good at not using my brakes." I almost told her I could do flips on tram-polines and diving boards, too, just to make sure the athletic abilities I did establish during the years I spent falling off the balance beam got some airtime.

Looking back, I'm afraid that my zooming confidently down that hill may have encouraged the others to speed up a little. For that stretch of road—mile twelve to mile nineteen, I'd say, between the chocolate–peanut butter frozen treats and the weird, doughy teriyaki burritos (really, more burritos?)

served at the first real snack stop, at a berry farm, I felt fast enough. My legs rejuvenated after the rest on the downhill, I found a rhythm that I more or less stuck with; it was quick enough to just keep up with the others but not so fast that I felt like I was overdoing it.

The next section of road, through mile thirty-five or so, felt about the same. Rolling over green pastures and golden hayfields, twisting and winding through productive Oregon dairy and farm country, I felt like I could ride forever—which, I now realize, may be the greatest and most dangerous feeling available in aerobic sport. Our group formed a tight pack, with me at the back, so I could draft off the stronger, faster riders to save energy. Normally, when cyclists ride together, they take turns at the front of the pack, which means each person gives about the same level of effort overall, resting (or at least working less hard) when they're riding at the rear. There seemed to be a general consensus among the others that I was to be pampered, and pamper they did. Aaron snuck up beside me on the steeper grades and, with his hand underneath my saddle, he essentially pulled me up the hills with him. Jim opened energy gels for me—smoked trout and burritos be damned—and Tracy encouraged me to drink, drink, drink. The air warmed, and the sun blazed, but during those miles, I thought about how lucky I felt to be healthy enough to ride, having spent many of the previous summers either injured or stiff with the joint problems that come with lupus. To be outside on a beautiful, cloudless day. To have made it so far already, at the very least.

Only, what I didn't consider when I was pleasantly wind-latched onto Tracy's or Aaron's or Jim's back wheel, was that, although I was having to do the least work of anyone at twenty miles per hour, I normally ride at only thirteen or fourteen miles per hour. So while I was given the prime spot for our journey together, I was still far outriding my usual pace. And when we stopped for lunch, a sprawling barbecue (complete with bluegrass band) set under a tent at a farm more or less in the middle of nowhere, I realized that, in every way, my body was finished riding a bicycle.

All at once, the idea that the purpose of riding the Gourmet Century seemed to be combining food and cycling seemed almost laughable. I didn't give a shit what there was to eat. It wasn't that I didn't feel capable of digesting food. It was that my body was so overtired and underfed and dehydrated, no amount of fuel, liquid or solid, seemed capable of returning me to an energetic state. I didn't care how anything tasted, as long as it was safe for human consumption. And having ridden almost two hours since the last stop, I realized that, without the breeze our speed created, the day had gotten hot. *Really* hot. I wasn't sure stopping was a good idea, but I also didn't know how I'd continue if I didn't stop. In the span of ten minutes, I downed an old-fashioned Coke and an Italian soda drink, sucking in the sugar like some sort of desperate hummingbird. I ate half a barbecued chicken sandwich and half a chickpea variation of the same, noticing halfway through that Jim had started pushing additional food onto my plate, perhaps realizing that his own day was going to be a lot easier if I was well fueled. It was there, padding across the farm's soft dust to fill a bottle out of a PVC pipe system that the organizers had set up to draw water off the farm's supply, that I started wondering why I was really doing the Gourmet Century at all. I believe exercise is good for everyone, but clearly my body doesn't need extra stress. I didn't *need* the physical challenge of riding a hundred kilometers. And since I spent a lot of my life at that point worrying about whether I was making the right choices for my child, I probably didn't need another emotional challenge, either. I drank my water and pushed the thought aside.

As soon as we'd left, we all noticed how the heat had started to puddle in still, stifling pockets in the bottom of each valley between the rolling hills. The road shimmered. Rumors about triple-digit temperatures floated between packs of riders. Now five hours into the ride—there was no way we'd be finished in six—I realized that although I'd already consumed a total of three liters of water and two sodas, I still hadn't peed all day. The route veered onto a gravel section, which I hadn't expected. ("Yeah, I didn't think you'd want to hear about that ahead of time," my brother said later.) I surprised myself by how well I could navigate the slippery, uneven surface, but it did require extra steering. And for about half of it, I did a very bad job of breathing, which meant that as the road shifted back to pavement, around forty-one miles in, I found myself gasping for air. And then, as we turned to head back toward where the ride had begun, the real hills started again.

At mile forty-three, I looked up at an incline that didn't appear to end. I looked at Jim. He looked at me. "Just take it slow," he encouraged, sensing my panic. For the first time on the ride, I went back to the "Cups" song I'd used as a motivational focus during my training. Using the beat to guide my pedal strokes, I started up. And up. And up. The road rolled by excruciatingly slowly, but I was still moving.

"So one time, I was on this killer two-hundred-mile ride," breezed Tracy, sidling up alongside me as the grade got steeper. She chatted on about how hard the ride had been, and about how hot it had been, and about how sometimes, she'd used word patterns to spur herself on. In this particular instance, she'd found the perfect combination of nonsensical grunting to get herself up the toughest hill. *Huh-HA, huh-HA.*

"And I got into this *rhythm*," she chanted. She said the word *rhythm* like she was referring to utter magic. I could tell Tracy was sharing an important moment with me, but it took an inordinate amount of effort to pedal and keep half my mind on my song and listen to her, all at the same time. My normally high capacity for multitasking had vanished.

"And then this girl who was in wayyyy better shape than me came up beside me and just started *talking*. Just talking and talking and talking, like it was taking her so little effort that she didn't even have to breathe," she said incredulously.

I let Tracy shake her head, still impressed and offended by the überathlete. Then:

"Tracy." My voice was very quiet.

"Yeah, how's it going now?" She was all cheerleader.

"Tracy, you're doing the same thing to me."

She blushed—if a person forty-something miles into a ride in one-hundred-degree weather can get redder—and apologized profusely before eventually leaving me behind.

I think she told Aaron that I was hurting, because the next thing I knew, he was back, hand on my saddle again, urging me to the top. I *loved* that he was next to me. I loved that I'd chosen to ride with people who were willing to put my own finish above their own personal goals because they knew the day would be a much bigger challenge for me. I loved that there were other people around us who were also obviously suffering in the heat, and that my husband was finally starting to look a little tired.

But in the middle of all that, I lost the internal tracker that tells one not to keep pushing harder when one runs out of breath. And the next thing I knew, I was stopped on the side of the road, hyperventilating with desperate, ragged breaths I'd lost the ability to control. My legs shook. My arms weren't strong enough to hold my handlebars, so my upper body collapsed over the bike, held up only by the physical structure of my arm bones, which were barely balancing where my hands normally go. The hayfields spun around me. I sensed Jim somewhere near, urging me to slow down each breath. It was the same boundless, twirling feeling I'd had during labor with Graham. After the doula had decided to leave, but before the operating room.

"You were going too fast," Jim said.

"Aaron was helping me," I countered, the words wheezing out in staccato barks. I was vaguely aware that arguing with my husband might not be productive in my current state.

"Aaron was helping you go much faster than you usually go, and you were still working hard," Jim explained in a calm, child-friendly voice. He tried to help me pace my breath. "Slow in," he said, hand on my back. "Then slower out."

"It's like with Graham," I squeaked to Jim over the course of two or three more spastic breaths, lungs still heaving. "I can't control it." I felt heat building behind my eyes. "What if I do too much?"

Aaron looked on, clearly wondering why he was being implicated in any way in my sudden falling apart. He left us to our recovery, signaling to Tracy that we needed space.

"It's not the same thing," Jim insisted. "This is you. This is a bike ride. This is for fun. Let's slow you down and get your breath back."

But no matter how hard I stared at the blackberries on the side of the road, and at how drying salt from my own sweat powdered the stomach of my orange bike jersey with white lines, all I could think of was our labor and delivery room at Seattle's Swedish Hospital. That was the time I was too tough.

The day Graham was born, rather than the beat of a bad pop song, it had been the lights on the buttons on the hospital bed that kept me going: one pointing up, one pointing down, raised blue circular buttons with glowing white arrows on the gray background of the bed's long side rails. I was on my left side, cradled in my own pain. For whatever reason, twelve hours of fevered labor had left those buttons as my focus, and during the final hour of constant contraction, I moved the bed up and down a centimeter at a time, willing the movement to translate somehow to relief. Jim was there somewhere, wide eyed and soft spoken, telling me to slow down and get my breath back. In what was left of my bewildered brain, I knew that the tough that had gotten me through the labor and the bed rest and the pregnancy—and issues with lupus before that—wouldn't be enough to save me from the Armageddon in my uterus. I knew that no matter what stories I'd heard about women birthing, what was happening in my belly at that moment was different. I knew instinctively that the someone inside my body was hurting in a way that felt like dying. Those buttons, though. The buttons could save me. They could save *us*, I thought. If only I could be tough enough to make it through the pain.

I wasn't. Despite the magic buttons and the gummy margarita-flavored Clif Shot Bloks and the beeping and the lights and the swarming doctors and my devoted sister and strong, capable Jim, I wasn't tough enough to make it through labor on my own, without pain medication, which had been our hopeful plan. Soon after the doula left—a classic blessing in disguise—I begged Jim between the same raspy, ragged breaths to ask a nurse for an epidural. I'd been unable to control my breathing for hours, and my baby's heart rate and mine had been in what the nurses kept terming "the red zone" for far too long. Neither of us were getting enough oxygen, and for reasons still unclear to us, the hospital was refusing to give me any from a tank. My adrenal system hadn't reacted the way it was supposed to, and my body hadn't released the hormones a woman typically depends on for normal childbirth. The anesthesiologist came, along with the doctor, who gave instructions to prepare me for a C-section. But to everyone's surprise, the epidural's relaxing effect turned a night's worth of what they called "ineffective" back labor into childbirth. Needle in to baby out, in under thirty minutes. There in the operating room, with neonatal nurses buzzing to prepare seven weeks' premature Graham for his trip to the NICU, Jim looked at me.

"You okay?" he asked. "You breathing?" I nodded, and pushed him off toward our baby.

While I was being stabilized and transported to a recovery room, my body having suddenly ballooned with liquid, Graham received extra oxygen and had a special intravenous device called a PICC line inserted into his chest, in preparation for a ten-day regimen of strong antibiotics. It wasn't until hours later that I rode in a wheelchair to meet Graham, and the nurse Marta. I was in the hospital for another week, and Jim bounced between us, logging minimal sleep in a blue pleather easy chair next to my bed, pacing the halls on his phone to manage his work from the hospital. When I had recovered enough to go home, our lives became a rotating roster of hand washing, baby watching, and breast pumping. The hospital released Graham thirty days after he was born. We went home with a five-pound nine-ounce baby boy, thrilled that we could identify him as "Graham" instead of "Baby Boy A Thomson," which had been his hospital name. Thrilled he'd kicked the *E. coli*. Thrilled he was healthy, and relatively huge.

It wasn't until months after Graham's cerebral palsy diagnosis—years, maybe?—that it occurred to me it might all somehow be my fault, or our fault. That on his birth day, after a lifetime of feeling like I would always be the slowest one and the weakest one, I'd vowed to be the toughest person in the room. And in that moment of complete resolve, I'd perhaps ignored the possibility that being tough might not be the safest choice given my body's unique limitations.

JULY

Of course, with a premature baby, there are lists and lists of factors that can contribute to cerebral palsy, which is more common than you might think. No one would ever assign actual blame for such a thing, and I can't say I assign it so directly myself. And in reality, calling for the epidural may have perhaps saved Graham from a much different, much harder, much more deeply affected life than he lives now. We will always be uncertain about exactly what caused the changes in our child's brain.

But I am totally certain that every time I feel a lack of oxygen, for the rest of my life, I will think of that moment. And each time, I will feel again the searing pain that came with the realization I was doing physical harm to myself and to someone else. And next to the blackberries, in the middle of Oregon on a bike, in a dizzying, asthmatic fit in the heat, I didn't feel sure that I could make a good decision about how much harder to push. What if I gave everything and it wasn't enough? Or worse, what if I gave everything, and it hurt me? Or hurt someone else? On the side of the road, in an effort-induced emotional craze, I felt almost relieved to know Graham was somewhere making lightsaber noises with my brother miles and miles away. To know that whatever was happening to me, I couldn't be hurting my child.

Minutes passed. Other riders passed. And slowly, the memory passed, too. My breathing slowed.

"Okay," I told my husband. "I'm ready. But I think I'm going to have to stop again soon."

"Good. You gotta keep it in the yellow," said Jim. "No red zone, understand? You won't make it if you push it into the red again."

And so for the next ten miles, we limped together, stopping literally every quarter mile in small patches of shade on the side of the road. Jim stopped with me every time. Every time, he'd offer me water or an energy gel and we'd stand, sweating, panting, breathing. Fighting fatigue and dehydration and heat and memory. Later, we'd refer to it as The Bad Hill.

Eventually, miles later, we found Tracy and Aaron at the crest of a hill. "Good work!" Aaron smiled, proud to also announce he'd found a sign for Dick Road. I realized that, as much as I was suffering getting the hills and the miles behind me, these people were suffering in the heat just waiting for me. At least they still had a sense of humor.

"Want this?" asked Tracy kindly. "I think I'll be good for the rest of the ride." She proffered a margarita-flavored package of Clif Shot Bloks, gooey green globs of bloodstream-bound sugar that would help me both recover from the previous hills and prepare for the twenty miles remaining.

"I can't eat those," I snapped, a little too quickly. Her eyes widened.

"Thanks anyway," I said, this time more softly, pushing back the dizzy, feverish feeling I kept noticing. "Go. We'll be fine." I doubt they'd have waited in any case at that point, but they seemed happy for official permission to ride on. We agreed to see them at the dinner.

Which was a good thing, because our pattern didn't change. I'd ride a distance—anywhere from a hundred yards to maybe five hundred, but never longer—until my legs didn't go around anymore. Then I'd stop, and try to drink, but after thirty minutes or so both Jim and I ran out of water. Then I'd go again, Jim trying to gauge how far I'd made it, his own body getting tired because no matter how fast you go, six hours on a bike at 101 degrees is still six hours on a bike at 101 degrees. I started emitting foreign, guttural moans every time my wheels stopped.

Ten miles and ten thousand small stops later (including one where riders lined up to dunk their heads under a spigot near a small rural cemetery), we arrived at our final pit stop, at Chris King's home. Outfitted with Portland's famous Salt and Straw ice cream, a massive charcuterie board, and a series of gorgeous salads (plus the same Stumptown coffee guys who'd been making lattes earlier that day), it felt like a triage unit in a culinary Shangri-la. Healthy, happy bikers streamed back onto the course with ice-cream-stained kits, while others, clearly finished for the day, dragged their machines to the road for pickup by the organizers' "sag wagon," the van that offered rides back to the factory. Some nursed wounds and injuries and broken bikes. In a matter of minutes, it became clear that I had both a distinct knack for consuming pork confit after fifty miles of riding and a willingness to finish that others did not, slow pace be damned.

"People are going home!" I slurred to Jim, stumbling into a shady garage. Mumbling something about heatstroke, Jim MacGyvered cold packs for me, knotting one end of each of the white arm warmers I'd used for the first part of the day (to deflect the sun) so they formed long tubes. He dipped the tubes into an icy trough of drinks, straining out enough ice to fill them to the brim and knotting their other ends, then shoved one tube down the back of my bike shorts and balanced the other across the back of my neck. Suddenly my whole body felt cooler. The shaking that had started on The Bad Hill, ten miles earlier, finally stopped. My body embraced another caffeine- and sugar-soaked cola. And somewhere between the first and second helpings of confit—my body told me quite clearly that the fat content of an ice-cream cone just wasn't going to cut it in the calorie department—I began to think I could finish the ride. And I began to feel, for perhaps the first time, that I might have found the difference between slowness and incompetence. I was going slowly. I was going terribly, painfully, awkwardly slowly. But I was still going. While others were quitting, I was still going.

THE GOURMET CENTURY

And there in the barn, staring at antique bicycle parts and piles of ancient tools clinging to the worn wooden walls, I wondered if that was why I'd signed up in the first place. I did have a decent reason *not* to sign up, after all. My body is not naturally designed for such endeavors. And since I grew up with a mother so much like Laura Marshall in that SoulCycle class ("Raise. Your. Standards."), I was terrified to ride. Not just scared to fail, like anyone might be, but more afraid of riding slowly, lest I let down the people who I felt always wanted me to go faster. Perhaps I'd signed up not to eat, but to find out if, after years of feeling like my best was never enough in athletic situations, I could learn to be okay with just being me. And if somehow facing that meant I could find a way to pass it on to our son. That, I reasoned, was far more important than passing on a love for any kind of food.

As I settled back onto the bike seat for the final time, I was suddenly no longer afraid of failing. I recognized an honest reality—at some point, my legs would simply no longer move, and I was getting closer and closer to that point with each revolution of legs and wheels—but when I let myself embrace the idea of being proud of finishing no matter how fast I went, and no matter how carefully my mother calculated my speed afterward, the ride suddenly got less hard. It felt less physically violent, because it became less emotionally difficult. I may not have "raised my standards" the way the spinning instructor had suggested months before, but I had found a way to change them.

Of course, we still had to go up the infamous Old Germantown Road, the seldom-used uphill version of what we'd descended hours and hours earlier with such speed. The tiny, tree-lined lane was just wide enough to allow me to switchback slowly up the ups, back-and-forthing enough to push our sixty-eight-mile course into more like seventy-two total miles, according to my bicycle's odometer. I ditched "Cups" in favor of a new little tempo chant: *Change. Your. Standards.* Up, and up, and up some more we went. It was no type of fun at all, but I did it.

My Gourmet Century was the opposite of a gallant effort. It was an ugly, heaving, sweaty, uncoordinated effort; it was a party to which I invited all the wrong feelings at first. In the end, the ride took us eight and a half hours, 9:00 a.m. to 5:30 p.m.

"All in a day's work," I cheered to Jim, lip quivering, as we rolled back into the Chris King factory parking lot. The first round of dinners had begun, and as unknown eyes lifted to watch us park our bikes—we were very close to the last to arrive—I bent my own eyes down to the pavement and let myself cry.

Chicken and Radicchio Salad

At T minus three days before the ride, in addition to being plain old nervous, I found myself in the awkward, unfamiliar position of not knowing what to eat. I instinctively assumed the carb-loading habits of my youth were no longer applicable. I wrote my coach.

"Fat and protein," texted Tracy. "And hydrate. Carbs not needed until day of."

I wrote my ultra-runner friend Lindsay, who *ran* one hundred kilometers the same day I rode them, to ask the same. "Eat your face off with carbs from lunch Thursday to lunch Friday," she countered. "Then normal easy-to-digest dinner Friday and regular breakfast Saturday."

Feeling paralyzed, I reasoned that, instead of thinking about what might show up on a nutrition label, I should eat for my foods' personalities. The Thursday before the ride, a salad came together in a tangle on my cutting board: I chose robust radicchio for toughness, spicy peppers for spunk, and preserved lemon for surprise, because I was sure I'd need to find all those things inside during the ride. I added chicken for sustenance, then handfuls of the arugula and parsley from my little front garden (they refused to stop growing, which seemed appropriate), and tossed it all together into a big purple salad.

I could eat this salad for a century—or more, if the parsley that perches on every edge of my little raised-bed garden was still growing well. It lands somewhere between a salad and a sandwich. If you prefer, throw in a handful of toasted walnuts and a little blue cheese, and balance a hunk of good bread on the edge of your plate.

To use the preserved lemon, cut a whole one in half, then halve it again—you'll just need a quarter of it. Using a small, sharp knife, cut the squishy flesh away and discard it. Then, with the peel flat on the cutting board, bright yellow side down, make cuts parallel to the cutting board to shave away any additional flesh and pith that remain on the peel, until only the yellow zest remains. That yellow zest is what you want sliced into thin strips for your salad.

Note that this is a recipe for one meal (in my stomach, anyway). Double or quadruple it as needed. For a crowd, you could plate the greens right around a roasted chicken, for something a little fancier.

MAKES: 1 GENEROUS SERVING

1 tablespoon finely chopped Mama Lil's Peppers
or similar spicy pickled peppers
1 tablespoon apple cider vinegar
1 teaspoon Dijon mustard
½ teaspoon sea salt
2 tablespoons extra-virgin olive oil
1 cup leftover cubed chicken
(about one breast, cut into ¾-inch cubes)
½ small head radicchio (about ⅓ pound), cut into 1-inch
hunks
½ cup baby arugula
¼ cup fresh Italian parsley leaves
Zest of ¼ preserved lemon, very thinly sliced

» In the bottom of a big bowl, whisk together the peppers, vinegar, mustard, and salt. Whisk in the olive oil until blended, then add the chicken, radicchio, arugula, parsley, and preserved lemon, and toss until all the leaves are coated with the dressing. Serve immediately, right out of the bowl or piled onto a plate.

Watermelon Gazpacho

In the end, the Gourmet Century's supposed crowning glory—the delicious dinner outdoors, served under twinkling fairy lights at the Chris King Precision Components factory in Portland—was for me an afterthought at best. I could hardly keep my eyes open, and walking to my seat was a serious challenge. But what still stands out is the taste memory of a watermelon gazpacho, served chilled and topped with smoked feta, poached prawns, and a tangle of ripped herbs. This version, which I made months afterward, is simpler—and, it so happens, delicious spiked with a bit of vodka.

If you love a spicy gazpacho, you can add a liquid hot sauce such as Tapatío for heat, but it will cover the watermelon's sweetness.

MAKES: ABOUT 8 SERVINGS

> About 5 pounds fist-size, ripe red tomatoes, chopped
> 2 red jalapeño or serrano peppers, seeded and chopped
> 1 red bell pepper, seeded and chopped
> 2 medium shallots, finely chopped
> 1 large clove garlic, finely chopped
> ¼ cup champagne vinegar
> 2 teaspoons kosher salt, plus more to taste
> 4 cups chopped watermelon (from half a 4-pound red water-melon), any hard black seeds removed
> ¼ cup freshly squeezed lime juice, plus more to taste

» In a large bowl, stir together the tomatoes, peppers, shallots, garlic, vinegar, and salt. Set the mixture aside to marinate for an hour, or refrigerate overnight.

» Working in batches, puree the mixture in a food processor or blender until it's evenly dark pink and smooth, then transfer it to a large bowl. Next, puree the watermelon with the lime juice, and add that to the tomato mixture. Stir to blend, then season to taste with additional lime juice and salt, if necessary. Serve immediately or refrigerate for up to 2 days, covered. (Stir well before serving.)

AUGUST

I've always had an unintentional bias toward the last five months of the year. In my head, I see months numbered in a circle as if I'm looking at a clock, instead of (as I imagine others do) as an organized stack of square monthly calendars. So my year is a clock, but August, the 8, is at the bottom, where a 6 for June should be, meaning more focus is on the months that fall between August and December. Those months get more space and more attention. It might be this way because I was born in August, and I'm just that self-centered. I can't think of another good reason.

But August, the halfway mark, is when I take inventory. It's when, dependably, I do a mental regrouping. And so I took out the Gantt chart again, reviewing what I'd planned to do by that point in the year, and comparing it to what I'd actually done. So far, besides the trip to California for a type of neurological therapy for Graham that was designed to allow his nerves to remap the way his muscles function, and that conference in DC, I noted that I hadn't left the Pacific Northwest. We'd embraced our region quite well, actually. Seven months filled with clamming expeditions and restaurant visits and lambing lessons didn't all quite feel successful, but we'd gone. Other adventures didn't go as well. Summer crabbing had been a total bust, twice; Graham had zero interest. My dad refused the fishing trip I'd proposed. I never made it to Eastern Washington to pick potatoes, as I'd planned. I'd spent the greater part of the year *right here*, working more or less on The Here List, but discovered that many of the things I'd listed held challenges I couldn't necessarily overcome. I couldn't change the way Graham ate. (And if I could, there wasn't a thing he could eat—nearby or far afield—that would change the way he walked or ensure the surgery would go well or affect how much I loved him.) I couldn't say when I'd have my husband's solid, comforting, Super Dad presence in Seattle, or when he'd be on a boat off the coast of Alaska or at some meeting in Virginia or at a conference in San Francisco. I also couldn't change my own body, or the fact that I would simply never be as strong or as fast as I'd always wanted to be. Maybe, I thought, I shouldn't try to change anything. Maybe I should just spend the rest of the year without a list.

In August, I took the Gantt chart off the wall in our little home office. I folded it up and put it somewhere safe, thinking perhaps I'd come back to it later, after the surgery. I knew there were things on The Here List I'd already booked—a salmon-fishing trip without my dad, for one—but I didn't want to commit to anything new before Graham had healed.

I also quietly started pining for a long ride on an airplane. I longed for a place where I could learn about the food I loved without also learning so much about myself or feeling responsible for sharing it with another person, big or small. Part of the magic of traveling farther than one can drive easily—especially traveling alone—is that you can leave the most dutiful parts of your adult self at home. You bring the right clothes and a good watch, maybe, but you leave the dishes and the laundry and the bills.

I started looking forward to our trip to New York as a temporary solution. Jim and I would take turns nursing Graham back to health after the surgery, we decided, and we'd each have some time alone in the city.

The Manhattan Project

WE knew that convincing our smart, brave kid that flying back East for his surgery would be in any way fun might be challenging—and a lie, really. Graham had been through muscle-relaxing rounds of Botox shots in his calves and hamstrings, and serial leg casts, which had succeeded in lengthening his calf muscles, but only until he grew again. He knew that changes to his legs usually meant hospital time and discomfort and therapy and therapy and therapy. We told him a week after kindergarten ended, after we'd seen the doctor who addresses his cerebral palsy at the farmers' market one bright Sunday morning.

"So, do you remember when we saw Dr. A?" Jim had asked casually that evening. "She said we should probably do surgery on your legs to make it not hurt so much when you walk. You'll have casts on your legs, but only one set, not casts that change every week like last summer." He'd left out the small detail that Dr. A didn't exactly approve of the surgical approach we'd decided to take.

"No, I talked to her, too," Graham had countered confidently. "I told her I don't think I need surgery. But we could still go to New York if you want." We knew he'd barely acknowledged her.

"Unfortunately, Graham, it's not your choice," Jim had responded. "We will be going to a place near New York called New Jersey for your surgery in August, and we will go to New York City afterward for therapy. We will all go together, and we will be able to see the skyscrapers and the dinosaur museum for sure, but we have to do the surgery first."

"Okay, fine," our child had conceded. Graham's lips had wobbled as he asked if he could be excused. Jim and I had exchanged worried looks. He's never been the kind of kid who can express sadness or emotion well out loud. He'd bolted from the dinner table on his hands and knees.

The first week of August, Graham was delighted to hop onto an airplane to New Jersey. We traveled with only his arm crutches, leaving his walker at home for the very first time while traveling because he seemed better than ever at using his sticks over long distances, and because we knew it wouldn't be useful on our way home. At the airport, he walked all the way from the curb to the gate by himself with those crutches, legs awkwardly bent the way they'd always been, like a young foal's at birth, always sticking out in random directions.

Graham was in no way excited for the actual operation. But when the anesthesiologist asked him which flavor he'd like for the drugged oxygen kids often receive to initiate the anesthesia process before surgery, he responded with complete certainty.

"I usually get bubble gum," he explained, nodding coolly. Like they'd asked his favorite color. "Yeah, I like that kind."

It wouldn't surprise me if Graham, who has only a relatively mild form of cerebral palsy, had at six spent more time in hospitals than many people do before forty. And as he settled onto the table in the operating room—for the first time, completely unafraid—it occurred to me that even though we'd told him he was having surgery on both legs, explained that he might be in some pain afterward, and described in kid-friendly detail that it would be a long road back to his version of normal, he had no clue what was happening.

Neither did we, really. Going in that day before dawn, we knew that choosing the New Jersey surgery, as we came to call it, meant travel to the East Coast and a few days' worth of recovery in a small town, then almost a week of therapy in New York City afterward. We knew that compared to the more traditional approach to hamstring and calf-muscle lengthening, the New Jersey surgery (really called selective percutaneous myofascial lengthening, or SPML, or sometimes just "percs" for short) required far less superficial healing and a significantly shorter recovery period. We also knew that none of Graham's Seattle therapists—a smattering of well-trained, intuitive, and effective physical and occupational therapists and alternative-medicine folks—had ever coached a kid back after SPML surgery. But ultimately, we didn't know what would happen in the operating room.

In theory, part of the reason SPML works is because the doctor doesn't know, either. Rather than completely anesthetizing the patient, the surgeon keeps the kiddo partially awake during the surgery so that he can make changes based on the patient's active muscular response rather than on assumptions about how the muscles work while watching videos of, say, the kid walking around in Seattle. So while we went in planning for Graham to have various "bands" of muscles lengthened (in ways not appropriate for detailed description in a book that also talks about food), we didn't know how difficult those bands would be to stretch, or how many bands might be affected, or exactly where the needed band lengthening might be located on his body. In he went at seven that morning, as clueless as his parents.

THE MANHATTAN PROJECT

While Graham was coming out of the lighter anesthesia (to be clear, he doesn't remember anything about the actual operation), the surgeon came to see us in the waiting room, briefly relieving us from the clash between the receptionist's gospel music and the emergency coverage of that morning's lightning storms on Long Island. Dr. N looked at us, then ran his palm down the entire length of his face, with all the fingers on one side and the thumb on the other side, like he was wiping a memory off his brain so he could give it to us. He was the kind of person who always seems to be sweating, and that morning was no exception.

The surgery had been more involved than Dr. N had expected. While he'd known Graham's hamstrings and calves were very restricted, he was quite surprised at just how tight they'd been, given Graham's relatively high level of function. He described how he'd had to perform basically double the amount of loosening he'd anticipated, meaning the optimistic predictions he'd given us the day before—he'd said, to our shock, that he expected Graham to be walking on his own without any assistive devices in two to four weeks' time— might have been overreaching. It made me wonder again just how much pain Graham had been in until that point, walking around with his little arm crutches day after day, toes on point like a ballerina's from the calf and hamstring tension his altered neurology caused.

"And we ended up doing the triple play," Dr. N added, describing like a sports commentator how he'd also loosened bands in Graham's adductor muscles. "The recovery will be longer than we talked about yesterday, but he'll do great." All I heard was his New Jersey accent. *Da recovery will be loingah dan we tawlked abouwt.*

Graham came out of surgery hurtling angry words and ultimatums.

AUGUST

"I'M NEVER GOING ANYWHERE UNTIL THESE CASTS ARE OFF," he hollered, sobbing hysterically, pulling at the new leg casts. "YOU CAN'T DOOOO THIS TO ME!"

He tore violently at all the various tubes and machines connected to his body. Nurses came running with needles. As the valium set in and the IVs came out, he calmed down, and we eventually made our way back to our dank, dark old hotel room to rest and organize all his various post-op medications. Seeing him so immobile was sad; watching him realize that he'd be depending on us to sit up and sit down and get to the bathroom was heartbreaking. I knew he'd worked so hard to be independent, but I don't think I realized how much pride he took in doing things himself.

At first, we thought getting him out might help. (I'd heard from other parents whose kids had undergone the same operation that some children are up to venturing back into the world the same day as their SPML surgery.) On a pizza-pro friend's recommendation, we took him to Star Tavern, in Orange, New Jersey, thinking a good, gooey slice of cheese pizza and an arcade-style video game—something he'd never done before—might lift him out of the doldrums for just a moment. But even with the doctor's warnings, we didn't realize that simply being picked up was painful for him; the weight of his own legs caused his hamstring wounds to gush blood when we carried him (gently, we'd thought) from the car to a table at the front of the restaurant. Piles of napkins and a wailing kid later, we excused ourselves and ate (very good) pizza in the rental car. I rode in the back with Graham, the way I did the first time we took him home from the hospital. Jim put him to bed while I scrubbed blood out of the rental car's pretty beige seats.

For the next few days, we stayed put. We ate room-service hot dogs and take-out Thai chicken satays and Starbucks boxed

THE MANHATTAN PROJECT

178

meals, all things Graham favored at the time. We watched the first six *Star Wars* episodes, adjusting and readjusting the cantankerous air-conditioning unit, coloring Graham's casts with a rainbow of new Sharpies, and generally coaxing our drugged little boy through his postoperative discomfort with the help of get-well notes sent generously by Seattle friends.

Once the incision sites had stopped bleeding and we'd passed the most acute recovery period, we moved into a small apartment on the Upper West Side of Manhattan. We rented one of those beefy off-road strollers—the kind we'd given away just the previous year, certain we'd never have a use for it again— and started in on a sad kid–unfriendly routine of twice-daily neurological therapy and supposed sight-seeing. The woo-woo alternative therapy, which theoretically (and in our experience, successfully) teaches kids' brains to map new neurological patterns as a means of solving often neurologically based physical problems like cerebral palsy, seemed to go well. We watched as Graham internalized that he could straighten his legs out in a sitting position for the first time. We watched him touch his toes where they stuck out at the ends of the lower leg casts, marveling in his six-year-old way that they didn't seem as far away as usual. We whispered excitedly when we realized he could flex his ankles to ninety degrees. He hated it all.

It was a different view of the Big Apple, to say the least. We thought spots like the American Museum of Natural History and the Liberty Science Center might distract Graham from his pain and annoyance, which they did—but only until they frustrated him more. Each time the initial excitement over a place like the Lego store wore off, he just got depressed. No child wants to be stuck in a stroller and on therapy tables all day. He was a sad sack, as an old Cape Cod friend used to say. In my head, the whole time, I called it "The Manhattan Project," despite the militaristic implications. But we *were* in

Manhattan. And we weren't sure whether the thing we'd just done was right.

On our last day, a week or so after surgery, we met some friends at a grassy park along the Hudson River. They brought their five- and two-year-olds, and much to our surprise, a game of hide-and-seek sprung up. Out of nowhere, our completely sedentary little patient was crawling around on the grass, even rolling down little hills, doing what he could to smear New York City mud into his unwashable casts and bruised little knees. The combination of friendship and dirt had finally propelled him back into the universe. There were grass fights. And even smiles.

After returning the stroller the next day, we took a car to the airport in Newark, New Jersey, carrying our minimalist two weeks' worth of luggage and a big, still mostly immobile boy. While my husband checked us in, I explained to Graham that we'd be borrowing a wheelchair to go from the check-in area, through security, to our gate. He burst into hot, frustrated tears.

"I can just *walk*," he insisted. (Since the surgery, he'd put a little weight on his legs to use the bathroom, but hadn't taken steps, even with assistance.) He tried awkwardly hoisting himself to his feet with his walking sticks, and promptly crumbled to the floor. We gathered him up and placed him back on the bench.

"OKAYYYY," he bayed into the ticketing hall, totally defeated. "I will sit in the chair. But I'm only using it until security. Then I'm *walking* to the gate." People stared from the nearby check-in lines. We nodded obediently.

We became the airport's art exhibit. I didn't mind the staring per se, but every time someone noticed Graham, it made me notice again, too. It reminded me how little I controlled: I couldn't control Graham's condition, regardless of what surgeries we chose for him. I couldn't prevent him from falling so hard, so many times each day. I couldn't know which days I'd feel like I led a very normal, pedestrian life, or when I'd feel like I needed a second brain to have a job and remember to feed the dog and make it through my medication infusion every month and still parent Graham well enough that he could turn into the most successful, independent seven-year-old he could possibly be. And I certainly couldn't look any further ahead than that.

The airport's security area was vacant, but its employees were dutifully cautious.

"Hi there, buddy!" cheered a friendly TSA guy with blue latex gloves. "We're going to wipe this piece of paper over your chair, and then you can go, okay?"

Graham was quick to spit back a response.

"This isn't *my* chair!" he protested. "I don't *have* one of these." He pushed one of the armrests away from him, like he was distancing himself from something smelly. "I don't even know how to use it."

It was oddly heartwarming to see my handicapped kid identify so strongly as not handicapped, but as we wheeled toward our plane, I could only wonder how long it would be until Graham was on his feet again. Days? Weeks? *Months?* We still didn't know. We'd arrived back East with a happy, increasingly mobile Graham, and we were leaving with a much-altered, much-dispirited, much less capable version of the same and no real known path back to normal (or better).

Ten days later, Graham's trajectory seemed positive, albeit bumpy. At home, he'd started crawling again and participating in life per usual if he had friends over; it was like the mere presence of another small body erased the physical memory of the surgery. (When they left, he collapsed on the floor in a teary heap.) In therapy, he started bearing weight on his legs, and even walking gingerly in short bursts between two parallel training bars. We got out the walker he used before his arm crutches, and he started taking a few steps at a time with that. He insisted over and over that taking the leg casts off would leave him magically new and strong. But predictably, those casts came off, and the proverbial rug was ripped out from underneath us. Each day was different. Every morning he was sore, often in new places. While we'd cheered the possibility of improved flexibility in certain muscles, we'd overlooked how hard it would be to put fifty-plus pounds of weight on spots that had never borne weight before. His heels, his ankle sockets, and his knees grew swollen and painful, with shadows of bruising spreading up and down his skinny legs. We iced and massaged and soaked that little body in Epsom salts, day after day. Every day he woke up asking to play, and every day we hauled him to therapy. And every day he got stronger. But he was definitely not walking again. And despite our best attempts at distraction, he was definitely not happy.

THE MANHATTAN PROJECT

Grilled Yellow Chicken Rice Bowl with Broccoli and Peanut Sauce

In our house, kid chicken consumption was erratic; Graham would eat chicken legs right off a roasted bird, but wouldn't eat plain chicken breast. One of his favorites, though, was the kind of turmeric-tinged chicken satay we order from our local Thai take-out spot. This version of "yellow chicken" was just for him—grilled over medium heat, not high, so the chicken gets marked but not actually charred, and served with a coconut-based peanut sauce that I made mild, then kicked up with a bit more sriracha for myself and my husband. During Graham's recovery from leg surgery, it seemed to make sense to stick with things Graham would eat—to things that we knew would fuel him—so I made this often, separating the ingredients out on a plate for him, and piling them into a bowl for the grown-ups.

Use this recipe as a guide for any similar dish—you could use soba noodles and leftover grilled peppers instead of the rice and broccoli, pork instead of the chicken, et cetera. It calls for red Thai chili paste, but green or yellow would also be great. (They're less spicy, so you may need to use a bit more.)

MAKES: 4 SERVINGS
SPECIAL EQUIPMENT: TWELVE 6-INCH BAMBOO SKEWERS

For the rice bowl
- 4 tablespoons canola oil, divided
- 2 teaspoons freshly grated ginger
- ½ teaspoon ground turmeric
- ½ plus ¼ teaspoon kosher salt, divided
- 1 pound boneless chicken breast, cut into ½-inch strips the short way
- 2 cups uncooked brown basmati rice

2 heaping cups bite-size broccoli florets
(from a ¾-pound head of broccoli)

For the peanut sauce
1 (13.5-ounce) can coconut milk
½ cup creamy peanut butter
2 tablespoons fish sauce
2 tablespoons lime juice
1 to 3 teaspoons red Thai curry paste,
   depending on your heat preference
2 teaspoons freshly grated ginger
1 teaspoon sugar
½ teaspoon kosher salt, plus more to taste

» Place the skewers in a shallow pan and add water to cover. Set aside to soak for about 30 minutes.

» To make the rice bowl, first marinate the chicken: In a medium mixing bowl, stir together 2 tablespoons of the oil with the ginger, turmeric, and ½ teaspoon salt, then add the chicken-breast strips and turn the pieces to coat them evenly. Cover and refrigerate for about 30 minutes.

» Next, bring 3¼ cups of water to a boil. When it boils, add the rice and the remaining ¼ teaspoon salt, stir, then reduce the heat to the lowest setting and cook, covered, for about 40 minutes, until all the water is absorbed.

» Meanwhile, in a small saucepan, after you start cooking the rice, make the peanut sauce: Combine all the sauce ingredients. Bring them to a simmer over medium heat, whisking until smooth, then continue to simmer for 5 minutes, stirring occasionally. Season to taste with additional curry paste and salt, and set aside.

THE MANHATTAN PROJECT

» Preheat a gas or charcoal grill over medium-high heat, about 400 degrees F. Drain the bamboo skewers. Thread the marinated chicken strips the long way onto the skewers.

» When the grill is hot, brush the grates as clean as you can. Grill the chicken pieces for 4 to 6 minutes, turning once, only when the chicken releases easily from the grill grates.

» When all the water has been absorbed by the rice, add the broccoli florets to the rice, cover again, and let both sit for about 10 minutes with the heat turned off, until the broccoli is bright green. Scoop off the broccoli and transfer it to a bowl.

» To serve, pile the rice into bowls, and top each with a little sauce. Top with the broccoli and chicken skewers, plus additional sauce to taste.

Trial by Fire

THE Manhattan Project knocked us all off balance, really. It was bigger than us. My husband's back went wonky from lifting and carrying Graham. I woke up with mysterious searing foot pain one day that was completely gone the next. It was the kind of month that takes you so many places, you no longer know how much strength to muster to close your own refrigerator. (At home, even weeks later, my husband and I kept swinging our fridge door almost closed, but not quite.) We might get our balance back, we thought, if we kept our plans to go through with the camping trip we made each year with a group of friends. Even though there were wildfires raging across the state that closed many campgrounds and blanketed others in a thick purple haze of ash. And even though Graham still couldn't bear weight on his legs.

If you ask Graham at the end of any given summer what his favorite part of it was, he'll invariably tell you about going camping. The summer after he turned two, we realized that he excelled at the necessary triad of components required for a kid to enjoy a weekend with his family in the forest: sitting in front of a fire eating marshmallows, getting good and dirty, and throwing rocks into a rushing river. Since then, we've made a conscious effort to spend parts of every summer completely outside, clean fingernails be damned, happily performing the same triathlon day after day, night after night, fire after fire. And as a result, each August, for my birthday weekend, we now host a group camping trip focused primarily on the same pursuits. We've become the de facto leaders of a pop-up summer commune, a weekend-long camping potluck laced with ripe peaches and booze and marshmallows, plus whatever has recently become legal in the fair state of Washington. And this year, save for the campsite location, we weren't planning on changing a thing.

In addition to the fire, marshmallows, and rocks, the ingredients required for a good camping trip, in my mind, are quite specific. First, you need to have a kid-friendly tent. The type of towering tent-vehicle one must plug in to both electricity and water and the kind of half tent that suspends a person precariously off the side of a rock wall are overkill and incommodious, respectively, for our situation. But a big regular tent—the kind with a rain fly for inclement weather, hanging pockets next to the ceiling seams, good sturdy zippers, and a size small enough for one semipracticed person to handle solo but large enough to cause her ever-useful husband to feel responsible for putting it up himself in time for a horde of children to climb in—that's where good camping starts. Because when you have a kid whose circumstances dictate that he spends the majority of his time on his knees, as opposed to running around in the woods, turning your own tent into the coolest hangout spot is crucial.

Next, you need some nice friends. In its past incarnations, the trip had involved a rotating roster of friends from Seattle, depending on who was available, mostly those with kids around Graham's age. It had been a few years since we erected portable cribs next to the campfire, and as the kids grew, it was fun to watch them develop from parent-dependent early campers, straining to figure out why they weren't sleeping in familiar clothes in familiar beds with familiar lights and sounds, to the dirt-crusted *Lord of the Flies* swarm they'd morphed into the previous year. Graham usually tottered toward the back of the flock with his walker, with the youngest siblings, as his peers scaled hills to build rope swings and scrambled over rocks to fish. Over the years, we'd learned that it was important to invite people whose children we could parent, if needed, and who wouldn't be afraid to parent our own kid, because inevitably, Graham would find himself in a situation he couldn't physically get himself out of, like an adventurous kitten up a too-tall tree. We'd learned that the best young camper friends were those who felt it might be just as much fun to map out an intricate imaginary monster battle inside the tent or sit in a stand of trees as it was to shoot makeshift stick-and-string bows and arrows at innocent flora while running at full tilt. More so than in previous years, because he still wasn't moving at all independently beyond a slow crawl, we hoped that this year's crop of campers would be empathetic to Graham's post-surgery situation. That, as is so often the case no matter where we are, he wouldn't be left sitting alone in the tent while the whims of the herd guided it elsewhere.

Then, good camping requires an interesting spot. Conveniently, Seattle sits within easy striking distance of a plethora of excellent campsites, many of which have big campfire rings, access to a burble or rush of water with the appropriate rocky accoutrements, and a pleasant view. Near the town of Leavenworth, a small Bavarian village whose covenants require that each building maintain a Germanic architectural style reminiscent of how Disneyland might design an Oktoberfestland for grown-ups, the Cascade Mountains' eastern slopes drip their snowmelt into gorgeous rivers, creeks, and lakes. There are campsites everywhere.

TRIAL BY FIRE

So, all these things are good to have. But the final part that separates my birthday camping trip from our other camping trips is that the setup also requires careful thought about the food, the idea being that each family (except mine) only cooks one meal, but cooks it for the whole crowd. This year wasn't any different. As usual, I assigned meals so that each family had one responsibility over the course of the long weekend, taking two dinners myself. My goal each year is not quite bacchanalia, mostly because packing heat-sensitive foodstuffs in late summer requires such extensive cooler space. But for camping, the food is extensive. I like camp cooking because when we're in the woods, I have as much time to cook as I want. I don't have to squeeze it in between homework and swim lessons. I don't have to twist it around our work schedules. I get to cook the way I fantasize people without kids do every night: slowly and intentionally, eating when the food presents itself as ready, and no sooner. For camping, it's cushy. I don't have anything against burned hot dogs and macaroni and cheese—I happen to love crunchy burned hot-dog skin, actually—but I aim higher and fancier for the sake of entertainment, and for the sake of my own enjoyment. And, admittedly, perhaps as a way of distracting myself from having to just sit still.

My husband Jim calls it rosé camping, because ultimately, when I assemble dinner for the fifteen or twenty people gathered under solar-powered lights, I cook something that merits a decent glass of wine, but also something that requires a little waiting, which also goes best with said wine in hand. And in August, that usually means rosé—this year, the sparkling rosé we'd saved from British Columbia's Bella Sparkling Wines.

The crowd this year was bigger than usual: seven families, each with a kid or two, planned to join us. I started plotting out the dinners a few days before, with a list in a notebook that leaked sticky notes across the kitchen counter like a milk spill, each topped with the kinds of words that make my husband crazy before we head into the woods, toward supposed simplicity. ("'Grilled lemons?' 'Twinkly lights?' Jess, we're camping!")

The awkward part about camping during a dry, fire-prone year is that nothing even remotely resembling a campfire can exist. And cooking for twenty on one small, weak gas camping grill plus one two-burner camp stove is a challenge, if you want a dinner that's layered with the flavors high heat can instigate. So I planned ahead, creating flavor with ingredients I could make in advance and bring myself rather than with live flame. For each meal, I shattered the cooking process into tiny pieces, with the intent of putting them all back together near Leavenworth. And, like every year, I discovered that I enjoyed making the puzzle pieces for a good group meal one by one as much as, if not more than, I'd enjoy making them all at once at home. I assumed that if I brought a smoking campfire in my mind's eye, I wouldn't be as disappointed in not actually having one.

For the first night, I gained permission to use the remaining fillets of pink salmon Jim had caught on a work trip to Alaska just before the Gourmet Century. I wanted to cook them as simply as possible, and serve them with grilled Caesar salad. At home, I whirled spunky preserved lemons into an eggless Caesar dressing tinged with sherry vinegar and as many pungent anchovies as I dared for a kid-filled crowd, and cut bread for giant croutons, and trimmed crisp romaine into halves I could theoretically snuggle together to mark on a hot oiled grill just before serving. I tumbled olives and parsley and basil together in a food processor to make a chunky tapenade-inspired sauce for the tomatoes my friend Hannah planned to rescue from her home garden deeper in the state, which she and her family were actively evacuating because of a fast-moving wildfire. I twisted baby orange tomatoes off my own backyard vines, for

TRIAL BY FIRE

good measure. On impulse, I whirled softened goat cheese and cream cheese together with a big scoop of pungent kimchi, for a dip intended to pair with Ruffles potato chips, to whet appetites in case I had to grill the salmon and the romaine in heats. I made coconut-oatmeal snickerdoodle cookies that somehow went terribly, terribly wrong, winding up all tacky on the top and sunken in the center, and that were subsequently served only to the children, who never noticed they were anything but a cookie in hand.

For the second dinner, I imagined a sort of Moroccan-inspired rice bowl. I made a fresh batch of spicy harissa, which I stirred into *shakshuka*, a North African tomato sauce sweetened with red bell peppers and enriched with swirls of olive oil. I hoarded our chickens' eggs for the trip and bought good chorizo, planning to grill the links and serve them with skillet-fried eggs over rice smothered by the spicy sauce, with perhaps a shower of sharp feta cheese and a pinch of the parsley about to bolt in my front garden. It was slated to be the kind of one-bowl meal that can quickly outgrow the size of the little neon-colored Ikea plastic bowls many of us bring camping, but I knew it would taste good. I packed up all the components neatly in jars and baggies, and labeled them with blue painter's tape.

This year, it did feel crazy, packing up between Graham's post-surgery therapy sessions to head into the mountains. For a while, it even felt impossible; there had been a major mix-up in the order for the orthotics Graham would need to wear the instant the leg casts came off, and for a week or so, we didn't think he'd be able to make the switch in time for what was inevitably a wet, messy weekend in any weather. Since camping with casts was out of the question, we debated canceling, right as I started cooking for the trip in earnest. But since the surgery, one thing had become clear: nothing motivates Graham like hanging out with his buddies. And despite his pain, we did expect him to have fun. So I drove an hour north of Seattle with him to fix the orthotics issue just in time, and the sweet orthotist let Graham help unwind the casting material, revealing shriveled white feet. Then off we went. Off we went, despite the fact that we weren't entirely sure how far the site was from active flames. Off we went, in search of friendship and dirt, with everything we needed (and a few things we didn't) for three delicious nights of camping.

We'd booked a site a ways west up the road from Leavenworth, on the shore of Lake Wenatchee, a miles-long tub of glacial water with a large state park at its southeast end. We knew ahead of time that the whole place was under a strict fire ban, so our friend Meghan plotted a grill-friendly Nutella-and-marshmallow version of s'mores, the idea of which managed to keep Graham occupied for at least a quarter of the two-hour drive there. He kept tabs with us on when each family would be arriving, like the conductor of a busy train station, trying to guess where each group would pitch their tent even though we had no idea what the campground looked like. For the first time since the surgery, we could see his brain start to spin with excitement. For the first time in weeks, he had something to look forward to.

When we arrived, Hannah was already there, with a van stuffed with everything one might expect from a family who had just left their home, possibly forever. There were ski boots and down layers, despite it being late August, and photo albums and favorite shoes and all the Legos her son could pack during their hasty evacuation from the fires. And nestled into the front seat, she'd made space for a new crate of the freshest peaches, still poufy with their cotton candy fuzz, intended for ice cream. She'd brought the bucket she brings each year for her old-fashioned ice-cream churner, but in the quite literal heat of the moment, between debating which bikes to save (all!) and whether to keep searching for her cat, she forgot the crank arm that makes the whole contraption work. But she had flowers for me, for my birthday, and fat German sausages from Leavenworth for that first night's meal, and her ever-present sense of adventure and devotion to fun, which, under the hazy gray sky and the still-sketchy threat of nearby fires, seemed much more important than the ice-cream maker's crank.

I thrilled at the discovery that the lake's beach was softish sand just until the edge next to the water, where it turned rocky; Graham would have his rock throwing and could theoretically also play in the sand, which often attracted other kids. But as families rolled in, and the sun's setting light reflected across the fire ash in the atmosphere so the whole sky lit up in an eerie shade of violet, we missed the campfire, which typically gave folks a place to gather, bugs-to-the-light style. Instead, the kid horde schooled from one activity to the next like tiny, nimble fish, and Graham wound up alone. He seemed content in his camp chair, like a cookie-crumbed old grandpa happy to watch and participate when the party came to him, but in my mind—using my own sense of what it must feel like to not be able to follow the crowd and to fear, as had been the case so much of the month, that any sudden movement might cause searing pain—I created a sadness for him that I couldn't seem to shake. Jim and I went camping to go forth, to go forward, to explore. We thought that by going, we were giving him the right kind of childhood. But watching him sit mostly in that same purple chair, I felt that we had sentenced Graham to a weekend of not feeling like a kid, or to always feeling slower than the rest—that feeling, at least in some sense, I knew well.

More friends came, all in good spirits. Jim pitched the tent. Hannah's husband, Joe, helped me hang solar lamps around the picnic tables we designated as our tribe's gathering site, and Tracy arrived with a glittery birthday sign and a set of delicate-looking twinkly lights, plus all the giving and kindness she stuffs into her pockets every morning. By the time dark came and stomachs wanted more than chips dipped in the soft, kimchi-spiked goat cheese we'd already opened, our string of sites looked like a *Kinfolk* magazine cover shoot staged inside a bow-and-arrow factory invaded by six-year-olds. I started to feel like the weekend might actually work.

Each year, the first night of the camping trip, traditionally, was not a *Kinfolk* dinner. It was usually a total mishmash, a rolling offering of sausages, leftovers, and gas-station staples that was never healthy and always included a bag of cold Dick's hamburgers and cheeseburgers, from the sixty-year-old iconic Seattle drive-in that still serves dinner for four for ten or fifteen bucks, depending on hunger levels. Aaron and Tracy had brought the bag of cold Dick's, a fact we insisted on repeating over and over at top volume to make sure the surrounding campsites understood our twelve-year-old humor.

As we settled in, it became clear that our friends had planned just as carefully, making a very concerted effort to include our kid. Tami and Dan brought face paints and their giant canoe, hoping to take Graham for a ride in it with their kids. Gina brought tempera paint, and gathered rocks for a surprisingly captivating rock-painting session. Meghan's Nutella s'mores were a hit, and the night faded into the glow of a flickering electric lantern. There were guitars and Neil Young, and a ridiculous Ween song called "Buenas Tardes Amigo," in which a jealous man frames someone else for killing his brother, then poisons a chicken's meat and feeds it to the accused. It was not camping per usual—there was no fire, and Maggie's family had moved, taking with them the intricate camping sink we'd all relied on, and my brother couldn't make it—but it was camping.

TRIAL BY FIRE

On Saturday morning, the day dawned bright and clear, with little trace of the smoke we'd seen the day before. Splinters of the group chipped off for canoeing and bike rides and swimming, but Graham, who wanted nothing to do with any friend that wasn't willing to sit and throw rocks, seemed to close himself into his own little bubble. Every time the activity changed, we did our best to help him join—which meant helping him change for swimming, helping him to the bathroom, helping him get on his adapted bicycle, helping him get off his bike, helping him to the table, helping him away from the table. Both the adults and the kids made constant efforts to include him, but he didn't want to be the one who needed help. And so he opted out of most things, to avoid it. And so it went for the next forty-eight hours.

The food was fantastic, I guess. There was a perfect picnic lunch, and great pancakes and French toast, and The Little Grill That Could got just hot enough to leave deep brown lines across the salmon and romaine lettuce. And on the last day, just when we'd all had enough, Tami and Dan appeared with the kind of kale-and-chickpea salad that makes one feel deeply self-righteous in the nutrition department.

But the food didn't matter to me, the way it normally does. Because every hour or so, I'd catch Graham sitting alone. He didn't seem particularly bothered by it, but he was alone—daydreaming, or drawing in the dirt, or absentmindedly munching on something—while the tribe of other children hopped nimbly out of trees, over rocks, between activities. And in those small moments, my heart was the crumple zone in a well-built car, folding in on itself until it felt like there was nothing left. We couldn't know how much the surgery would eventually help him, or whether he'd ever walk independently, or whether he'd one day be able to just get up and start running, Forrest Gump–style, with the other kids. But I knew then that the food, which had always fueled me in body and spirit when I needed lifting up, was not enough for Graham. I could make other people smile with what I cooked, but no matter how silly or messy or fun I made it, food didn't heal him. I couldn't say *I made you salmon just the way you like it* to cheer him up. I couldn't cook him out of his doldrums. And I didn't know how else to help someone heal, except wait.

Tomato Salad with Olive Sauce

Part tapenade, part vinaigrette, the herb-flecked olive sauce I use to dress fat chunks of the season's best tomatoes would be equally delicious over cucumber slices, grilled salmon, or butter lettuce.

MAKES: 6 SERVINGS

½ cup pitted kalamata olives
½ cup lightly packed fresh basil leaves
½ cup lightly packed fresh Italian parsley leaves, divided
2 tablespoons extra-virgin olive oil
Freshly ground black pepper, to taste
1½ pounds fist-size ripe tomatoes (about 5),
    any color, sliced or cut into wedges
Chunky sea salt, to taste

» In the work bowl of a food processor, combine the olives, basil, half the parsley, olive oil, and pepper. Pulse about 15 times, so the olives are chopped but still a bit chunky, scraping down the sides of the bowl after the first 10 pulses. (If you're taking this on the road, transfer this mixture to a sealed container, and assemble the salad just before serving.)

» In a large bowl, combine the tomatoes, the olive sauce, and the remaining ¼ cup parsley leaves. Season with a shower of salt, and serve immediately.

Preserved-Lemon Grilled Caesar Salad

The success of grilling romaine lettuce head halves on a grill while camping depends a lot on the shape of the grates you'll be grilling over; dirty or rusty or uneven grates are not ideal. If you're not using nicely cleaned grates or a gas camping grill, line the grill's grates with oiled foil, or the heavy-duty nonstick foil specifically designed for grilling.

For ease, it's nice to purchase the kind of romaine lettuce that comes three heads to a bag; the roots tend to hold together well when grilled. This recipe makes one cup of dressing, so if you want, you can drizzle it over fewer grilled romaine halves for a smaller crowd, then save the dressing to enjoy over multiple days.

This recipe omits egg yolks because I make the dressing ahead of time, and it's often hard to keep things really cold when you go camping. But if you make this at home, by all means, please whirl a fresh yolk into the dressing.

MAKES: 6 SERVINGS

For the dressing
1 whole preserved lemon, rinsed, halved, and seeded
4 anchovy fillets
2 tablespoons sherry vinegar
1 tablespoon Dijon mustard
1 large clove garlic, smashed
Freshly ground black pepper, to taste
¾ cup extra-virgin olive oil
Kosher salt, to taste

For the salad

3 medium heads romaine lettuce, halved lengthwise

About ¼ cup extra-virgin olive oil, for grilling

¾ cup freshly grated Parmigiano-Reggiano cheese

» To make the dressing: Combine the lemon halves, anchovies, vinegar, mustard, garlic, and pepper in a blender or food processor, and whiz until completely smooth. With the motor running, add the olive oil in a slow, steady stream, processing until the oil is completely combined. Season with salt (this will depend on the saltiness of your preserved lemons), whirl to blend again, and set the dressing aside. (If you're taking this on the road, transfer it to a sealed container, and grill and assemble the salad just before serving.)

» To make the salad: Preheat a gas or charcoal grill over medium heat, about 350 degrees F. Brush the cooking grates clean. Brush both sides of each romaine half with olive oil, then grill, cut sides down first, for 3 or 4 minutes per side, or just until the lettuce begins to brown but hasn't yet softened.

» Transfer the grilled romaine to a serving plate, cut sides up. Drizzle with the dressing, scatter the cheese on top, and serve immediately.

Smoky Campshuka with Chorizo

Shakshuka is a classic North African dish, made by simmering eggs in a spicy tomato and pepper sauce—similar to *oeufs provençales*, but with more heat. When we were camping with kids who all happened to love chorizo, we added that too, and served it over rice, which seemed like a successful way of satisfying a big variety of ages and palates. I made a sort of North African rice bowl by piling my eggs on top of my rice, then topping them with sauce, hunks of spicy chorizo, and feta cheese. You can follow my example, or allow each person to plate up a combination of eggs, sauce, and condiments that works for them.

Look for *pimentón de la Vera*, or smoked Spanish paprika, in the spice section of a large grocery store. The harissa—a red-hued North African paste made with dried chilies, spices, and sometimes lime and/or rose—is usually hiding in the ethnic food aisle. Note that not all harissa is created equal, so add less at first, then add more toward the end based on how spicy you like things.

MAKES: 6 TO 8 SERVINGS

For the sauce
¼ cup extra-virgin olive oil
1 medium onion, diced
3 large cloves garlic, finely chopped
1 teaspoon smoked Spanish paprika
1 teaspoon kosher salt, plus more to taste
1 (28-ounce) can diced tomatoes
1 (28-ounce) can ground peeled tomatoes
2 large red bell peppers, diced
2 to 3 tablespoons harissa

To serve

4 chorizo sausages

4 tablespoons extra-virgin olive oil, divided

1 dozen eggs, divided

4 cups cooked rice

1 cup crumbled feta cheese

1 cup lightly packed torn parsley leaves (optional)

» To make the sauce: Heat the olive oil in a large, heavy pot over medium-low heat. Add the onion and garlic and cook, stirring occasionally, for 5 to 10 minutes, or until the onion is soft. Add the paprika and salt, and cook, stirring, for another minute or so, until the mixture is fragrant and the spices begin to stick to the bottom of the pan. Add both cans of tomatoes, the peppers, and the harissa. Stir to blend, then increase the heat to bring the mixture to a strong simmer. Reduce the heat to low and cook at a bare bubble for about 30 minutes, or until the peppers are completely soft. At this point, you can either leave the mixture as is, or blend all or part of it. (I use an immersion blender to blend just some of it, so it still has some chunkiness.) Set it aside. (If you're taking this on the road, let this mixture cool, then transfer it to a sealed container. Before serving, gently rewarm it in a pan while you cook the eggs, rice, and chorizo. If you'd like, you can also cook the rice a day or two ahead, and just warm it before serving.)

» To serve: Start by cooking the chorizo. Heat a gas or charcoal grill over medium-high heat, about 400 degrees F. Brush the cooking grates clean. When the grill is hot, add the chorizo and cook, turning occasionally, until the sausages are browned in spots and cooked through, about 10 minutes total. Set aside to cool for a few minutes, then cut the chorizo into 2-inch chunks and transfer them to a serving bowl.

» Meanwhile, heat a large skillet over medium heat. Add 2 table-spoons of the oil, then crack six eggs into the skillet and cook them to your desired doneness. Transfer them to a platter and repeat with the remaining oil and eggs.

» Serve the campshuka like a taco bar, allowing people to fill their bowls with plenty of sauce, then add chorizo, eggs, rice, feta, and parsley.

The Opposite
of Ilwaco

IT was hard, at that point, to avoid feeling like we'd never live normally again. Every day we let Graham watch a television show to distract him while we rubbed arnica into his surgery wounds and massaged his black-and-blue legs, and every night we soaked him in Epsom salt baths. We began a nightly rotation of removable leg splints intended to help him retain the flexibility the surgery had achieved. One night we'd put a knee splint on the right leg. The next night we'd do the left leg. The third night we'd put a different kind of splint on both ankles. Somewhere in the process, we'd remember that while the New Jersey doctor had insisted the splints were absolutely necessary to ensure proper healing, the alternative therapists didn't want us to use splints at all. And so on the fourth night, we took a night off. Then we'd start the rotation over again, waking at varying times each night except the fourth, removing the splints when Graham started screaming because his legs had cramped. There was more therapy. He was still not happy.

However, he wasn't actually in any danger. So rather than canceling the salmon-fishing trip we'd booked two months earlier, we parked Graham at his grandparents' house for a night. They were more than willing to continue with the massaging and soaking and splinting, and he adores them. *Maybe*

we'll just do some of The Here List without him, I thought. The
list sat in a big file-cabinet drawer under my desk, invisible
to the naked eye but somehow always still seen. It made me
sad to think of changing it so that I could do more without
my child, simply because it was easier. On the other hand, I
wanted to go fishing.

My father's family has a history of fishing out of Ilwaco,
Washington, a dirty burp of a town near the dangerous sand
bar that separates the Columbia River from the Pacific Ocean,
right between Washington and Oregon. The truth is, he grew
up fishing everywhere, so his brain is mapped with the rivers
of the United States. But the way I remember my father telling
it growing up, it was Ilwaco—they referred to fishing there
using just the town's name, often with the same knowing, por-
tentous tone my veteran grandfather reserved for saying "Viet-
nam" or "Korea"—that served as a Howe family rite of passage.
The boat ride was rough, but the salmon were unbeatable. My
great-grandfather Henry used to say he was going salmon fishing there as a euphemism for gambling and drinking whiskey,
and when his wife, Dolly, suggested the family start coming
along, there was a permanent palpable tension between the
two. But off they went, yearly in my own mind, for the family
fishing trip.

As far as I knew, Ilwaco had been what had inspired my
father's lifelong love for trout fishing. I'd assumed, my whole
life, that my father fished in rivers because we lived in Boise,
Idaho—because fly-fishing for fat rainbow trout a three-hour
drive from home with my brother had been much more convenient than driving the ten hours to Ilwaco and chartering
a boat and a captain for salmon fishing on the frothy Pacific.
Since, growing up, I'd usually been the one to stay warm
and dry with my mom, who harbors a notoriously strong dis-
taste for all creatures finned, I'd missed the mostly father-son

adventures on the Idaho streams that provided most of the fish I ate growing up. I was a fish eater in a family of recreational fishermen, but I'd only been fishing myself a handful of times. And so early in the summer, I had called my father, suggesting our own family fishing trip to Ilwaco for Father's Day and providing, I thought ingeniously, an out for my mother, who wouldn't enjoy it if it involved looking at fish: she could stay on shore with Graham. We'd catch fat king salmon during the fish's fattest weeks of the Pacific Northwest season, in a famously fantastic fishing spot.

"No way," my dad had responded, launching into a tirade about the area's deadly conditions. "That is just so *stupid*. Knowing what I know about Ilwaco, it's ridiculous to even imagine us trying to fish there. In fact, fishing there is my idea of hell."

My father—who, as his brother, Ken, puts it, "has always had his differences with open water"—scolded me for asking for trouble. As if I'd called to let him know I'd planned to march on Jerusalem with an anti-Semitic graffiti team, or wanted to wander naked with hungry polar bears in the Arctic. I'd known his earliest fishing trip had been a stomach-jolting combination of too many candy bars for breakfast, the smell of diesel fuel, and rolling seas, but I'd thought perhaps having outgrown a Hershey habit had made seasickness a problem of the past. I'd suggested Ilwaco might have changed for him by then.

"You're wrong. There isn't an ocean salmon-fishing trip I've been on that hasn't made me sick," he'd promised, his voice rising on the other end of the phone, like he was instinctively trying to speak over the sound of a motor. "I'm sorry to be such a Debbie Downer on this particular subject, but I'm speaking from experience. It's a very bad idea. I do love to eat salmon, but I only fish from the shore." Then he hung up.

THE OPPOSITE OF ILWACO

It is perhaps worth noting that I come from a family of social Neanderthals. That may be a slight exaggeration, but my clan typically doesn't say much that isn't necessary for everyday function. No one says nice things just to be nice. And more than that, though we are kind folks, we can all of us get a little sharp, if you hit the right buttons. It would have been completely uncharacteristic, for example, for my dad to say that the trip had been a nice idea.

Still, I'd flinched, and spent the rest of the afternoon stunned by his coarse dismissal. Sure, my husband, who had recently chartered an Ilwaco fishing captain's boat (and accompanying area knowledge) for an oceanographic research project, had said the waters were rough. In fact, he'd gone there during the worst storms he could find precisely because the waters were rough. He'd fished with the captain in his off-hours, but he hadn't said anything about real danger. I couldn't tell whether I should have saved my hurt feelings by believing my dad's version of the story, or relied on my husband's typically dependable (and usually cautious) assessment of an area's wave conditions and absorbed the paternal rejection. I'd pouted around for an evening, feeling frustrated that my clever Father's Day plan had been foiled.

My dad's last comment had stuck with me, though, reminding me that I thought I cared as much or more about *eating* the fish as I did about *catching* the fish. It didn't really matter to me how far from the shore I went for said fish, as long as I came home with them. So I'd abandoned my brilliant plan and switched tacks. And in a quick squall of e-mails that resulted in much less planning and driving than an Ilwaco trip but probably the same amount of money, I arranged spots on a salmon-fishing charter with my husband and our friends Anne and Ben, leaving from a dock less than three miles from my home in Seattle. It was advertised as a "classic Pacific Northwest saltwater fishing experience." If my dad didn't want to come salmon fishing, I'd just go fishing myself, I figured.

Jim and I dragged ourselves out of bed before dawn, excited to fish but dizzied by another up-and-out. I overstuffed black-bean breakfast burritos, wrapped them in foil, and drove them down to the docks at Seattle's Shilshole Bay Marina, the floating parking lot next to Golden Gardens Park that hosts the city's year-round population of motorboats, sailboats, and fishing boats for people who hire other people to help them fish for salmon once a decade.

The morning of the trip, in the dark, I was the salmon-fishing equivalent of loaded for bear. We donned waterproof gear head to toe, like we'd be heading out for an experience à la *Deadliest Catch*, and brought a cooler of beer for good measure. Anne and Ben were giddy, overflowing with recipe ideas for our presumed catch; they planned to rev up their little home smoker for half of whatever they brought home. The other couple on our charter, a building supply–store owner from central Washington and his new bride, were starstruck by the city and excited to board the boat. As we waited for the guiding company to unlock the dock-access doors, I shifted nervously from foot to foot. The man chomped down a bag of Reese's Pieces for breakfast, and I grimaced, wondering whether the forecasted rain would come with wind, and whether the wind would come with waves, and whether we'd see those Reese's Pieces again, like at Ilwaco circa 1960.

Only, our captain—a tight-lipped, weatherworn guy much more focused on doing his job than on getting to know us (or, say, ask our names)—didn't go very far. In fact, rather than crossing Puget Sound toward the islands just appearing on the horizon in the misty dawn, as Jim and I had done once on a different charter boat years earlier, he cut the engine about ten minutes from the dock. And without ceremony, he let the boat drift within a very good stone's throw of the shore and busied himself setting up the fishing rigs we wrongly assumed we'd be learning how to use ourselves.

Ben and Anne and Jim and I exchanged glances.

"This is it?" Anne mouthed.

"I guess so?" I mouthed back, turning my palms to the sky with a shrug. We had anticipated an adventure. We'd imagined waves sloshing over the sides, knuckles whitening with the effort of holding rods and rails tight in bad weather. The captain had given us a brief demonstration on how to reel fish in properly, offering no more detailed information than one might glean from being a human in a world full of fish eaters for thirty-some years. We had to pry for details about what bait he was using, and where he thought the fish might be, and what exactly we should anticipate catching. The answers came in short, almost militaristic reports: "Herring." "Here." "Salmon." We couldn't understand why someone so unwilling to talk held a job that theoretically required talking. Thirty minutes in, it became clear we'd paid to hang out on a boat together and watch someone else fish.

We sat in the half-light, not even slightly shivering, comfortably drinking still-hot coffee out of a fancy Japanese thermos, as Captain Quiet bustled around the wet aft deck casting off his piratical glare, only grunting occasionally toward us if one of the four fishing lines wiggled a little. I wondered if the weight of his bushy mustache made it hard for him to open his mouth. For an hour, we caught nothing. I started to feel guilty for dragging my friends out for an experience we might have given ourselves in a rented pool raft. I imagined them imagining better fishing.

Then, from inside the cozy little cabin, we heard a hiss and a pop, and turned to find my husband had cracked open a Rainier beer, the regional equivalent of Budweiser. "This is the best way I know of to catch a fish," he announced. It was ten past seven in the morning. We all smiled. And, as if on command, the lines started hopping. "FISH ON!" he hollered triumphantly, pointing. And then came another.

For a moment, Mr. Mustache was overwhelmed—with a fish on one line and another flopping on the boat's deck, a third line wobbled, and he nodded to me, suggesting it was my turn to reel one in. I stepped forward and reeled, surprised by the wonkiness of the rod and the strength of the salmon. As I brought the fish in closer, I felt what must be the rush fishermen refer to when they have a live thing attached to their palms via braided microfilament line; the moment I saw the fish's fin glint in the soft morning light, I grasped the rod tighter, and spun the line-winding widget faster, blood hot in my arms.

But I was too hasty. Too desperate. In a blink, not ten feet from the boat, the fish disappeared. I had reeled him in too fast.

"Now look what you've done!" roared the captain, suddenly articulate and plenty loud. "You've ripped the poor guy's lip out!"

I cowered with mock guilt, thinking he was mostly joking and that perhaps he did have a personality after all, until he leaned over to dangle a large hook with a bloody fish lip attached to it about six inches from my forehead. "You did this," he yelled again. He was right. I'd de-lipped a sockeye salmon. And since in all our sibling photographs, I was the sockeye— my brother, my sister, and I have an uncanny ability to frown deeply, drop our lower jaws, and bug our eyes out, to such good fishy effect that we sometimes go by Bassface, Tunaface, and Sockeyeface, respectively—it felt a little like ripping out my own lip. It made me never want to catch a fish again. I moved to the soft little bench inside the boat's cockpit and opened a beer.

THE OPPOSITE OF ILWACO

And so the morning went: silence and slow lines, followed by the hiss-pop of a beer, then the wiggle of a preset fishing line, and sometimes a catch (once, begrudgingly at first, by me). The captain radioed other boats, who all asserted it was one of the slowest fishing days of the season. In the end, we collectively drank twelve cans of beer and caught fourteen fish—just over half our boat's daily catch limit, which was a major disappointment for some on board, but still fourteen salmon more than we had at the start of the day. There was nothing close to the threat of seasickness. Save the four seconds of excitement one finds in bringing a live salmon into a gently rocking boat, there wasn't much thrill, either.

I couldn't help thinking that between the dead-calm seas and the very light drizzle and the cantankerous captain and the scanty catch, I should be frustrated with our day. But as we bobbed for silent minutes at a stretch in plain view of Seattle's foggy downtown, I realized that despite missing the so-called exciting part of ocean fishing, the part I'd previously connected in my mind with the legend that was Ilwaco—the bumpy seas and the foamy air and the threat of seasickness and, in my mind's eye, copious quantities of fish and fish guts flying across the boat's stern—I was having a very good time. In our spurts of conversation, we made plans for future adventures with Anne and Ben, and delved deep into the existential merits of the midmorning chili-cheese Fritos meal. We googled the differences between various salmon species. When silence came, we let it stay as long as it felt comfortable sitting next to us. I sat still and quiet for minutes at a time. And hours later, I knew the waiting and the friendly time-passing banter and the plaintive hiss of cold morning beers, combined with the magic of occasionally pulling something alive and edible from the sound's black depths, were enough. I realized that, in my urge to do something with my dad that would appeal to him, I'd failed to recognize that the waiting part is, perhaps, what makes salmon fishing such a strong pastime in the Pacific Northwest. As they say, it's called fishing, not catching.

Back at the dock, the captain zipped through the filleting process, separating fat pink slabs from backbones, unceremoniously dumping guts into the water between the docks while gulls squawked over who got what for lunch. It seemed like they were celebrating a miracle—food had appeared from the dock gods! again!—and their excitement was contagious. Anne, Ben, and I immediately noticed the captain jettisoning the salmons' slick bright-pink egg sacs, and scrambled to open zip-top bags to collect them, planning to prepare them as *ikura*, traditional Japanese cured salmon roe.

We walked off the dock with nine pound-size salmon fillets per couple. We were each about $200 lighter, which translated, I figured, to fresh-caught salmon at almost fifty dollars per pound—twice the cost of king salmon at my local grocery store that week. From a home-economics standpoint, it was a terrible way to buy dinner.

But I got other things, too. Memories of a morning on the water, for one. A few hours with friends, uninterrupted by work or worries or any of my other paltry stressors, which helped me understand what my father loves about fishing. Salmon with a story, which we saved and shared for Christmas dinner. A lesson in doing nothing. And the thought that perhaps when it came to Graham's recovery, I needed to focus more on the fishing than on the catching.

Roasted Sockeye Salmon with Savory Plum Jam

My dad would have loved to try the cured salmon roe we attempted to make after fishing. But after misgauging the water temperature required to clean our roe, their milky-white sac residue remained, so we wound up with a lackluster version of traditional Japanese *ikura*. (We did, however, succeed in transforming strips of raw roe temporarily into beautiful pink pearly bracelets. Really, fish eggs make great jewelry.)

In lieu of roe, we ate lots of salmon. We roasted the final two fillets, which weighed in at about a pound each, for Christmas, served with a smear of a savory Italian plum jam I'd made over the summer. If you have the foresight to make the jam in August or September in anticipation of the holidays, it makes a lovely main course on a well-dressed table. (See the following recipe for suggestions on how to make the jam with cranberries.)

I cook sockeye and pink salmon mostly naked; because the fillets of those particular breeds are relatively thin, they cook quite quickly. When the small white beads of fat that signal salmon's doneness begin to form on the edges of the fillet, I want to be able to see them.

You can use other types of salmon; just keep in mind that the thicker the fillet, the longer it will take to cook.

MAKES: 6 SERVINGS

> 1 tablespoon extra-virgin olive oil,
>   plus more for oiling the pan, if desired
> 2 (roughly 1-pound) sockeye or pink salmon fillets
> Sea salt and freshly ground black pepper, to taste
> 1 cup Savory Plum and Rosé Jam with Mustard
>   (recipe follows)

» Preheat the oven to 425 degrees F.

» Oil a baking sheet if you want to keep the skin on when you serve the fish. The skin should lift off it when the fish is done, which means you'll have more luck transferring the fillets to a serving platter in one big piece. But if you want the skin to stick to the pan, don't oil it. You'll be able to lift the cooked fish right off the skin, albeit probably not in one piece, unless you have a long, fancy fish spatula. I like doing this and serving the salmon in pieces on top of the jam.

» Place the salmon fillets side by side on the baking sheet. Smear them with the olive oil, season with salt and pepper, and roast for 4 to 8 minutes, depending on the thickness of each fish. (If your fillets are bigger, 1½ pounds each, for example, it'll take more like 8 to 10 minutes.) You'll know the fish is done when the entire top of the salmon has turned a lighter shade of pink and you begin to see small white beads of fat forming on the lower edge of the thickest end of the fillet.

» Serve the salmon immediately, along with the jam.

Savory Plum and Rosé Jam with Mustard

In the dog days of summer, when dark, oblong Italian prune plums begin appearing on your neighbors' trees, make a plea for a big handful and make this savory jam, which is as delicious on pork or chicken (or on toast with a slab of sharp cheddar melted on top) as it is on salmon. In the fall and winter, substitute cranberries (frozen are fine) for the plums, which will give you a thicker, more substantial jam, but one that is also lovely on fish, pork, or poultry.

If you have an abundance of plums, this recipe can be doubled or tripled and canned according to your jar manufacturer's instructions.

MAKES: ABOUT 3 CUPS JAM

1½ pounds small Italian prune plums, halved and pitted
1½ cups sugar
½ cup dry rosé wine
1 teaspoon yellow mustard seeds
1 teaspoon kosher salt
1 bay leaf

» In a medium saucepan, combine all the ingredients over medium-high heat and bring to a low boil, stirring occasionally, and cook until the sugar has dissolved completely. When the liquid is clear, let the jam cook for an additional 12 to 15 minutes, skimming the foam off the top occasionally, until the bubbles become thick and the plums are falling apart. Let the jam cool for a few minutes on the stove, then pack the jam into three half-pint jars and let it cool. Cover and refrigerate until you're ready to use it, up to 3 weeks.

AUGUST

Breakfast Burritos with Bacon, Onions, and Pickled Padróns

Looking back, the fastest I had to move the day of our fishing adventure was actually early in the morning, making these hearty burritos. Each element is quite simple, but getting the eggs, black beans, onions, and bacon into the tortilla while each is still hot requires a little orchestrating. Please note that the whole operation works best if you use big (ten-inch or larger) flour tortillas, as opposed to whatever sort of unique alt-grain tortilla might have flirted its way into your cart at the grocery store, because the gluten in the flour tortillas is a crucial part of keeping these babies closed.

If you prefer, you can substitute store-bought pickled jalapeños for the pickled Padrón peppers (which need to be made the day before) or skip the peppers altogether. Add sour cream and cilantro, if you'd like.

MAKES: 4 LARGE BURRITOS

8 ounces sliced bacon
1 large onion, thinly sliced
1 teaspoon ground cumin
Juice of 1 large lime
2 cups cooked black beans (home-cooked,
    or from one 15-ounce can, rinsed and drained)
½ cup chopped Pickled Padrón Peppers (recipe follows)
Kosher salt, to taste
8 large eggs, whisked to blend
Freshly ground black pepper
4 (10-inch) flour tortillas
8 ounces sharp cheddar cheese, such as Beecher's, grated

» Heat a large, heavy skillet over medium heat. Add the bacon strips and cook to your desired doneness, turning them occasionally and adjusting the heat as necessary. Transfer the bacon to a paper-towel-lined plate to drain and set it aside. Scoop a tablespoon or two of the bacon grease into a little bowl and save it for cooking the eggs.

» Add the onions to the bacon pan with the remaining grease and cook, stirring occasionally, for about 10 minutes, until they are soft and browned in spots. Stir in the cumin, lime juice, black beans, and peppers, season with salt, and cook for another 1 to 2 minutes, stirring once or twice. Remove the pan from the heat.

» Meanwhile, heat a medium skillet over medium heat. When it's hot, add the reserved bacon grease, then the whisked eggs, and season with salt and pepper. Cook the eggs, stirring frequently with a rubber spatula, until they are just set.

» Place 1 tortilla on each of 4 plates, and divide the cheese between the tortillas. (If you want, you can heat the tortillas briefly in a dry pan or in the microwave to make them more pliable.) Divide the eggs and the bean mixture among the four tortillas in little piles, then immediately roll the tortillas around the ingredients, tucking in the edges, and letting the burrito rest, seam side down, for a minute to steam itself closed. Serve as soon as possible. (If you need to travel, you can wrap the burritos in foil, but they are best eaten within 10 or 15 minutes.)

Pickled Padrón Peppers

Made with little Spanish Padrón or Japanese *shishito* peppers, which sometimes (but not always) have a bit of kick, these refrigerator pickles are the perfect bite when you're just browsing through your kitchen for a snack, but they're also an awesome punch atop one-bowl meals—think rice bowls, Smoky Campshuka with Chorizo (page 199), or even ramen or pho.

MAKES: 2 QUARTS PEPPERS

2½ cups apple cider vinegar

1¼ cups water

1 tablespoon sugar

2 teaspoons kosher salt

½ teaspoon black peppercorns

½ teaspoon coriander seeds

1 bay leaf

¾ pound Padrón or *shishito* peppers

» In a medium saucepan, combine the vinegar, water, sugar, salt, peppercorns, coriander, and bay leaf. Bring to a boil and cook for 1 to 2 minutes, stirring as the sugar and salt dissolve. Add the peppers, and cook for about 5 minutes, turning them occasionally, until they have lost their bright-green color and have softened. Remove the pan from the heat, cover it, and let the peppers sit until the pan cools to room temperature.

» Using tongs, transfer the peppers to 2 clean quart-size jars with tight-fitting lids. Divide the liquid and aromatics evenly between the 2 jars, cover them, and refrigerate until you're ready to use them, up to 1 month.

THE OPPOSITE OF ILWACO

SEPTEMBER

A full month after the surgery, Graham was still making progress, albeit slowly. He returned to using his arm crutches, with the much-different and healthier walking gait we had hoped for, but he was still nowhere near as strong as he'd been before we boarded the plane to New Jersey. While public-school kids citywide ironically stayed home for an extra two weeks to accommodate a teachers' strike, Graham's private school began the week after Labor Day, as usual, which was weeks earlier than he was ready. He could walk with his sticks again, but he had very little stamina.

"Maybe he shouldn't start right away," I said to Jim, half begging. We'd taken distinctly different approaches to helping Graham heal, and I was definitely the softie. "I mean, how much are they going to do the first week?"

"Look, he's not where he was in May, but he's more functional than he was at this time last year," countered Jim. "He wants to see his friends. And he still has Austin this year," he added, referring to the patient, caring aide who had stayed by Graham's side for most of each school day throughout kindergarten.

And so we allowed Graham to start school. The twenty-five-second walk between the parking lot's handicapped spaces and the first-grade classroom—a slow trek we'd always accommodated by arriving at school fifteen minutes before all the other kids—became a despondent slog. Graham suddenly refused to let us use the handicap-parking pass we'd had since he was three, so we parked farther away than we had the previous year. Jim and I began swapping strategies for getting into the classroom in under twenty-five minutes. From singing to storytelling to imaginary karate, Graham did anything he could to distract us so he could stop and rest. When I picked him up at the end of each day, he'd dissolve into tears, hiding his eyes with the seat-belt strap so I couldn't see him—an outburst caused more by the emotional buildup of having been tough all day in front of friends, I assumed, than actual acute pain. It wasn't until a full month into school, until the warm-up weeks we'd thought he'd need had passed, that we realized Graham wasn't strong enough to both make it through the school day and attend the various activities he normally did afterward. Austin ferried him across the campus in a fat-tired wagon. His teachers reported him spacing out during lessons. Some days, he'd actually fall asleep in the middle of the day. Eventually, the bomb dropped.

"I *hate* school," Graham told me emphatically one morning, just before Jim left for a seven-week work trip on an ice-breaking research vessel in the Arctic Ocean. "I only like the weekends in my life. I never want to go back." That the recovery was causing the kid to hate anything seemed like a giant red flag.

Feeling the odd sense of power I usually associate with buying Ikea furniture when Jim is at sea, I started rearranging Graham's fall schedule. On the weekends, I began trying to let him take it as easy as possible, hoping to infuse him with enough energy that he could make it through the school week in one piece. I rescinded our fall sign-up for his adaptive soccer league. I loosened our movie-watching policies, intentionally encouraging him to spend more time on the couch, massaging his legs when he'd let me. Without telling Graham, I ordered the small high-tech manual wheelchair Dr. A had recommended anew (much to our horror) the week before school had started, suggesting that we consider again how much more Graham might learn if he actually had enough energy to pay attention all day. And when it became clear that Graham still needed daily emotional bolstering, I began canceling trips—the hunting trip with my brother, a trip to Oregon with a friend to learn about honey, and a huckleberry-picking trip with Graham in the Cascade Mountains. I decided that no matter how much I wanted to leave Seattle to explore, how much being "right here" might mean the Pacific Northwest to me, for Graham it meant having me around to take him to school and pick him up from school, and take him to therapy and tuck him in at night, every night. It meant I should be the one to scoop up fiftysomething pounds of crying child and carry him to the car, when he dissolved in the hallway outside the therapy gym so that I could be the one to decide whether he needed a firm voice or a soothing one. I learned quickly that if I was going to have enough energy for him, I'd need energy for myself, gathered by focusing on the things I did while I was *not* mothering. What Maggie had told me at the Inn at Langley about needing time to stare at a wall suddenly came into focus.

For a while we did school and therapy, and not much else. I cooked very simple foods that Graham would eat. We watched more *Star Wars*, and learned about bats. While Graham was at school, I became almost completely unproductive. I couldn't write coherently, which made me cranky. I roamed online, reading everything and nothing about children and pain and cerebral palsy, and the new *Star Wars* movie and chicken molting and kitchen lighting. It felt like going nowhere.

SEPTEMBER

OCTOBER

In late September, Jim left for the far northern part of the Arctic Ocean. We were proud, knowing he was in charge of a massive scientific effort. Graham told everyone that his dad was looking at how the ice is melting near where Santa lives. We received photos of polar bears, arctic foxes, and the northern lights in e-mails sent via the ship's Iridium satellite connection, but we didn't speak with him on its emergency phone. Jim became, in a strange way, a sort of ghost. It reminded me of our junior year in college, when I lived in Paris, and Jim lived in Adelaide, Australia. We used a prepaid phone card to talk once a week for thirty-two minutes over a spotty landline connection—Wednesday nights for me, which meant Thursday mornings for him—and wrote each other long, sappy notes on the kind of flimsy prestamped post-office stationery that folded up on itself, so you saved money on the cost of postage because the letter became its own envelope. He signed every letter with one word: *Always.* We were miserably in love.

Except that, whereas our separation in college had felt like an unhappy rite of passage, I really hated my husband for going to the Arctic. I felt like he was abandoning me during the hardest part of Graham's recovery, when Graham and I both needed emotional support. One day Graham got his arms caught up in his jacket while he was on his knees at his school locker, and wound up taking a face-plant into the floor hard enough to give him a mild concussion. In the emergency room, I e-mailed Jim, frustrated that he couldn't help, and couldn't tell me in his calm, reassuring way that kids hit their heads every day without causing any lasting damage. My brain knew Jim had to be at sea—that he'd been planning this particular research trip for years, literally—but my heart saw him as the lucky one, leaving us for greener pastures because it seemed anything, even hauling icy machinery on and off boats in below-zero weather, would be easier than watching Graham stumble through his days with so much melancholy effort.

For much of the fall, I let Graham sleep in my bed next to me, where I could smell his hair after he fell asleep, and be just inches away when he woke up in the night with leg cramps, and pretend my presence could actually help him heal.

I started daydreaming about the presumably possible but infuriatingly unpredictable time when Graham might suddenly seem better. My Internet roaming turned to an imaginary trip to Mexico—specifically, to going on an all-inclusive vacation, the kind where so much of normal life is done for you that you almost cease to exist.

But that's exactly what I wanted: the kind of travel where you can think about a different place, so you don't have to think about your own.

What Would Jesus Brew?

IN college, I bought Jim a beginners' beer-brewing kit on the half-price rack at a bookstore. In his typical all-in style, he decided upon graduation that brewing would become a hobby, and that he would be good at it; he claimed a sort of manifest destiny for making beer. In time, we amassed the appropriate tools and equipment for making a batch of two dozen bottles at a time. And over the next decade, as promised, he became a bona fide homebrewer. With whichever friends he could coerce into helping—that part was never difficult—he toyed with various combinations of grains and malts, learned how and when to add different hop varietals for flavor, bitterness, and aroma, and mastered the all-important sanitization process. Carbonation was always his Achilles' heel, but with the adoption of a box of old-school green-glass Grolsch bottles, which seemed stronger and more dependable than regular ones in the capping department, even that became easy for him. Jim's twentysomething challenge hobby turned into a thirtysomething source of pride and happy distraction. When we moved to Seattle, I planted Cascade hops (which are still the only thing on our property that flourishes consistently despite the persistent abuse they suffer from dog paws and bicycle tires), and Jim learned to use fresh hops, instead of the more traditional dried version, in his beers. He aged batches in old wine barrels, and began guiding his graduate students at the University of Washington through the process each fall.

Which is why every year, sometime around Labor Day, he now invites his whole lab to our house to brew. Each year, the same robust hop bine—which is what the climbing, vine-like plants hops grow on are technically called—spirals up a web of plain white strings from the ground to the pergola above the French doors on our house's sunny back porch. While the soft, verdant, pinecone-shaped hops themselves aren't difficult to pluck from their plant, there are fifty or so of them on each bine, so having help turns the process from a three-hour chore into a quick half-hour task. It's a casual affair, always including Jim's ever-rotating stable of graduate students. (In addition to providing labor for whatever research Jim is doing at a particular time, they happen to make excellent pickers.) And every year, I cook for them.

After an exceptionally warm, dry summer, the party had been slated for Labor Day itself, and the hops were drier than usual, having rested on the bine a good three weeks longer at full size than they usually did. But as usual, the plan stipulated our respective responsibilities: I would prepare most of a dinner for twenty or so, and the students would bring snacks, drinks, and desserts, which we'd dive into after Jim and his low-wage laborers unhinged the bine from the pergola, splayed it across the back patio, and relieved it of its fragile payload.

Like every year, the dinner was lovely on the surface. When ten pounds of hops had been gathered in bowls and brown paper bags, I laid out flash-grilled zucchini, draped with a loose walnut-parsley pesto and curls of lemon peel. I served roasted porchetta, stuffed with garlic, rosemary, and thyme, and a big bowl of black- and white-spotted orca beans tossed with tiny tomatoes, olives, and herbs. I guarded the thermometer for Jim while the wort for the beer came to a boil, watched his lovely Chilean student pour pisco sours for everyone, and watched my child fall in love with the Chilean student's husband because he was wearing a T-shirt with Chewbacca on it. ("Oh, Jesus!" said Graham excitedly when the shirt walked in, showing off the language he'd recently adopted from his grandfather.) I marveled at how Jim, who is usually so busy at work, could relax and show his students a good time in his own home, with his own family. I saw how his lab at the university made up its own kind of family.

But when the dinner ended, something nagged at me, like it always did. I felt unsatisfied. The food wasn't enough. It certainly wasn't that I'd put forth so much energy to cook for my husband's crowd and they hadn't appreciated it. (No one appreciates a good free meal like a grad student.) It wasn't that Jim spent the remainder of the night pitching yeast into the wort to jump-start the fermentation process, or that, from the corner of the guest-bedroom closet, I'd hear the burble of the beer (as that yeast did its job) for the next week or so. Nothing annoyed me about his beer-making process. But I began to understand that nag: Every year, Jim got to undertake a project I didn't fully understand because I had never been part of all of it. I got to cook the food, as is always my role in our house, but the point of the thing was the brewing, which happened in my kitchen, right under my nose, but still remained shrouded in complete mystery to me. I finally recognized that I was jealous Jim was cooking something and I didn't get to help. That every year, he gets to be the beer doer. And I realized, after he'd gone north to the Arctic with some of those same grad students and I began to miss him terribly, that in all the years we'd spent doing different things in the kitchen but never really cooking together, perhaps I'd missed an opportunity to spend time with him there simply because I prefer drinking wine.

See, the truth is, I don't really like beer all that much. Each time Jim brews, I taste the final product. Since he now usually brews roughly the same kind of American fresh-hopped IPA, whose flavor changes with the year's hop harvest, I know what to expect. It's good, as far as hoppy beer goes, but it's not my thing. He knows my disinterest in the drink has nothing to do with him or his talents as a brewer. But ultimately, I think he takes on the brewing and fermenting and bottling and aging processes himself because he knows I'm not going to actually drink the stuff. *But what if?* I thought. *What if there was beer I'd enjoy drinking, and therefore, making?*

Soon after he left, I began plotting a surreptitious takeover of his brewing equipment. (I am my mother's daughter. She taught me that when a partner leaves the house, one must undertake large projects during his absence.) Seven weeks was exactly enough time to brew a full batch and age it before his return. I wanted to find out whether I should hone in on what had always been his thing, and whether I was capable of finding a beer I liked enough that we could begin brewing together. But really, I wanted to find out if, after spending almost none of our two decades as a couple together in the kitchen, and after making so little time for ourselves as a couple that spring and summer, we could brew something new together without talking about our kid.

But what to make? I began by combing through the William's Brewing catalog online, wondering whether the combination of their equipment guide and *True Brews*, a book my friend Emma Christensen had recently published, might be able to guide me through the process successfully. I narrowed my choices down to a *Weizen* (wheat) beer and a *Kölsh*; both choices were light on hops and body, which I preferred. Still, I didn't love either enough to drink it every day. I procrastinated my decision.

Driving down the road the next day, I saw a junky old Honda with an oversize, battered white bumper sticker plastered slightly off-kilter on the trunk. "*What Would Jesus Do?*" it asked in puffy blue font. I started to roll my eyes, wondering, as I often do, what the driver might say if I asked her to make her own choices instead of asking Jesus. But then the rhyme hit me: What would Jesus *brew*? It was a valid question.

And as if on command from above, the phone rang. It was a number I didn't recognize, but I answered it while driving, feeling that strange impulse that inspires one to do something totally unsafe even when one knows better. It wasn't Jesus.

"Hi, this is Duncan," said the caller, who sounded very far away. *Duncan*, I thought. *Duncan who?*

Duncan, it turned out, was the parent of a kid at our son's school. He was the same parent who owns an apple orchard in Washington's Methow Valley. The same parent who, the previous March, had contributed five gallons of fresh fall cider to the school auction. I'd gleefully purchased it after sharing a bottle of champagne with my husband, then I'd completely forgotten about it. But the previous weekend, Duncan said, they'd harvested the apples and pressed the cider. He'd be delivering it to my front porch the next day.

"Hold on," I interrupted. "Tomorrow?"

"Yeah," he said. "I hope that's not a problem? Isn't that what we'd arranged?"

"No problem," I said, wondering how long it would take just Graham and me to drink that much apple cider.

"What are you going to do with it?" he asked.

"I'm going to make hard cider," I said, deciding on the spot. Because Jesus would brew cider, if apple juice fell onto His porch from above. And cider, unlike beer, had a place in my heart.

WHAT WOULD JESUS BREW?

When I'd arrived in Paris as a bouncy college student, on January 2, 1999, the host family I moved in with was preparing for the wedding of one of their four children. There had been drama my French skills couldn't identify: it was clear that the Jacqueau family was content about the marriage but not mad about the man's family. On my first night, a heated discussion had erupted between Monsieur and Madame regarding, I think, whether or not the groom's mother would appreciate the milk bottles Madame had planned to craft for the occasion.

I remember sitting in my newly appointed spot in the grand dining room of their top-floor Beaux-Arts apartment, trying to figure out how an Hermès-clad Parisian society woman from the seventh arrondissement knew how to *make* milk bottles. Since the flat sat directly on the Champ de Mars, I'd had an unimpeded view of the Eiffel Tower. (How I got to be the student who claimed the spot in that particular family is still a mystery.) While scooping pumpkin velouté from a delicate bowl in the form of a cabbage, it had occurred to me that my room's positioning toward *la tour*'s light might make it difficult to sleep. And as I sipped on yeasty hard cider I understood to be from their working farm in Normandy, I couldn't convince my brain to comprehend why the cider, which I became sure was to be served at the wedding, would be served in those homemade milk bottles, which was what I'd thought I was hearing.

Only with time—the prompter of so many discoveries when one travels—did I understand that saying *bouteilles de lait*, which I had naively translated directly as "milk bottles," was Madame's way of describing the cider bottles based on the way she'd be labeling them, not on how they were made or what was inside. (She'd planned to hand-letter each paper label for the wedding and dip each one in milk before laying it on the bottle, hence the name. The milk apparently acts as a natural adhesive.)

OCTOBER

During those six months, when a lovely, kind French woman had made my dinner four nights each week and brought me cookies and tea when I'd cried over Jim, I'd pretended that it was totally normal to drink alcohol with dinner at age twenty back in the States. I'd grown to love hard cider. Once I'd gotten used to the way the word flowed off Monsieur's tongue—*cidre* in proper old-man French sounds like someone emphatically saying the word *see* in English and then choking on a fly—I'd known to accept when he offered to pour from a bottle of their farmstead stash. I'd known to listen when he pontificated on how their cider was better than other nearby farms' ciders because of the way the salty maritime wind blew through their property's trees. I never did learn how the cider bottles for the wedding came out, but back in the States, with a newly useful identification card, I'd practiced being legal by buying cider.

Even at twenty-one, with a novice palate more suited to sweeter drinks, I'd known America's relationship with cider wasn't the same as France's. American cider seemed young and restless, pumped with sugar and bottled in individual portions, as if we didn't have the same patience the French do for sharing a full-size bottle with friends. I hadn't been in the position to spend the time or money seeking out good French or British bottles, so it was usually Woodchuck cider. And so, along with my French skills, my love for cider had faded. Until I moved to Washington.

We'd bought a house in Seattle after Jim finished graduate school and after I'd stopped working as a private chef in peoples' homes. We'd established permanent jobs and had a child and became Grown-Ups, and somewhere along the way, we'd started choosing our beer and wine with care. And as Washington cider circles blossomed from a smattering of glorified hobbyists to a full-fledged industry, we'd started buying cider regularly. Our refrigerator had developed a his and hers section in the back of the bottom shelf—beer in one row, cider in the other. I didn't see why our designated beer-aging cubby, under the stairs, couldn't also have two rows.

Over the next twenty-four hours, I learned as much as I could about making cider. I pressed my friend Ben, a hard-cider hobbyist who makes an excellent brew from apples on Lopez Island each year, for his favorite strains of commercial yeast and details on the most reliable methods of controlling the sundry wild yeasts that inherently show up in unpasteurized cider. He outlined a schedule for me that detailed when I should add the pasteurizing tablets, when I should activate the yeast, and when I should add it to the cider, and I copied it all down on a sticky note next to the coffeemaker. I raided a local homebrew store for new bottles—I knew Jim was territorial about his Grolsch bottles, which a store in Boston had given to him for free a decade earlier—and I chose the liter-size clear kind with flip-top caps, because they reminded me of the bottles my French family had used for their own cider in Normandy. I bounced around the store, selecting an ounce of this and an ounce of that, hoping my air of pretend confidence would translate the unpronounceable, unrecognizable powders Emma and Ben had suggested using into a batch of fermented, carbonated hard cider. And without more hesitation—because five gallons of cider did arrive, and I had to act immediately, or else dump out half the fridge—I became a cider brewer.

At first, I felt like a too-small child copying a parent's big movements. I knew from watching Jim that at least half the time required to make any successful batch of beer should be spent sanitizing equipment. And so one afternoon while Graham was in school, I began the scrub-down. On rickety tiptoes, like a kid stealing cookies, I extracted the buckets and lids and spoons and siphons and hoses and tubes Jim stores carefully on the top shelf in his shop. Eventually, I combined the raw cider and the powders and the yeast into a five-gallon bucket, struggling to close its impossibly tight-fitting lid. It took me three tries to plug the hole in the top with a little contraption called an air lock—the thing that, when the yeast gobbled up the sugars in the cider, would expel bubbles of carbon dioxide gas without letting any impure air in—and then I put it in the corner in the guest bedroom.

For a second, I just stared at it. I was the six-year-old wearing her grandmother's makeup, wondering in the mirror whether it looked any good. I tried to remember what Jim did at this point in the process, but he was, at that moment, literally getting himself stuck in ice (on purpose) halfway between the northern Alaskan coast and the North Pole. A quick conversation with him wasn't an option, but I didn't know how to call anyone else and ask about good-luck charms. *Did the cider have a soul yet?* I wondered. It seemed an appropriate time to pray, but I didn't have any idea how to, or where such a prayer might be directed. I hadn't heard of cider gods, and Jesus must certainly know I'd disrespected his role as a bumper-sticker celebrity and would probably opt out if I tried to chat him up. So I rubbed my hand along the top of the bucket's lid, politely asked the cat not to jump on top of it, and waited.

Sure enough, a few days later, the air lock jiggled and bounced, the same way it did for Jim's beer. *At least the first step is going okay*, I thought.

A week later, I transferred the cider to its second fermentation stage. There was more washing, more sanitizing. More wishing I had bigger, stronger hands. I discarded the sludge of apple particles and yeast by-product that had precipitated out of the deep golden liquid and accumulated on the bottom of the first bucket. I used a hydrometer—a thermometer-like doohickey that measures how much sugar a liquid contains—to help me determine later how alcoholic the cider would end up, bursting with pride once I established that my cider was behaving, in a word, normally.

Some ten days later, the day after Halloween, I simmered corn sugar with water until it formed an innocuous-looking clear solution, which I then mixed with the cider, giving the yeast enough additional food that the cider would carbonate once I bottled it. Again, I dove into the sanitization process, scrubbing down the entire kitchen before I began siphoning the now-alcoholic but flat cider from its fermentation bucket into the big, clear (and now very clean) bottles. It took me a few tries to learn how to pause the siphoning hose's flow between bottles; for the first few, I simply didn't, and the cider sprayed in a big golden arc across the kitchen. I swore, and mopped up the floor, and sat down to rest.

Why was I doing this? I certainly didn't need to make cider myself; Washington State now enjoys as healthy a population of excellent cider makers as grocery stores do tomato-sauce makers. But I wanted to try. And I wanted to find something more in common with my husband so I could stop being so mad at him each time he left. As I sealed the last of the bottles, I congratulated myself on making something that, while nothing close to efficient or financially advantageous, would taste good simply because it was alcoholic, and because I made it myself.

The night Jim came home from seven weeks at sea, I chilled a bottle of the cider, along with a bottle of his fresh-hopped beer. I'd made spaghetti and meatballs I wanted him to try, but as his plane skimmed over the clouds between Anchorage and Seattle, Graham and I accidentally finished the meatballs with friends. So near midnight, once our son had talked out all his excitement over seeing his dad and passed out, Jim and I opened both bottles.

The cider, having aged just two weeks instead of four, was not ready. It was destined for greatness—it had almost no residual sweetness, which is what I'd wanted, and an effervescence just shy of champagne's, which had been the hope—but seemed somehow unripe, or even raw. It was alcoholic, but my calculations said it was only about 4 percent alcohol. The beer, on the other hand, was sharp and novel. It had the green freshness and the bitterness I usually anticipated from the yearly fresh-hopped batch. It also had the distinct and undeniable flavor of a flower that seemed too common to guess.

"This tastes like roses, doesn't it?" I half asked, half declared.

Jim nodded, and smiled. "It does. It's amazing," he swooned.

I hated it. To me, it tasted like beer crossed with fancy soap. But he was smitten.

I put my glass down.

"Jim, I have to tell you something," I said. He looked up, alarmed. "I want to make beer with you. But I want to make beer that I like."

And in a crush of words, I breathed out the air that for so long I hadn't known I was holding—the air of jealousy and need created by all those years when he did something important to him without me. The air built up by the pressure of being a wife who sometimes felt like she didn't have a husband. He looked blown over at first, and then overjoyed.

"Let's do it," he agreed instantly. "We can do it tomorrow. Or now if you want." His eyes filled with mischief, like I'd asked him to swing by a lingerie shop with me.

Over the next moments we agreed that soon we'd try a batch of fresh-hopped cider, and that perhaps the next year we could use our own backyard harvest to dry-hop a batch of cider together, which I might actually help drink. And that, like so many people who work very hard to become partners in parenting have to when part of life gets hard, we'd found a way to rebrew the friendship that had brought us together in the first place.

Grilled Zucchini with
Chunky Walnut-Parsley Sauce

Because there aren't many ingredients in this dish, make the ones you use count; use a high-quality olive oil, if you can.

To toast the walnuts, place them on a baking sheet in a preheated 350-degree oven and bake until fragrant and toasty brown, 8 to 10 minutes.

MAKES: 12 SIDE-DISH SERVINGS

For the zucchini

12 medium zucchini, ends trimmed,
    halved lengthwise
¼ cup extra-virgin olive oil
Kosher salt and freshly ground black pepper, to taste

For the sauce

1 packed cup fresh Italian parsley leaves (with stems),
    plus ¼ cup leaves only (for garnish)
1 large clove garlic, smashed
2 tablespoons capers
½ teaspoon kosher salt
½ cup plus 2 tablespoons extra-virgin olive oil,
    divided, plus more for drizzling
2 tablespoons walnut oil
2 cups walnut halves or pieces, toasted
Zest and juice of 1 medium lemon
Crunchy sea salt, for serving

» Preheat a gas or charcoal grill over medium-high heat, about 400 degrees F.

» To make the zucchini: on a large platter, toss the zucchini halves with the olive oil, then season with salt and pepper and set them aside.

» To make the sauce: In the work bowl of a food processor, buzz together the cup of parsley, garlic, capers, and kosher salt until finely chopped and pasty. (You may need to stop and scrape down the sides of the work bowl to incorporate all the parsley.) With the machine running, add ¼ cup plus 2 tablespoons olive oil and the walnut oil in a slow, steady stream, processing until blended. Add all but a handful of the toasted walnuts, then pulse the mixture 8 or 10 times, so the nuts are chopped but still a little chunky. Transfer the mixture to a bowl and stir in the remaining ¼ cup olive oil. Set the sauce aside.

» Brush the grill's cooking grates clean. Grill the zucchini for 5 to 7 minutes, cut side down first, turning about halfway through cooking, only once the flesh is marked on the first side. Transfer the zucchini to a platter, and top with the sauce. Scatter the remaining ¼ cup parsley, the reserved walnuts, and the lemon zest on top, then squeeze the lemon's juice over the whole shebang. Serve warm or at room temperature, with an extra drizzle of olive oil, if you'd like, and a little shower of sea salt.

Emma's Dry Apple Cider

When I dove into cider making, I used Emma Christensen's *True Brews: How to Craft Fermented Cider, Beer, Wine, Sake, Soda, Mead, Kefir, and Kombucha at Home* (Ten Speed Press, 2013) as my general guide, with occasional input from friends who had also brewed cider. This is her recipe. I multiplied this version by five, using a five-gallon fermentation bucket instead of the two-gallon type Emma recommends, to accommodate the volume of cider left on my porch, but I agree with her: a gallon is a good place to start. Remember that, as in beer brewing, it is luckiest to drink cider while brewing cider.

Says Emma:

> This cider is dry in the sense that it is not very sweet tasting. All the naturally occurring sugars in the apple juice become yeast food. We're left with a hard cider that has a snappy-tart flavor, a refreshing bitterness, and an astringent edge. The balance of these flavors, as well as any lingering sweetness, depends on the apples going into your cider. If you are buying your own apples for pressing, get a mix of different apple varieties (15 pounds of apples will give you 1 gallon of juice). If buying juice, choose one with a nice complexity of flavors. If the cider ends up a bit too dry for your taste, you can sweeten it up just before bottling.

Says me: I didn't use the sweetener in the recipe, or when bottling, and my cider was very dry.

Please note that Emma's book comes complete with pages and pages of great ingredient, equipment, sanitization, brewing, and bottling information. I trust you'll do your homework and read her information (or something similar) before embarking on your own cider journey.

WHAT WOULD JESUS BREW?

If you want to label your cider when it's finished, simply cut pieces of paper to your preferred label size, label them with ink that won't run, and paste them onto the bottles with milk: pour a small amount of milk onto a dinner plate, then, one label at a time, submerge the label into the liquid and press it neatly onto the bottle. Once it's dry, it should stay there indefinitely!

I purchased many of my ingredients online, including the yeast, at www.williamsbrewing.com.

MAKES 1 GALLON

SPECIAL EQUIPMENT: 2-GALLON FERMENTATION BUCKET, HYDROMETER, 1-QUART CANNING JAR, 1-GALLON JUG, RACKING CANE, SIPHON HOSE, TEN 12-OUNCE BEER BOTTLES OR SIX 22-OUNCE BEER BOTTLES WITH CAPS, AND A BOTTLE FILLER

Target Original Gravity Range = 1.055–1.060
Target Final Gravity Range = 1.000–1.005
Target ABV = 7 percent

1 gallon apple juice, preferably unpasteurized
1 Campden tablet
1½ tablespoons (½ tube) liquid cider yeast
1 teaspoon yeast nutrient
1 teaspoon acid blend
½ teaspoon pectic enzyme
¼ teaspoon tannin
3 tablespoons (1 ounce) corn sugar, dissolved in ½ cup boiling water and cooled, for bottling
1 cup (1 ounce) Splenda or other nonfermentable sugar (optional)

» Sanitize a 2-gallon bucket, its lid, the air lock, and a spoon for stirring.

» Pour the apple juice into the 2-gallon fermentation bucket. Take a hydrometer reading to determine and record the original gravity. Crush the Campden tablet and stir it into the juice. Snap on the lid and attach the air lock. Wait 24 hours for the Campden to sterilize the juice. (If using pasteurized juice, you can skip this step.)

» After the juice is sterilized, prepare the yeast starter. Sanitize a measuring cup, a 1-quart canning jar, and a stirring spoon. Scoop out 1 cup of juice and pour it into the canning jar. Pour the cider yeast over the top and cover the jar with a piece of plastic wrap secured with a rubber band. Give the jar a good shake and let it stand for 1 to 3 hours. It will become foamy, and you will see tiny bubbles popping on the surface of the liquid. Once you see some sign of activity, the starter can be used.

» Pour the starter into the juice along with the yeast nutrient, acid blend, pectic enzyme, and tannin. Stir vigorously to distribute the yeast and aerate the juice. Snap the lid back on and reattach the air lock. You should see active fermentation as evidenced by bubbles in the air lock within 48 hours.

» Let the cider ferment undisturbed for at least 3 days or up to 7 days, until fermentation has slowed and the sediment created during brewing has had a chance to settle. At this point, the cider is ready to be transferred off the sediment and into a smaller 1-gallon jug for the longer secondary fermentation.

» Sanitize a 1-gallon jug, its stopper, the racking cane, its tip, the siphon hose, and the hose clamp. Siphon all of the cider into the jug. Tilt the bucket toward the end to siphon all of the liquid. Stop when you see the liquid in the hose becoming cloudy with sediment. Seal the jug with its stopper and insert the air lock. Let it sit somewhere cool and dark for another 2 weeks.

» To bottle the cider, sanitize a stockpot, a hydrometer, ten 12-ounce beer bottles or six 22-ounce beer bottles, their caps, the siphon hose, the racking cane, its tip, a measuring cup, and the bottle filler. Siphon ½ cup of cider to the hydrometer and use to determine final gravity. Drink the cider or pour it back into the jug once used.

» Pour the corn sugar solution into the stockpot. Siphon the cider into the stockpot to mix with the corn sugar solution, splashing as little as possible. Scoop a little cider with the measuring cup and give it a taste. Add Splenda if a sweeter cider is desired.

» Siphon the cider into bottles, cap, and label.

» Let the bottles sit at room temperature out of direct sunlight for at least 1 month or store for up to 1 year. Refrigerate before serving.

NOVEMBER

Graham's world changed in early November. Slowly, over the fall, he'd graduated back up from using a walker to using his little yellow arm crutches again to very occasionally—in therapy at least, and sometimes at school—walking independently, with heels flat on the ground, rather than on tippiest toes, as he'd done before the surgery. Although his mode of transportation hadn't changed at home, where he still always crawled everywhere, and he certainly hadn't started using the handrails we'd installed in our basement when he was four as aids for pulling himself up to stand, as we'd envisioned, he had much more energy. One week, school parents started reporting their kids coming home gushing about Graham's improvement.

"Your child is going to be tired tonight," Erica texted me one day. "Someone in the class figured out that if they gave Graham a pencil, he'd walk to the pencil sharpener solo, so the kids just asked him to sharpen pencils over and over all day, so they could watch." All the pencils in the first-grade classroom were now sharp, she said. And Graham had become first-grade famous.

Casting aside any concerns I should have had about my child learning to walk with a bundle of newly sharpened pencils in his fist, I started looking for ways to encourage his progress without actually asking him to walk alone, which always made him whine or roll his eyes heavenward with his mouth half agape, the way some invisible teenager had taught him. He wanted nothing to do with my suggestions.

As parents, we are not above bribery; we lure our kid to act nicely, do his homework, and finish dinner by proffering gifts and sweets and extra screen time. But having a child with a handicap adds an additional layer to the perennial parental-bribery question. Each time a friend suggested I reward him for trying walking at home, which happened often, I explained our theory—that while a doughnut or movie screening might somehow reinforce, in a child's mind, that dutiful homework habits or prolonged kindness might give one certain lifelong advantages, we didn't want to teach Graham that he would be a better person if he could walk the same way the rest of the world does. We wanted him to know we'd love him no matter what.

And so, at home, I just kept waiting. And while Graham only crawled inside our house, he continued improving at school. One day at physical therapy in mid-November, he and his therapist, Hunter, got into a heated pool-noodle-as-lightsaber battle. The goal of the genius exercise was to occupy one of Graham's hands with the saber so that he could only use one stick for balance, instead of two. But Graham suddenly realized that because the Force is so strong, real Jedi use both hands on a lightsaber when the fighting gets really intense. So as if it were the most natural thing, he ditched his second stick and used both hands to grasp the blue foam, still walking upright on two flat feet. And then, realizing what was happening, he grinned, and simply turned around and walked out of the room, leaving Hunter and me behind, wiping away tears.

That same night, Jim came home. The next day, Graham walked across the living room on two feet. A few days later, I canceled the wheelchair order. Somehow that one action— "Please cancel the order for now," read my e-mail—was the moment when the whole world brightened.

Chronicles of a Coffee Lover

ALTHOUGH I assumed, as Graham grew older, that his developmental pattern meant I'd forgo that magical moment parents report feeling when their kids learn to walk, I didn't miss it. That day with Hunter, even though Graham had taken many tens of steps in a row before, the walking was different. His new steps looked natural. And at the very moment he took those steps, I felt my shoulders relax. I didn't know what combination of therapy and home treatments and time had led to the neurological catharsis, but it didn't matter. Suddenly I could think again. When I sat down at my computer, I could focus on something besides Graham. I went back to making the rounds, working at coffee shops, and when I was writing, the words came back.

Edie was a new writer friend. We'd set up our computers side by side in a coffee shop we both frequented, a classic example of the "work date" that precedes actual friendship among working-from-home moms. When I offered to buy her the mocha she typically drank around ten, she accepted.

"But oh, I get decaf," she said quickly. "And soy." She was apologizing, with the same tone she'd probably use if she spilled said mocha in my lap. "Because I'm that kind of lame," she added sheepishly. I tried to smile forgivingly.

In Seattle, coffee culture is as dependable as the rain and the tides; any deviation from regular consumption is circumspect. Since three young entrepreneurs opened the first Starbucks in Pike Place Market in 1971, the city as a whole has become synonymous with its darling drink. Seattle unquestionably redefined the way the world approaches the morning buzz. But that coffee habit—the one that started as careful brewing of higher-quality beans, then blazed across the world under Starbucks CEO Howard Schultz as an espresso-drink trend—has matured. Coffee connoisseurs have developed bean-flavor preferences the way wine geeks take to grape varietals, and today in Seattle (and even at Starbucks, depending on the location), rather than asking for a light- or dark-roasted coffee, it's more common to see beans defined by their origin. Asking for a cup of Ethiopian Harrar means you probably like coffees with a complex, fruity flavor. It also means you'll probably know how you want it brewed—in a French press, for example, or in an AeroPress, a plastic contraption that forces hot water through ground coffee and an impossibly thin paper filter. And if you're cool, you'll probably ask for a pour-over.

There is a certain portion of the population for whom the term "single-origin pour-over" has deep, important meaning. In Seattle, this specimen is easy to identify if you permit yourself some unabashed stereotyping. Pour-Over Paul is the guy in the sharp slim suit with expensive pointy loafers, a full handlebar mustache, and mirrored Warby Parker sunglasses. Pour-Over Penny is the girl with the artful ombré-dyed hair cascading down over her grandmother's vintage dress, which mismatches perfectly with handmade four-hundred-dollar clogs that, she's happy to tell you, she got for ten bucks at a local thrift shop. They both probably like Ethiopian Yirgacheffe, a fruity bean whose brewed flavor reminds most people of blueberries, and sometimes lemon.

NOVEMBER

At some spots in Seattle, ordering coffee feels like nothing short of an insider drug deal. I have nothing against drug dealers, but I want more tranquility. I want more ease. When I need coffee, I often find it challenging to speak English, much less converse in a language unfamiliar to me. I don't want to consult a map before I caffeinate. Coffee is more about sitting at a table by myself, headphones humming, while I make sense and order out of words, rather than out of, say, our son's therapy schedule. It's having two hands wrapped smugly around a warm cup, knowing I won't drop it, instead of one hand outstretched under an IV containing my monthly supply of lupus medications while the other organizes a playdate. Coffee is about the time that's mine, rather than the time that belongs to my family or my pets or my illness. That fall, as Graham improved, other things fell apart. We had a dog at death's door, a cat wounded from a tangle with a raccoon, and a cranky neighbor who hated our chickens and wanted us to replace them with a quieter breed. Coffee really needed to be simple. But as I retreated into my work, which usually takes place at coffee shops, I found those places felt unsafe because coffee in Seattle as I knew it had changed.

Historically, as a French-Press Fannie, I've been coffee chic. When I'd left for New York in early August, ordering a short latte still felt cool. But suddenly, one misty gray day in Seattle, where my regular order (short latte, whole milk) had always passed as an acceptable secret handshake in any coffee shop, I began feeling inadequate. I don't really fit in with The Pour-Over People. I wear mostly sensible shoes (often bought new) and relatively boring eyeglasses. I have no tattoos. I'm the kind of girl who thinks having a single-origin pour-over just means getting a cup of coffee that comes with a side of pretension. I felt uncool because I didn't want any goddamned blueberries in my coffee. Felt no less than uneducated, because while the latent leaders brewed their quiet takeover, introducing fanatics to a new way to enjoy the nuances of coffees from around the world, I was busy coaxing my kid out of his own small personal hell. So when I started working in earnest again in November, I had a coffee crisis.

Take my initial experience at Slate Coffee, a sunny hiccup of a shop in the no-man's-land between Seattle's Ballard and Phinney Ridge neighborhoods. It's a place you go to prove you're a real coffee snob. First, you have to get there—it's a barely signed spot in a cozy neighborhood convenient to nothing if you don't live next door—and park, which is in and of itself proof that you are devoted to the bean in a way that makes you more special.

The first time I went, I made the mistake of walking straight up to the counter—there was no register, so I had to be creative about defining where the proper ordering location might be—and ordering a latte to go. The barista's neck tattoos quivered with disgust. I'd involuntarily violated every shop rule.

"Do you mean an *espresso* with *milk*?" he asked. His tone suggested I'd been speaking a distant Amazonian dialect. "I'd be happy to make you one. Have a seat and I'll bring you a menu."

Of course. I should have known. At Slate, standing stock-still at the counter to order your coffee is like ordering your steak directly from the chef at a restaurant. Ordering to go is gauche and shows you're too hurried a person. And at Slate, there are no lattes. There are various forms of espresso, served with steamed milk measured by the ounce in the kind of glassware usually reserved for cocktails. Once I'd been seated and plied with a glass of water that made me feel guilty about intending to do anything there but appreciate the vibe, I was permitted to order a six-ounce "espresso with milk" for $3.88, which was brought to me ten minutes later in a pretty, petite sherry glass. It was one of the best lattes I've ever had—probably the result of someone being very careful with some part of a process I'll never fully understand, and of a smaller quantity of milk, which made the coffee taste more pronounced—but it left me with the aftertaste of pure shame. In a world of tasting the bean itself, I'd apparently ordered the coffee-culture's equivalent of a wine cooler. And I'd loved it.

Traipsing across the city on small magazine assignments, I found myself cowed by my preferences over and over. The kinds of coffee shops I'd always assumed would feel completely welcoming became intimidating, almost scary. (Whether the fear was a reflection of my general self-doubt that fall is another story.) In any case, every morning, sitting in the humming car after school drop-off, I'd weigh my options. I hated that getting to work seemed to require considering how much I wanted to feel like an asshole for drinking a latte. Until I settled in at Vif.

At Vif Wine|Coffee, a morning-meeting outpost and wine shop housed in a bright, airy former burger joint in Seattle's Fremont neighborhood, the coffee lexicon flows freely, but without the snobbery. There are three pour-over setups. The first time I arrived, they didn't seem to judge me for drinking the coffee-world's version of mom jeans. My latte always came with a genuine smile. I started going there two or three times a week, ordering a latte and often a bowl of slow-cooked white beans topped with a perfect six-minute egg.

And then one day, surprising myself and them, I ordered a pour-over.

"Really?" asked a barista named Raelyn, putting away my latte mug. "Which kind?"

"What are my choices?" I tried to sound confident as I clenched and unclenched my cold hands in my coat pockets.

"Ethiopian or Colombian?" she asked brightly. It was the Seattle coffee-shop analogy to a diner's list of toast flavors. She was going to give me coffee beans from one place on the planet, and she wanted to know my regional preference.

She tipped perfectly ground Colombian beans into a conical silver bottomless teacup that had been fitted with a filter and poised over a small glass pitcher. The whole setup rested on a scale so that she'd know she was adding twenty-three grams of coffee to the filter (no more, no less). She poured water from a delicate-looking teapot at around 202 degrees Fahrenheit over the beans in a circular motion, until the total water weight measured 391 grams, or roughly seventeen grams of water per gram of ground coffee. Mahogany liquid dripped through the filter into the bulb at the bottom of the pitcher. I waited, realizing that adding my usual half-and-half to the science experiment I'd just paid $3.75 for would be a travesty. I wanted to ask whether my coffee would be ruined if someone opened the shop's door during a stiff breeze and cooled the water down by a degree or two on its way to the ground coffee.

When the cup of Colombian came, steaming at the temperature likely predetermined to be the most perfect for my particular cuppa, I resisted the urge to add anything. It was astringent to me, despite the varietal's common reputation as a relatively mellow bean with low acidity. From the moment it coursed across my palate, I was proud of identifying the nutty, caramel-like flavors, but the moment I'd swallowed, I knew I'd need a latte. Or something with cream in it. I'd grown so accustomed to doctoring my coffee with dairy that even Colombian, the bike-with-training-wheels bean, was too bitter for me. I was a pour-over failure. Which I'd known, but for some reason had had to relearn.

I got halfway through the cup before sheepishly slinking back up to the counter.

NOVEMBER

"Would it be possible to add some steamed milk to this?" I smiled my sweetest and apologized for my lack of sophistication.

The barista demurred. "I have a secret for you," said Raelyn quietly. "I've been doing this for seven years, and I still always put cream in my coffee." She offered to make me my usual, then presented me what she called "my shameful latte" with a wicked grin. I knew I'd found my forever coffee shop.

Weeks later, we had a long dinner with Ben and Anne, the friends we'd gone fishing with, and another couple, Erik and Kate. As homemade pizza faded into wine and whiskey, someone asked me to name my favorite coffee.

"I love Herkimer's espresso roast," I quipped, plugging the bean roaster just up the hill from our house (as opposed to the one a handful of blocks away, or the one a whopping two miles away). "But honestly, I'm kind of a coffee whore at home," I admitted. "I usually try to buy a darker roast from somewhere nearby, but whatever's on sale."

Ben gawked. I'd clearly said the wrong thing. Erik ventured that the espresso roast from Lighthouse Roasters in Fremont was their go-to, which led us into a conversation about hearsay that one Lighthouse barista's nipples theoretically make the wheel hubs for the giant bicycle tattooed across her chest. But in any case, no one just buys whatever's on sale, they agreed. I shrunk, deciding not to tell them that Jim had bought me a Nespresso machine before he'd left. That Jim knew what I needed most was to hold a warm caffeinated drink in my hands and not do much to get it there.

"So what about just regular coffee?" Ben asked. "For pourover, I mean."

"I only make espresso," said Erik.

"I use the same beans for everything," I said. "I just grind them differently."

"You make coffee with an espresso roast?" Ben asked incredulously. (Poof! Gone was any legitimacy I'd gained by putting my name in print. Eight cookbooks, flushed to the sea.) "You should try a Yirgacheffe," he counseled gravely. "It makes such a good cup."

A few minutes later Anne was telling us how their morning coffee setup consists of a hand grinder, a scale, a thermometer, and a scientific process in which they add sixteen grams of water per gram of ground coffee. It used to be that "fancy" coffee was the kind of coffee you could make with the press of a button. Now fancy coffee means doing everything—including the grinding, in their case—by hand.

"Sixteen grams?" I challenged. "Don't most places use seventeen?" I said it with the same authority I might use to change degrees Fahrenheit to Celsius. These were facts. Ben's furry eyebrows hit the ceiling. I'd gotten sharp, and he was wounded.

"You are missing out," he said, his normally sweet demeanor turning defensive.

Then plans were hatched, under the guise of getting our children together on the ski hill, to rent a cabin near Leavenworth later in the winter. Ben would be responsible for the coffee.

"I'm going to make you the best cup of coffee you've ever had," he promised.

Soon after that, I went to Lighthouse for espresso beans and a glimpse of the bicycle, which was present but not so excitingly placed. The next morning I plunged the French press, had an eye-opening cup of very good coffee with my husband, and then went to Vif for a latte in front of my computer. I didn't ask where the beans were from, or when they were roasted.

And in that moment, sitting in a warm sunbeam, I resolved to be okay with loving my coffee in whatever way fit me best. Though we may be two different breeds of coffee drinkers in

Seattle, Ben and I aren't alone in our addictions—his to the process and to the bean, mine to cream and simplicity. My writer friend likes her soy and her chocolate. In the end, it may not be that Seattle does coffee so well because we are such innovators. It may be that we are simply human, trying to keep warm in the rains life brings, each waking up every morning to see if the day brings a new path forward.

Beans with an Egg

At Seattle's Vif Wine|Coffee, in the winter and summer alike, there is always a breakfast bowl on the menu—often slow-cooked beans or pulses, sometimes mixed with the tender vegetables of the season, always topped with a six-minute egg and served with a fat slab of garlic-rubbed toast. It's my new definition of the ideal breakfast.

If I can time my appetite and work schedule accordingly, I eat it twice a week. I've grown to prefer the lentil version, often served with kale or soft radicchio and chunks of soft carrots, plus a tangle of pickled fennel on top. But occasionally, if my lentil craving falls on, say, a Monday, when Vif is closed, or in the evening, I make my own bowl at home—minus the fennel, but with a little bacon, for good measure.

Use home-cooked beans and homemade stock, if you have them; those two ingredients make a world of difference. Garlic-rubbed toast is a plus.

MAKES: 2 SERVINGS

> 2 tablespoons extra-virgin olive oil
> ½ cup thinly sliced leek (white part only) or onion
> 3 leaves lacinato or other kale, or radicchio, chopped
> 1 carrot, chopped into 1-inch chunks
> 1 small clove garlic, smashed
> ½ teaspoon kosher salt
> 1½ cups chicken stock (homemade, or unsalted
>   or low-sodium store-bought chicken stock)
> 2 eggs
> 2 cups cooked lentils or beans (home-cooked,
>   or from one 15-ounce can, rinsed and drained)
> 2 slices thick bacon, cooked and crumbled (optional)

NOVEMBER

1 teaspoon roughly chopped tarragon

Champagne vinegar, to taste

Crunchy sea salt, to taste

» In a medium saucepan, heat the oil over medium heat. Add the leek and cook, covered, stirring occasionally, until soft, about 5 minutes. Add the kale, carrot, garlic, and salt, and cook for a few minutes more, stirring occasionally. Add the stock, bring to a simmer, and cook until the carrots are completely tender, 10 to 15 minutes more.

» While the vegetables cook, fill a small saucepan with enough water to cover the eggs, and bring to a boil. Carefully add the eggs to the boiling water and cook for 6 minutes. Transfer the eggs to ice water, let them cool until comfortable to handle, then carefully peel them.

» When the carrots are soft, pull out and discard the garlic, add the lentils, bacon, and tarragon to the pan, and season the lentils with 1 or 2 dashes of champagne vinegar.

» Pile the lentils and liquid into 2 bowls, top each with an egg (sliced in half, if you prefer), and serve hot, showered with crunchy sea salt.

Chocolate-Covered Candied Oranges

Despite the twee leanings that sometimes turn me off, the coffee-drinking experience at Seattle's Slate Coffee Bar is undeniably perfect—especially when you order a latte and a so-called chocolate orange, which is an entire orange slice, candied until chewy and sweet, coated in perfect dark chocolate. This is my own approach, which I often pair with coffee from the Nespresso machine my husband bought me (to replace himself, because he's the coffee maker in the house) when he left for seven weeks at sea. If I put the drink in a bespoke cocktail glass, I can pretend I'm at Slate and enjoy the combination without worrying about whether I'm ordering correctly.

I start the oranges using only one round of blanching so that some of the peel's bitterness remains, and coat it with the best chocolate I can find in my baking drawer. You'll have a little chocolate left over, but I find the oranges much easier to dip in a larger quantity of chocolate. (Plus, good melted chocolate makes amazing hot chocolate.)

MAKES: ABOUT 20 ORANGE SLICES
SPECIAL EQUIPMENT: ICING GRATE

- 1 medium navel orange (or a grapefruit, if you prefer)
- 1 cup water, plus more for blanching oranges
- 2 cups sugar
- 4 ounces (about 1 cup) semisweet or bittersweet chocolate, finely chopped, or high-quality chocolate chips

» Cut the orange vertically, through the poles, then cut each half into ¼-inch-thick semicircles. Place the oranges in a medium saucepan. Add just enough water to cover, bring to a simmer, then reduce the heat and cook the mixture at a very bare simmer for 5 minutes. Drain the oranges and set them aside. Give the pan a quick rinse.

» In the saucepan, combine the sugar and 1 cup of water, stir, and cook over high heat, swirling the pan occasionally, until the mixture turns clear and all the sugar has dissolved. Gently add the oranges back to the pan and cook at a gentle bubble, stirring occasionally and carefully turning the oranges over and rearranging them once or twice during cooking, for 40 minutes, or until the peels start to become translucent. (The flesh will turn clear and begin to disintegrate a little.)

» Set an icing grate over a rimmed baking sheet. When the oranges are cooked, carefully transfer them to the grate. (They will be quite fragile, so be gentle—a slotted spoon works well.) Arrange any oranges that have lost their shape back to semicircular form, so they dry back into their original shape. Set aside to firm up for 30 minutes.

» Line another baking sheet with wax or parchment paper (I like to tape the paper down so it doesn't budge) and set aside.

» When the candied oranges are completely cool, melt the chocolate: in a double boiler, or in a small saucepan set over the lowest heat setting, slowly melt the chocolate, stirring often, until it's fully liquefied. Working with one orange at a time, using the pointy parts of the peel as a handle, dip the orange peel side down into the chocolate, going about halfway down the orange slice. Allow some of the chocolate to run off, then transfer the orange to the paper-lined baking sheet. Repeat with the remaining oranges and chocolate, then let the oranges sit for about 90 minutes at room temperature, until firm. (If you're not in a rush, cover them loosely with another sheet of parchment at this point, and let them sit at room temperature overnight.)

» Store the cooled chocolate-covered oranges between layers of wax or parchment paper in an airtight container, and share soon thereafter because the chocolate will start to sweat after just a few days.

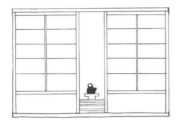

Slow Dog
Noodle

THANKSGIVING is my favorite holiday. Almost every year, we travel to a different place to meet my relatives, each family unit taking turns to play host. We're a far-flung group fairly taken with an American sense of mobility; in past years, the destination list has included Kansas City, Sun Valley, New Orleans, Park City, Colorado Springs, San Francisco, and Boise. There is always turkey. There is always homemade eggnog, made from my (now Beijing-based) uncle Ken's rum-heavy recipe and aged in a garage for at least one month. There is always too much cranberry sauce. And I am always in the kitchen, thrilled by the ever-present challenge of what goes into which pot, pan, or oven at what precise time to produce a piping-hot spread of foods people completely ignore the rest of the calendar year.

This year, though, we planned a departure from the norm. Because schedules didn't permit, it was clear we couldn't pull off our family Thanksgiving in the usual sense, with grandparents and cousins. And, theoretically, I had made a vow not to get on any more airplanes until January 1. With the Canadian dollar practically in free fall, I booked a two-bedroom hotel suite in Whistler, British Columbia, and sent an e-mail to my parents and siblings inviting them, with their significant others, to gamble on an early-snow year five hours north of Seattle with us. It might not have been on The Here List, I thought, but it would likely be fun, at least.

A few weeks before leaving, my brother tried to talk me out of cooking a turkey.

"You know our family," he chided over the phone. "If the snow is good, people aren't really going to be into making food. It's Whistler. Everyone will want to ski. We could go out. Or if you want to stay at the hotel, we could just skip the turkey and have a nice dinner that we can make ahead the night before. Or eat whatever we feel like eating. Pulled pork tacos?"

Josh knows that I carry a lethal genetic mixture of type A planner, multitasker, and chronic overachiever, which usually comes with a dash of martyrdom. When it comes to cooking for a crowd, that combination can be tiger-loose-from-the-circus dangerous. It gets especially acute when I feel unnecessarily compelled to impress hypothetical future family members as a means of welcome, and when I intrinsically expect help in the kitchen from people much more interested in exercising outside than in cooking inside once snow starts falling.

But as much as I knew he was right—that I'd be cooking alone until the slopes closed if the conditions were even marginally decent—I couldn't stand the thought of not having Thanksgiving dinner. In the end, we compromised: We decided we'd cook turkey for dinner, knowing that it wouldn't follow the typical Thanksgiving afternoon meal pattern, and we'd limit the dishes to things we could collectively pull off after a full day of skiing. And he'd cook dinner the next night.

"We can pull that off, right?" I texted my sister, Allison, the youngest, who at the time made her living cooking, among other things, but is more committed to fresh tracks than me. She didn't text back immediately, as she usually does. I felt my grip on tradition begin slipping away. So for good measure, as Thanksgiving neared, I did what any turkey-happy control freak with an addiction to her yearly feast-making habit would do: I organized a surreptitious pre-Thanksgiving insurance Thanksgiving the night before we left for Canada, when Maggie would be visiting with her family. There was a gleaming roast turkey and shredded, sautéed brussels sprouts tossed into a salad with bacon and preserved lemon. There was even gravy. It was the culinary equivalent of downing a cup of very hot coffee too quickly when you have to leave the house before dawn, just in case there's not more coffee wherever you're going: it works in theory, but you still need the real thing.

On our first night in Whistler, before getting settled in, we decided to assess our bird options. Whistler is a European-style pedestrian ski town gathered around a long twist of heated flat cobblestones. It has the self-aggrandizing impor-tance of a place that the winter Olympics has called home. (If reality television has any base in truth, those Olympics seem to have upped the late-night sleaze factor intrinsic to a town essentially populated by twentysomething male ski bums.) But in late November, as the trees lining the quiet village lanes were coming to life under the power of thousands of pious-looking holiday lights, walking to the town's IGA supermarket felt like walking through a skiers' Disneyland before the opening bell. It was cute, quaint, quiet.

Graham hadn't spent a lot of time in grocery stores—he'd never had the stamina for or interest in making it all the way around a room that big, even before the surgery—so we as-signed him a short list of fruits for our suite's kitchen, which he sought out with Jim as I dove into the meat section. There were blueberries and raspberries and strawberries and black-berries, but there were no turkeys.

"How could there not be a single turkey?" I asked Jim. "Isn't this place overrun with Americans this weekend?"

"I bet they just order a limited number," he said. "Or maybe they're not in yet." It was the Sunday before Thanksgiving. We left without a turkey, talking about getting a chicken later in the week. Celebrating with small poultry seemed better than celebrating with no poultry at all.

We walked into our hotel room, expecting to see the kitchen in the two-bedroom unit we'd been able to splurge on with the resort's fall rate specials and a sinking Canadian dollar. Only, it wasn't a kitchen. It was a wet bar. It was a two-by-six-foot counter punctuated by a sink, counter space approximately the size of a toaster, and a two-burner stove. The refrigerator seemed designed to fit a box of wine and six sodas, and not much more.

"Guess it's good we didn't buy the chicken today?" quipped Jim positively. I was unsuccessfully trying to Tetris the eggnog I'd brought from Seattle into the fridge, trying to keep my cool. After four weeks of carefully aging and stirring it, I refused to serve it warm. I began to panic. The table had four chairs, and we were going to be nine for Thanksgiving dinner. There were only four of each place setting. All the variables I'd double-checked with a reservationist three days earlier were wrong for what I wanted to do three days later. But I wasn't the only one who was upset.

"PELiiiiiii," wailed Graham, prostrating himself on the floor in front of his toy bag.

"Where's your pelican?" I asked, searching for signs of a small white stuffed animal. "Can't you find it?"

"He's not heeeeere." In times of desperation, Graham does a good job of approximating an emergency vehicle's siren, but it's the European kind—more of a two-toned *wee-noo wee-noo* than a variable-pitch American *woo-woo-woo*.

"Has he eaten since the waffle?" asked Jim, pointing to the puddle of child at my feet. We'd stopped in Richmond, near Vancouver, British Columbia, on the drive up, for bubble waffles.

"Oh no," I gasped. "He hasn't. And that was a long time ago." I turned to Graham.

"G, you slept with him last night in Seattle," I said (I thought) kindly. "We must have left him in your bed."

"Noooooooo," went the siren, its volume increasing as the severity of the situation sunk in. We texted Maggie, who was still at our house, and it was confirmed: Peli the Pelican had stayed in America. Maggie texted us a video of her daughter holding Peli by the neck, assuring Graham that she would take good care of him. We told him that it was well past dinnertime, and there was just no way Peli could make it to Whistler that week. The news did not go over well.

Once Graham started breathing again, he went about hurling things at me, because it was my fault, and he was six, and throwing books fixes things at six. Then he grabbed a piece of paper and a pen, and began writing a heartfelt apology to the stuffed bird—which, before that evening, had held no special spot in his heart that we'd been aware of. *I am sarry but I left you. I stil have the orange blankit,* said the letter, referring to a fleece blanket he used every night. On and on it went, instructing other members of the Seattle-based stuffed-animal crew how to use their special powers to get Graham back to Seattle so they could be reunited. I wasn't sure it would be a good idea to point out that, although he was sad, at least he was learning to write lowercase letters in first grade. We put the eggnog on the snowy porch and unleashed the only dinner option we knew to be a sure distraction.

"Graham," said Jim softly. "There's a sushi restaurant downstairs. Should we go have avocado rolls?"

Graham peeked up from behind the arm he'd been using to

hide his wet eyes. He seemed to be judging whether we were playing a trick on him.

"Okay," he said. And the pelican was forgotten.

Ka-Ze Japanese restaurant is a small ski-town hotel lobby sushi spot run by a Japanese guy known locally as Tokyo Tom. (*Kaze* translates as "wind" in English, which we thought appropriate given the fleeting storm we'd just experienced with Graham.) Tokyo Tom, in his youth, was a very good freestyle skier. Along with decorations like *noren*, the vertically slit curtains that traditionally cover the door of most sushi restaurants in Japan, and the sliding bamboo shoji screens that obscured the group dining tables, the restaurant was plastered with signed, framed photographs of a freestyle skier named Wayne Wong.

It turns out that in the 1960s and '70s, Tom skied with Wong—a man who was famous for, among other things, creating a specific style of freestyle skiing called the "slow dog noodle." Initially created as a method of skiing bumps (turning on top of the bumps after an early pole plant, instead of in the troughs between them, allowed skiers to avoid getting the era's long, stiff skis caught in the troughs), it devolved into the equivalent of dancing *Saturday Night Fever*–style on snow. (Along with a generation of young skiers who competed in what was then called "hotdog" skiing, Wong is also credited with inventing something called the "worm turn." Terminology is important in skiing.)

In my family—one more devoted than most, perhaps, to skiing lore—the slow dog noodle is an heirloom ski turn. My mother and father can do it quite naturally, having grown up with Wong and the same stiff skis. My sister and I are okay at it. But my brother does the family's best slow dog. On the ski hill, it's like calling a white-pants-clad John Travolta your sibling. Every time he does it, he unearths a wiggle that even the most novice skiers recognize as a vintage style, and the whole chairlift watches, and I feel famous by proximity. Which is why entering a restaurant devoted to Wayne Wong felt akin to cultural kismet. We made a reservation for nine at Ka-Ze for Thanksgiving dinner, thinking that when the time came, we just might feel like eating sushi again instead of turkey or chicken. I was sure Josh would approve.

Still, the hotel room's "kitchen" taunted me. I decided to sample the kind of cooking experience it offered by making breakfast.

Determined to celebrate the bubble waffles I'd learned to love in Richmond, I'd purchased online an electric bubble-waffle maker, a contraption that looks like a cross between a chain hotel breakfast room's Belgian waffle maker and an *ebelskiver* pan. I balanced it on the wet bar's miniature stove top.

The recipe and directions that came with the device seemed simple enough. First, I needed to melt butter. I melted it in the little overhead microwave without making it explode—typically the sign of good things to come, for me. But there, things stopped seeming so simple. I needed to whisk egg yolks and whites, separately, until the yolks were simply blended and the whites were stiff, which meant I'd need two different vessels for mixing. There were no bowls. The yolks went into a large, shallow roasting pan, where they eventually submitted to the idea when I chased them around the pan with a serving fork. The whites weren't having it. No matter how hard I whipped the whites with a fork in a saucepan, and no matter which fork size I used, they refused to become anything beyond frothy. Ditto for shaking them in a drinking glass with my hand over the top, which was a misguided suggestion anyway.

In the end, it all worked out: I nixed the idea of whipping the whites, which, added right at the end, give typical bubble waffles their signature airy, shattery texture. I blended the egg yolks and whites back together, and stirred them into a buttery batter until it smelled rich, like crepe batter—except that it also smelled like coffee because in order to pour my siblings' coffee into empty mugs and heat up the bubble-waffle iron and make bacon, I had to balance the brownie pan full of waffle batter on *top* of the coffeemaker's domed lid. It was like playing vertical kitchen Jenga with water balloons; no single vessel had the kind of sharp, square edges that would let it partner with another vessel in the same space, and any wrong move would have catastrophic consequences. I was sweating before any of us started eating.

But I cooked the first waffle, and it puffed and browned in all the right ways. In a swarm of plates and napkins and powdered sugar and timers and green and red readiness-indicator lights, we ate bubble waffles and bacon for breakfast, taking turns at the little breakfast table. And instead of being light and shattery, they had the weight, in the belly, of traditional crepes—which was perfect, because no one can ski on a breakfast of air. Especially when you're skiing with a family of former collegiate ski racers.

The problem with planning a Thanksgiving in Whistler, of course, no matter where you eat, is that there is nothing particularly sexy about fall skiing, the way there is for spring skiing. No one waxes poetic about the tumble of loose rocks, or about rough grasses gliding across the edges of one's least favorite pair of skis. No one took photographs of Wayne Wong skiing in the fall. And so we had a day that was satisfying from an athletic standpoint, because those addicted to aerobic challenges still had to work hard to ski the icy slopes, but it was not in any way a glamorous adventure. It was weaving through crowds and stepping over rocks and waiting in holiday chairlift lines, punctuated by the occasional family dance moves that keep us interested in such conditions. It was practical skiing. Which is why it seemed right to forgo the Jenga and abandon the chicken idea and eat Japanese food for Thanksgiving dinner, even though my mother doesn't eat fish. It was the practical answer.

Tokyo Tom greeted us like family. "I hear we're supposed to feed you only fish, right?" he teased my mother, as his crew poured us Asahi Super Dry, and then warm sake, and then unfiltered sake, and then a sake none of us remember much about, except that it came in a very small brown bottle.

And this time, on a day when the food is usually paramount but we'd made a conscious decision not to let it matter, it was the food that became our adventure. We took our shoes off and crawled to our spots at the table, which Graham assigned happily.

"We're eating under the watch of Wayne Wong," I reminded everyone, when we'd all stopped giggling about squeezing ourselves down to a table set almost at floor level.

"Can we order slow dog noodles here?" asked Jim.

We shoveled in freshly made gyoza, and taught my parents how to eat edamame beans by biting into the shell instead of picking the beans out by hand, one by one. My mom, who normally avoids Japanese cuisine because it tends to be fish-heavy, tasted shabu-shabu, gaping at the mix of vegetables the server plunged into the boiling broth in the center of our tables, and at how fast the beef cooked when she dipped it into the liquid with her chopsticks, and at how much she liked the sesame-tinged sauce we used as a dip for the beef. She squealed at the long, elegant enoki mushrooms because they're cute. After two hours, little scoops of green-tea ice cream replaced our sake cups. And Graham ate it, even though it was foreign and green.

Nobody mentioned turkey that night. If my siblings' significant others ever thought we were heathens for not cooking a bird, they didn't show it. They seemed to just smile and enjoy what we enjoyed: an adventure created not by extreme travel or exotic plans, but by the willingness to make a different turn off a path we'd all taken before.

Ken's Eggnog

Based on my uncle Ken's recipe, this eggnog is the real stuff. We typically favor a combination of dark rum and cognac, but one year, when I substituted bourbon for the cognac, we loved the change. You can do it either way—just make sure you mix it up at least three weeks before you plan to drink it (four to six weeks is best), as the flavors mellow and blend over time. And the further ahead you make it, the more opportunity you'll have to taste it. As Ken says, "Stir and taste, every day if you can. Consequent shrinkage may argue for doubling the recipe."

This nog is an excellent rationale for owning two bowls and two whisks for your stand mixer. It may also be a rationale for owning two refrigerators, although stouter constitutions might allow the nog to age in a chilly garage if it's made for the winter holidays.

MAKES: ALMOST 2 GALLONS EGGNOG
SPECIAL EQUIPMENT: 2 GALLON-SIZE OR LARGER
SEALABLE GLASS OR CERAMIC CONTAINERS

> 12 large egg yolks
> 1 pound confectioners' sugar
> ¼ teaspoon kosher salt
> 1 cup bourbon (such as Bulleit)
> 3 quarts half-and-half, divided
> 1 quart (about 4 cups) dark, black, or spiced rum
>   (such as The Kraken Black Spiced Rum)
> 6 large egg whites for making the eggnog,
>   plus 6 more for serving
> Freshly grated nutmeg, for serving

» In the work bowl of a stand mixer fitted with the whisk attachment, whip the egg yolks on medium speed until light, about 2 minutes. With the machine on low, slowly add the confectioners' sugar, and mix until blended. (No need to sift the sugar.) Add the salt and bourbon, whisk to blend, and use a rubber spatula to scrape any sugar off the insides of the bowl, whisking on low and scraping until the sugar is totally absorbed into the liquid. Add 1 quart of the half-and-half and the rum (the liquid should come up almost to the top of the whisk), whisk on low speed to blend, and transfer the mixture to a large mixing bowl. Clean and dry the work bowl and whisk attachment.

» Next, pour 6 egg whites into the bowl and whisk until thick and opaque but still soft (soft peaks). Add the remaining 2 quarts half-and-half, and whisk again to mix. Transfer half of this mixture to each of the 2 gallon-size vessels. (I store my eggnog in 2 ceramic crocks with lids that seal closed.) There will be about 6 cups in each, including the foam.

» Finally, stir the reserved mixture with the alcohol in it, and divide it between the 2 crocks again, pouring about 6 cups into each. Stir to blend, and refrigerate for about 1 month, stirring (and tasting!) the eggnog once every few days, and ladling liquid from 1 crock to another, if you'd like the 2 crocks to taste identical.

» To serve, whip 6 additional egg whites to soft peaks, and fold them into the eggnog. Serve it cold, dusted with freshly grated nutmeg.

DECEMBER

My friend Kate is also a freelancer and a mom who works part-time. One morning at Vif, as we set up our computers for our weekly Battleship work date, I realized how much I'd ignored about her life while I was busy worrying about my own.

"How was France, anyway?" I asked brightly. When we'd gone to New York, she and her family had left to go spend two luxurious-sounding weeks at a rental house in the Dordogne, followed by a week in Paris. I was jealous. Somehow, I'd never even asked her about it.

"Great. Paris was amazing," she said vaguely. She smiled, then lowered her voice. "I had a great time. I just wish I could go back again and have a different trip without my kids."

Kate loves her children as much as any mother. But I understood her point immediately: there's only so much vacation a parent can have with her kids in tow. She told stories about her three-year-old's wild, hair-pulling fit that landed them in a Paris Starbucks, and about the vomit count they developed for both car-sickness-prone and jet-lagged children. Kids act like kids no matter where they are in the world, which means the kind of travel most adults imagine changes vastly when kids are involved.

"I hear you," I empathized. "When I was in France with Jim and Graham a couple years ago, I had this running fantasy that I'd come back someday and sit in a different café every morning with my computer, and just write. Just sitting there, with nowhere to be. No dishes to do. Just let every parental responsibility stay in Seattle for, like, a *week*."

"*Exactly*," she sang. "Imagine if you could work all day, and then just drop your computer off and wander."

"And you never had to wait for someone to stop and pick their nose, and no one ever complained," I agreed. "You could chew that Hollywood-brand gum without sharing it and then having to hold it when your kid wants to spit it out into your hand."

We laughed, and sighed, and then we each went back to our work. I felt a little ashamed to want to leave, but I couldn't deny it: the great nearby was beginning to feel uncomfortably small. I couldn't stop asking myself whether my kid was in pain. I hated wondering if and when Graham would reach a point at which he'd just plain stop progressing. I wanted to get on an airplane. I wanted any sort of escape I could find. Not forever. Just for . . . a while.

That night, after Graham was in bed, I texted Kate.

"How's your stash of airline miles?" I asked. Her husband, Erik, travels as much as Jim. He'd also just returned from weeks and weeks away.

"Wait . . . Paris?" she responded. She had apparently shared our coffee-shop conversation with Erik already. Her brain had taken the same path.

"What if we went in January, after the kids go back to school?" I asked.

"Erik emphatically supporting the idea," she texted back. "Can't see why not." He'd assured her that he and Jim were quite capable of taking care of our combined brood while we were away.

And so late into the night, we coordinated a trip to Paris via text, each commandeering our families' airline miles to travel inconvenient routes across the Atlantic, and we found a good deal at a small hotel not far from where I'd lived in college.

DECEMBER

To Market, to Market

THERE'S an international product-delivery company based in Seattle, which once just sold books, that is named for a swath of territory in South America famous for hosting the largest variety of plant and animal species on the globe. After an initial beta test in 2007, the company started delivering groceries and other sundry items in Granny Smith–green refrigerated box trucks, which crisscrossed the city to drop off groceries on peoples' front porches in certain Seattle zip codes. True to the company's standards, there were a vast variety of products that appealed to the kind of generally kid-busy, double-income families that people our own neighborhood. For some, it changed grocery shopping in Seattle. You could order organic grapes and king salmon and a new bike tire and a bath mat and an emergency birthday gift, all with the click of a mouse, and a grocery elf would drop them on your front step in the dark of night, at little to no charge. Sometimes he left muddy footprints on the porch.

It was an embarrassing habit. But taking a child who hasn't really learned to walk independently to the grocery store is a little like bathing a cat—it's awkward, it's messy, and someone always ends up crying or bleeding—so ever since Graham had grown out of the small seat that folds out of the front of each metal grocery cart, I relied on AmazonFresh when my husband left town. When Jim was home, I went to the grocery store alone. But when he was at sea, I opened the little green iPhone app with a tap of my finger, and, with an implicit agreement to forgo personal approval of anything I'd normally touch or smell or take part in buying, I grocery-shopped from my couch. The druggish high of finishing a task without expending either time or effort outstripped my need to touch my tomatoes before buying them.

But when Jim left for his Arctic trip, the unthinkable happened: rather than delivering groceries for next to nothing, as they'd been doing for years, AmazonFresh began charging a yearly $299 membership fee. I took advantage of the new system's free thirty-day trial, but when we came home from Thanksgiving, the gig was up. I decided that, having made huge strides recently in physical therapy (no pun intended) but still hesitant to use his new walking skills in the wild, Graham was ready to come grocery shopping with me. And so the first weekend in December, when he'd had a week's worth of good sleep, I cooked a big breakfast, made a shopping list in my best fat first-grade handwriting so Graham could read it, and drove us to Ballard Market in the rain.

December is an overwhelming time to visit the market for anyone. But for a child who has rarely considered sky-high piles of underripe avocados and mountains of shiny clementines from his three-foot-eleven stature, the sheer square footage of edibles is mind bending. Add in towers of gingerbread-making kits, pricing signs that he could now read, and the cacophony of normal Sunday-morning grocery-store traffic, and you wind up with a kid standing stock-still in the center of the floor mat just a foot or so beyond the building's automatic doors, wide eyed and stunned.

"Keep walking, please," I ushered. "There are people behind us."

"I forgot that this place is seriously *big*," Graham said casually, coming to.

"Do you want some clementines?" I asked, eager to make room for other shoppers to enter the store. "We could put them in your lunch this week."

"Yeah!" he cheered, making a beeline for the baby oranges. "Here." Close to the display, he handed me one of his yellow crutches so that he had a hand free to probe the bin. And in one too-quick motion, he tried to scoop up five or six little orbs at once from the corner of the display, sending most of them skittering across the linoleum floor before I could catch them all.

"Oopsie," he said lamely, watching them roll. "Guess that's why they come in those blue bags."

And so he grabbed a bag, and froze under its weight. As I purposely busied myself picking up clementines, he wrestled with how to make sure his little clutch of treasure made it home with us. He still wasn't used to moving with only one crutch, and he had the three-pound orange bag grasped in the hand closest to the display, not the hand closest to the shopping cart. First, he made a move to lob the package overhead and behind him, across his crutch hand toward the cart. But he quickly realized both that the oranges were too heavy for him to lift above his head, so there was no way the rocket-launch approach would work, and that the cart was still too far away, even if he managed a good toss. And so, working slowly, he improvised: He shuffled each foot a few times, using the remaining crutch for balance, to turn his body so it was facing the cart. Using the oranges as ballast, he moved the crutch toward the cart, then scooted his feet toward the crutch. He did it again, theoretically applying the one-crutch walking drills he'd been doing with his physical therapist for weeks. By then, I'd gathered all the wayward clementines, and glanced up to see people watching me watching him, wondering whether I'd help him. Or perhaps they wondered how long they'd taken for granted the reflexive, mundane task of loading a bag of oranges into a grocery cart. Ours made it into the bottom of the cart with a cluster of dull thuds.

"What's next on the list?" Graham asked. I wondered how many items would make it home. We'd spent five full minutes on the clementines.

"Fruit strips," I invented, pointing to the nearest display, which held the kind of packaged fruit leather he loves. I stretched the second crutch out to him so that we could move across the produce aisle toward them.

And without hesitation, he turned his back on me, and on the wagging stick I proffered, and moved forward on just one crutch again, taking the few hobbling steps that remained between him and his favorite snack. As if it were totally normal, he crouched down (instead of falling to his knees to access something low on a shelf, the way he'd always done), snagged his favorite flavors, and tossed them into the cart nonchalantly.

"What now?"

I took out the list, trying not to congratulate him, trying not to interrupt the long neurological chain reaction an emphatic expert had once told us must finish on its own for each new skill to be fully integrated into a cerebral palsy patient's life. Trying not to reach into my pocket for my phone, so I could take a photograph, in case it never happened again. Trying to pick the most enticing items first, so whatever magical force had convinced him to walk happily with one crutch in the real world would stick around.

"Apples and red bell peppers," I read. "They're—"

But before I could finish directing him, he interrupted, holding his free hand out in front of his face, palm out like a Supreme, asking me to stop in the name of love.

DECEMBER

"Mooommm," he moaned, annoyed.

"Yes, Graham?" I was missing something, clearly.

"You don't have to tell me where everything is in this store," he whined. "I can use the Force to find it." And as much as a kid with one crutch and a precarious sense of balance can, he stomped off in search of apples with one hand outstretched, clearly upset with me for my limited faith in the powers bestowed upon him by his recent Luke Skywalker Halloween costume.

We developed a pattern: Graham wandered the produce aisles on one crutch, with one hand thrust out in front, using the Force to find things, occasionally toppling displays unknowingly until I taught him, amid much objection, to use the Force to find the highest item in each pile. ("Find the tallest apple, you should," I said in a raspy Yoda voice, after he'd unhinged a few apples from the lowest line in the Honeycrisp display.)

He zigzagged around in search of berries with that same arm flailing, pausing occasionally to close his eyes like a Jedi might if the Force was guiding him through the grocery store, causing a veritable traffic jam between the peppers and the potatoes. (I think shoppers wondered whether he was, among other things, also blind.) It was hard not to direct him, but his sense of accomplishment was palpable. He could buy *anything*, I'd said, as long as it was a good choice for his lunch, and as long as he helped me gather everything I needed for dinner.

"Blueberries don't grow here in the winter," he admitted, piling two cartons of pricey winter blueberries in the cart. "But I found some that grew on [the Forest Moon of] Endor, so we can buy them." I had trouble arguing with the agricultural patterns of a fictitious *Star Wars* planet.

At the far end of the produce section, we stopped to scan the list.

TO MARKET, TO MARKET

"Okay, so when I say a thing, if we have it, you say 'Check,' okay?" I instructed. "Potatoes?"

"Check," he said.

"Brussels sprouts? Carrots?"

"Check and check."

"Lettuce?" I asked.

"Is that what goes in salad?" wondered Graham, eyeing the fluttery green section next to us. It seemed like a terrible oversight, but I couldn't remember ever having asked him to eat lettuce, as opposed to eating salad. I nodded.

"I'll get it," he said importantly, returning with a head of romaine that dripped its recent thunderstorm-on-command down the back of his little hand. I worried that the stick still being used would slip on the mess he was making and we'd wind up in the same emergency room we'd visited a few weeks earlier.

"Lettuce?" I asked again, smiling. I loved how seriously he was taking this; he was performing an adult's physical equivalent of shopping while hopping on a balance beam on one foot. I could see sweat beading up on his temples.

"CHECK!" he yelled, thrusting it toward my face. A man at the meat counter forty yards away turned around. We turned the cart toward him.

"Should we buy a whole chicken?" I asked, pointing to a neatly wrapped bird in the poultry case. "Or should we buy a chicken that's been cut up into all different parts?" I pointed to the cut-up version.

"Chicken costs three hundred and forty-nine dollars?" he protested, again very much out loud, misreading the label for the parts. "This store is so expensive! That's more money than a really big Lego set!"

"Three dollars and forty-nine cents," I explained quietly, indicating the decimal point. "And that's the price for every pound, so every package costs a different amount. So this package is sixteen dollars," I added, "because the chicken weighs almost five pounds."

Relieved, he combed his hand across the five-pound bird, fingers seeking purchase in the packaging. He realized he couldn't pick up a whole chicken with one hand.

"Parts," he answered matter-of-factly. He poked a thumb through the plastic packaging surrounding the cut-up chicken, grasped a raw leg, and used the leg's secure spot in the wrapping as leverage to pick up the whole package with one hand.

"Here," he said, handing me the package, which now dripped raw chicken juice onto my shoes.

"Thanks," I said, wincing. Because my kid was standing next to me at the grocery store, and he was helping me pick out food for dinner, and there was nothing more to say.

And so we progressed, up and down the aisles, Graham exploring his own Amazon's worth of edibles with the same curiosity and fervor and energy I recognized having had myself when I'd gone to the grocery store for the first time in rural France, gaping at the roasted-chicken-and-thyme-flavored potato chips and the wide variety of mustard colors and the fact that one could buy six different kinds of store-made pâté. That time, almost exactly two years prior, Jim and Graham had just stayed in the car to play, because that was what made the most sense to us then. This time, Graham learned that a Buddha's hand smells like lemon, that the chicken sausages I'd been feeding him for years have apple in them, and that the price for popcorn was listed on the shelf below the popcorn ($2.99), not the shelf above. ("Holy moly, $8.99 *for popcorn*? Mom, that's way more expensive than I thought popcorn would be.") Graham literally climbed into the cold case to select the pound of butter he deemed most appropriate and chose eggs from chickens he told me were

TO MARKET, TO MARKET

actually friends with our own hens. And he did it all with just one little yellow crutch for balance. We made our way to the deli.

"A pound of the roasted turkey, sliced thin, please," I asked. "And half a pound of Jarlsberg, sliced thick."

"Can you get the Jarlsberg with the most holes in it?" Graham asked me.

"I can't choose the holes, bud," I apologized, laughing a little to myself. "No one knows how many holes are in it until it's already sliced."

While we waited, Graham busied himself by tracing patterns in the grease other children had left on the glass deli casing, jettisoning his one crutch into the access aisle so he could really get into it. Between his body, my body, his crutch (which I wanted him to pick back up himself), and the shopping cart, we effectively monopolized the entire ordering area in front of the deli's two slicing machines.

I didn't mind. It was the same deli counter, I realized, as other shoppers strained to form a cohesive line around us, where I'd once run into a woman who was also buying salami for her little boy, who seemed to me at the time to be very large to be sitting in a grocery cart. Graham had been ten months old, and I'd just plunked him into the cart's seat for the first time, even though he still hadn't been quite strong enough to sit upright on his own. Seeing the orthotic helmet he wore then, the woman had scanned me with the kind of X-ray vision that makes one happy to be wearing nice underwear. "We used to have a helmet, too," she'd confided reassuringly, touching my arm, nodding toward her own two-year-old. She seemed to know something I didn't. "It does get easier," she'd said.

I'd blathered something about it being Graham's first time in the seat, and about how he still couldn't quite sit up at ten months old. She'd smiled, patiently and encouragingly, and told me how her two-year-old wasn't walking yet, which was why he was still in the cart. I remember wondering, in that moment—before we had our own cerebral palsy diagnosis—whether Graham would be walking at two. And not knowing how to ask what made her child different, or how different mine would be.

As I drifted back in time, daydreaming about what her kid might be like now, and realizing that I was living the future I'd been afraid to imagine that first time I'd put Graham in the cart, Graham somehow snuck away. The next thing I knew, I was grabbing my paper-wrapped packages and starting the frantic child-lost-in-grocery-store search most parents learn to cope with much earlier.

I found him not far away, cruising back to me with a box of Cheez-Its in his free hand and Christmas on his face.

"Look!" he squealed, dumping the box into the cart. "I got Cheez-Its! And you can't put them back because"—here, he pumped his free fist into the air—"We're! Done! Shopping!" He was so focused on the prized box that he didn't realize the bottom end of his crutch wasn't using the ground for support. He was *standing*.

Volume control has never been Graham's strength. I could feel other parents watching, wondering whether saying no to a handicapped kid went any differently than their own battles did. I made a mental note to organize our next trip for less popular shopping hours.

"Graham," I clucked, wanting to show him I controlled what went into the cart, but not wanting to take away his moment of independence, both physical and edible. Wanting to shake him and tell him out loud that the box of Cheez-Its was why we'd gone through the surgery and its aftermath, but not wanting to knock him over. He'd made it easy.

TO MARKET, TO MARKET

"Read the box, dude," I said. "Those are the hot-and-spicy kind. See the hot-sauce picture on the front?"

He peered into the cart and stared at it, a sort of horrified shock spreading over his face, like he was watching some sort of poisonous insect. I handed the Cheez-Its back to his free hand.

"Please put that one back and get the box with the bunny on it," I said. "You can put those in your lunch." He fetched the bunny box and put it into the cart, and handed me his second crutch absentmindedly. And then he suddenly stopped again, eyes closed, both hands out, again right in the center of the aisle, so a man had to veer his cart to the side at the last moment to avoid hitting us.

"We're done, G!" I prompted. "Now we can go to the front and check out."

"We aren't quite done," countered Graham at top volume. The deli line noticed. "I'm feeling something. I'm feeling for what Dad wants." His outstretched palm moved slowly from one side to the other, like a fly swatter ready to attack.

"I'M USING THE FORCE TO FIND BEER FOR DAD," he yelled, eyes still closed.

Eventually, we shuffled our way toward the front, where I handed Graham his crutches, so the checker could load the groceries into the cart. He gazed at a chocolate display without asking for any as I finished paying, and without a word, he shoved both crutches into his left hand—carrying them side by side, like a pair of ski poles whose tips pointed backward, rather than down toward the ground for balance—and walked behind me out of the store and across the parking lot to the car.

DECEMBER

One-Pan Chicken Dinner

For whatever reason, Graham began eating chicken legs first, eschewing the breasts completely. Dumping bone-in chicken into a bowl with whatever vegetables we had on hand; tossing them with olive oil, salt, pepper, and herbs; and roasting them became my default quick weeknight dinner.

If you want the skin to be extra crispy—Graham likes it as dark as possible, and I happen to love deeply browned vegetables—you can pump the temperature up to five hundred degrees F at the end for a few minutes.

MAKES: 6 SERVINGS

> 3 pounds bone-in chicken parts (legs and thighs)
> 1 pound large brussels sprouts, ends trimmed,
>   halved if larger than a golf ball
> 1 pound small red or purple potatoes, halved lengthwise
> ¼ cup extra-virgin olive oil
> 3 slices bacon, cut into ½-inch pieces
> 1 tablespoon chopped fresh thyme
> Kosher salt and freshly ground black pepper, to taste

» Preheat the oven to 450 degrees F.

» In a large bowl, mix together the chicken, brussels sprouts, potatoes, olive oil, bacon, and thyme. Spread everything but the chicken on the bottom of a large roasting pan, and season with salt and pepper. Add the chicken, skin side up on top of the veggies, and season the chicken generously. Roast for 45 minutes, or until the chicken is browned and the potatoes are totally soft. Serve immediately.

TO MARKET, TO MARKET

JANUARY, AGAIN

I woke up in Paris on the third day of January. It had been a bleary sleep after the kind of travel the body must endure to get from one continent to the next. Re-sorting night and day always feels to me like assembling a bowl of cereal and then trying to recuperate the dry bits from the milk. Plus, I'd made the terrible error of sending myself and Kate to bed with large pots of what I thought was a soothing, grapefruit-tinged, detoxifying tisane, but which had really been a soothing, grapefruit-tinged, detoxifying caffeinated green tea. We lay awake in our respective miniature hotel rooms, me thinking the kind of oversize thoughts one imagines in a city recently hit by major terrorist attacks.

That morning I got an e-mail from Jim. It included a transcript of a conversation he'd had with Graham at the counter where we eat breakfast:

> G: *Dad, show me your eggs, so that I can tell you who they're from.*
> Dad: *Okay.* [Shows eggs, cooked over medium.]
> G: *Suki. You should thank Suki before you eat them. That's very important.*
> Dad: *Good idea. Thanks, Suki.*
> G: *Wait, I should thank an animal for this bacon, too.*
> [Pause.]
> G: *Where does bacon come from?*

Dad: *Pigs.*

G: *Really?*

[Pause.]

G: *Wait, do they kill the pigs to make the bacon?*

Dad: *Yes.*

G: *Then how do I thank them?*

Dad: *Well, if we buy bacon from good farmers, they thank the pigs for us before they kill them.*

G: *Okay, that sounds good. I am very thankful for this bacon.*

[Pause.]

G: *What part of the pig does the bacon come from?*

Dad: *The belly, I think.*

G: *Delicious.*

I wondered whether he'd have ever said those things if it had been me across the table, and I was happy Jim had been there instead when Graham wanted to talk about his food. Happy I was halfway around the world.

To be clear, I didn't go to France to be rid of Graham. I went to be worry-free, which is different. For months, I hadn't been able to let go of Graham's pain. The memory of choosing to allow him to go through the surgery tangled me up in competing feelings of guilt and hope and impatience and fear, like a very long, very sharp-edged Slinky that sprung back toward me when I least expected it, slapping me with how much he'd been through every time I stopped wondering whether we'd done the right thing. I'd hoped that, from my window seat on the airplane, I'd be able to drop my entire list of things to do, along with that goddamned Slinky. Just watch the remnants of our fall fly off into the atmosphere, never to be seen again, like emotional jetsam that would be absorbed eventually by an empathetic ozone layer. Somehow, in my mind, being at thirty-five thousand feet would make me tall enough to just let it go.

"*Vive l'insouciance!*" wrote a friend, congratulating me on the trip. In my memory of the French language, *insouciance* translated quite literally, so she was basically saying "Long live worry-freeness!" which was certainly appropriate. But I asked Google to translate from my hotel room, to be sure, and it told me *insouciance* meant recklessness.

Found in Translation

I N the decades since I'd spoken French more or less fluently, some of the words had gotten confusable, like crayons that have all lost their wrappers. At first, before French seemed more at home in my mouth again, I felt like I was watching the most common phrases come out on a printer that had been misfed. It was the old-school printer I grew up with—the kind that sprays words onto connected sheets with removable perforated strips on each side—so the words came out rumpled and slightly off-kilter. My comprehension was just as wrinkled.

I'd sent Madame Jacqueau my phone number and a family photo in a Christmas card that vaguely described our upcoming trip, hoping that she would receive it, hoping she would call. It was the closest I'd come to asking someone on a date in decades, but it felt the same. From Seattle, I'd been too timid to call her directly. I'd blamed it on the wrinkly French, but deep down, I knew it was because I'd have been able to hear it in her voice if she didn't remember me as well as I'd remembered her. She'd hosted literally dozens of students over the years. It was as if I'd wanted to give her an excuse in advance if it turned out I hadn't been as important to her as she'd been to me.

The call came while Kate and I were working at two small, cracked tables at L'Éclair, a hipsterized version of a classic

French café on Paris's rue Cler. It was a Paris phone number. I stood in the street in the wet January wind, and over the crackle—I imagined the call being routed from Paris to Seattle, then back to my phone in Paris—I heard that Madame's voice was still strong.

"Madame!" I exclaimed. "How wonderful of you to call!"

"You'll come to lunch on Thursday," she informed me. I was glad to hear her bossiness hadn't faded. "Bring your friend. Monsieur will be there, and the four of us will eat well. We'll work on your French again."

I didn't know how old she was. In college, when I'd lived with her for six months, she'd seemed grandmotherly. Seventeen years later, she couldn't be much younger. I sat back down in the café feeling shaky and more nervous than I'd been in years. A woman in her eighties who cooked and entertained better (and more often) than anyone I'd known was going to make us lunch.

Kate and I arrived thirteen minutes early and walked in circles around the building, wondering how I'd landed a host family in the tony seventh arrondissement, one short block from the Eiffel Tower. I didn't remember it hurting to look all the way to the top of the tower from such close range when I was twenty.

Madame ushered us into her apartment on the top floor in a rush of kisses and fussing, assuring us that lunch was ready, but that we were waiting on her husband. She gushed politely for a moment about my child's stunning good looks, and said she was tickled to learn that the same Jim who had visited me there in her apartment, years earlier, was the man I'd married. Then she stopped dead in her tracks.

"You have rouge on your cheek," she admonished, reaching over to scrub at my unrouged wind-red skin with a licked thumb. It occurred to me that the last time I'd seen her, I hadn't had a lupus diagnosis, or a postbaby body, or constantly flushed skin. Mothering managed, she went back to chattering away in French, quite aware that Kate wasn't fluent but much more intent on updating me on her husband's health, and on her children and grandchildren and seven great-grandchildren. ("Seven! Can you imagine?" she crooned.)

Then we sat in the formal salon I'd never been allowed in as a college kid, drinking viscous muscat from the thin green-glass jiggers always reserved for grown-up guests, gazing out at the Eiffel Tower and the yawning lawns beside it at midday, when, as a student, I'd always eaten lunch out. Kate and I took in the table: forks laid out like *matryoshka* dolls, each one more petite than the next. Lines of antique crystal glasses. Layers of pale linen. Ancient holiday-themed china. Steak knives, supported by small ceramic wiener dogs. Madame plied us with waxy cured black olives, placing them on a little coffee table so overrun with trinkets that we weren't sure whether the plates in front of us were meant for the olive pits, or whether they were part of the decor. I began to collect olive pits in my cheek like a rodent.

When Monsieur arrived (tall and lanky as ever, with mysterious small bandages plastered across his bald pate), we started with a sort of smoked-salmon timbale, made, I suspected, by whirling together smoked salmon, crème fraîche, cream, and chives. Topped with paper-thin layers of smoked salmon, the flat little cylinder also sported an antiquated garnish of chives tied in a cute bouquet. We smeared it all onto triangular white toasts.

Monsieur still spoke English quite well, but Madame didn't seem interested in pointing her efforts toward getting to know someone new. The conversation became a doubles' Ping-Pong game with two balls (one French, one English), both of which rocketed across the table as Monsieur interrogated Kate in

English on her work as a Japanese translator and I strained to find the words to describe my husband's work as an arctic oceanographer. ("They had specially trained men posted to watch for polar bears each time they were stationed on the ice" isn't a phrase one ever runs across in a French class.)

When we'd piled our plates with *blanquette de veau* (a classic French veal stew where meat simmers slowly into complete submission and then gets smothered with a rich white cream sauce) and buttered, peeled potatoes showered with fresh parsley, I fixed Madame with the most serious gaze I could, given that I knew I might butcher what I was about to say.

"You know, I think my semester here may have affected me more in the long run than I anticipated at the time," I started.

"In what sense?" she asked, scooping *blanquette* sauce over my potatoes for me. I loved that she still treated me like a child, and still corrected my French. Still decided how much I needed to eat and how.

"I think you awoke in me a love for food that I might not have found otherwise," I said carefully, realizing as I said it that she was the one I, as a mother feeding her child, had been trying to imitate.

"Me?" she said. "I only cooked you dinner four nights a week."

"But you cooked *this*," I responded, gesturing to our veal, and the overflowing bread basket, and the red wine Monsieur had begun pouring for the meal—a third bottle, after the muscat and a white. (We didn't have any cider.) "You cooked things I'd never known existed—leeks with vinaigrette, and goose from your farm, and pumpkin soup. And you served me almost all the different cheeses from Normandy. Remember when we visited that cheesemaker in Camembert?"

I also reminded her that I write about food for a living now. And that when I'd visited her, I'd been an economics major. And that just after, I'd gotten a job at a fancy restaurant, because it served something I actually wanted to learn about.

"I forgot we went to the cheesemaker!" she exclaimed. "You have a good memory. But I wouldn't have cooked today if I'd remembered what you did for a living. You must think this is so pedestrian."

I knew she was lying, because she had my cookbooks, which I'd sent her over the years, stacked up in a presentable little pile on a pink settee in the corner. And I knew she was fishing for compliments, because she'd always liked to say she'd just cooked up *un petit quelque chose*, "a little something," instead of fessing up to having cooked a beautiful three-course dinner.

"Madame, it's incredible," I promised. Although she professed only a rudimentary understanding of French, Kate did a very good job of keeping track of what was happening on the court in both directions, and she nodded immediately in agreement.

"Do your children cook?" I asked Madame, trying to glean more information from a woman I knew wasn't any better than I am at accepting compliments.

"One daughter is a true cook. She's much better than I am," Madame assured me, wagging her pointer finger toward the sky, like there was a casserole of some sort on the ceiling that might prove her point.

"That's not true," barked Monsieur in French, right on cue. "She's a good cook, but she's not as good as you."

"She's better," said Madame, nodding at her own pronouncement.

"She's not," said Monsieur. And that settled it. He'd said enough.

"It was a good goose, though, wasn't it?" she remembered. Evidently, there had only been one goose on the farm in Normandy that they'd ever brought back to Paris to cook.

FOUND IN TRANSLATION

The conversation trotted off toward *la ferme*, which, along with the cider-apple orchard, they had recently sold, and toward having chickens in Seattle. Madame celebrated the presumed joy of hearing the chickens' gentle clucking in an urban environment.

"No roosters!" objected Monsieur, when I explained Seattle's chicken laws. "But then how would you enjoy the wonderful noise that they make?" I could feel my neighbor, who hated hearing the girls' clucking each morning, cringing from five thousand miles away.

When we finally left, Kate and I twirled down five twisting flights of stairs as if chased by a wave of pleasure. There had been cheese, and then poached pears with homemade ice cream, and then tiny bites of chocolate cake, and then little *orangettes*. But I was most elated by the high that comes from connecting in a different language with people who are important to you, and from telling them how much of an impact their food, their language lessons, and their kindness has had on you, and still has today. I was reeling because I was somehow able to tell a woman I might never see again how deeply important she is to me, but simultaneously unable to order lunch for myself without saying something ridiculous.

Back outside, we decided to walk off the meal. I announced that the visit had felt like a reset for my French; Monsieur, who hadn't ever handed out free compliments, had told me my language skills had hardly seemed rusty. On our way to the small antiques store Madame had recommended for good linen hand towels, we passed the Institut National de Jeunes Aveugles. There were derelict-looking kids wandering down the street in front of us.

"Ooh, interesting," I said to Kate. "It's the national institute for young thieves. It's France's juvie." We exchanged impressed, worried glances and kept walking.

JANUARY, AGAIN

Five minutes later, I clasped my hand over my mouth.

"Oh my God, Kate, I'm terrible," I said from behind my fingers. "*Aveugles*. Not *voleurs*. Blind people, not thieves. It was a school for blind kids." She shook her head.

I continued making fabulous mistakes. I poured water into the mugs meant for cider at La Cidrerie du Marais, because I hadn't understood that the thick, wide-mouthed mugs were meant for the actual drink, and the server hadn't brought us water glasses yet. More than once, I asked to try on *ces boîtes*, "these boxes," instead of *ces bottes*, "these boots," because, under the dizzying influence of shoe shopping, my once pitch-perfect pronunciation skills seemed to fail me. At a delicious, swanky bistro called Lazare, I mistakenly ordered *moules de bouchot*, a tiny species of mussel cultivated on big wooden poles on the Atlantic shore, by asking for *moules de boulot*. (*Boulot* means "job"; since *moules* could also refer to molds, such as the kind made out of wood that are used to manufacture something, asking for "job molds," which presumably made more sense than "job mussels," caused some confusion.) We went to dinner at L'Ami Jean, a casual spot known for its *riz au lait*, which (uncharacteristically for the French) is served in a bowl that could feed eight (at least). The American woman at the table adjacent to ours made an overdramatic hand motion that swept her full water glass, and its contents, into our vat of rice pudding, which we'd only just begun eating. In my exasperated confusion, when the server asked if we'd like a replacement, my internal printer spooled out *c'est bien*, very unspecific French for both "that's nice" and "it's fine," which meant our soggy dessert stayed put, when I'd meant to ask for another one. At the end of most days, I couldn't worry about whether I was doing the right thing for my child or whether my husband was remembering to feed the dog because I was too busy unwinding whether I'd worn boxes on my feet or told people I liked my rice pudding just fine with a splash of Perrier. Since I couldn't control the little things, I gave up controlling the big things.

We left Paris just in time—before I'd blown my entire budget, and before I turned into a chocolate croissant with legs, and before I'd recuperated enough French to stop benefiting from all the wisdom we gain when things get lost in translation. After we'd relearned how to be the kind of people who make their own decisions and know how to ask themselves when they're hungry, instead of always worrying about who else needs something, but before the warped marble stairs in our little hotel in the seventh arrondissement stopped being interesting every time we used them. When I told a taxi driver we were going to the airport, he asked me which route I'd prefer. He seemed to think I knew exactly where I was going.

JANUARY, AGAIN

Mussels with Curried Cream

Moules de bouchot—a type of mussel that grows in sacks attached in a spiral pattern to big wooden poles that jut into Atlantic beaches—taste different from the mussels of the Pacific Northwest. They're sweeter, and much, much smaller, and the flesh has a stronger yellow color. But like the mussels we see in our region, they love a good bath in curried cream.

I had *moules de bouchot* for the first time at Lazare, a ritzy bistro in the eponymous Paris train station. I was as taken with the color of the cream pooling at the bottom of the copper bowl—a sunny hue somewhere between buttercup and mustard yellow—as I was by the mussels themselves. As soon as I got home, I found myself trying to re-create that cream, which seemed to have hints of garlic and wine, but a smoothness I found alluring.

I strain the aromatics out of the cream, as directed below, but if you prefer, you can skip that step.

Also, for the record, this is lovely with clams instead of mussels.

MAKES: 4 SERVINGS
SPECIAL EQUIPMENT: FINE-MESH STRAINER

> 3 pounds mussels
> Kosher salt, for cleaning the mussels
> ¼ cup (½ stick) unsalted butter
> 1 medium (½-pound) leek, white and light-green parts only, rinsed thoroughly, halved and thinly sliced
> 2 large celery stalks, thinly sliced
> 2 cloves garlic, smashed
> 2 teaspoons curry power
> 1½ cups dry white wine
> 2 cups heavy cream
> Good crusty bread, for serving

» Rinse and scrub the mussels, then pile them into a bowl filled with enough salted cold water to cover them (about 1 teaspoon kosher salt for every cup of water). Let them sit for about half an hour, to remove any sand and grit they may have brought inside with them. (*Moules de bouchot*, if you can find them, typically don't carry any sand.)

» Start the curried cream: In a soup pot, melt the butter over medium-low heat. Add the leek, celery, and garlic and cook, stirring occasionally, until soft, 8 to 10 minutes. Add the curry powder, stir to coat all the vegetables, then add the wine and bring to a hard simmer. Cook, stirring once or twice, until most of the wine has evaporated, about 8 minutes. Add the cream, bring to a bare simmer, and cook 5 minutes more. (Watch the liquid carefully. If it comes to a full boil, it can climb up and over the sides of the pot, so lift the pot off the element and turn the heat down if the bubbles seem to be getting aggressive.)

» Strain the sauce through a fine-mesh strainer into a bowl, pressing on the solids to extract as much golden liquid as possible. Return the liquid back to the pot.

» Finish cleaning your mussels just before you cook them: Use your thumb and first finger to grasp the furry mussel "beard," which connects it to the natural world in the ocean, and pull hard, perpendicular to the mussel, to remove it. Discard any mussels that refuse to close or those with broken shells.

» Bring the sauce back to a simmer over medium-high heat. Add the mussels, cover the pot, and steam until all the mussels have opened, about 5 minutes. (Discard any mussels that won't open.)

» Divide the mussels among 4 bowls, pour the sauce over the top, and serve hot, with hunks of bread for mopping up the sauce.

JANUARY, AGAIN

Epilogue

A YEAR RIGHT HERE

O NCE, I allowed myself to think that if I'd written this book in a different year, I might have come away with the experience I'd expected. I might have landed, twelve months after starting, with a sense of exactly what defines Pacific Northwest food. I might have found the red beans and rice of the Pacific Northwest, the grits-and-collard-greens menu I could plop down in front of an eater new to these parts, saying, *Here. This is what this part of the world tastes like.* Knowing me, I'd probably have the components of an official food profile written out by hand on a nice thick piece of paper, with boxes and check marks. I'd organize the shit out of it.

It's true, of course. In a different year, I might have traveled more *right here.* I might have gone deer hunting with my brother. I might have picked blackberries until my arms and legs bled, like I'd planned, with Graham tottering in my wake. I might have spent a weekend digging potatoes at Olsen Farms, in Washington's far northeast corner, because twice, it was on my calendar. And twice, I canceled.

In hindsight, I laugh at myself for thinking I had a year's worth of control over my own calendar. For assuming that any of us could know what's bound to happen at any particular point in our lives, much less a whole year in advance. But we can't choose our years like that. We can't plan our own emotional paths. We can't just *know*.

And choosing to do this in another year—in a different year—would also have meant missing out on the things that, in the fall, the not-going allowed me to embrace. I won't ever regret staying close to home while Graham recovered. I won't regret staying close to home so I could recover, too.

While some excursions worked out exactly as I'd anticipated—keeping chickens was indeed the necessary inroad our son needed to begin eating chicken, and the Inn at Langley was an adventurous restaurant experience that re-created, as I'd expected, the smells and textures of the Pacific Northwest writ large—others really didn't. I thought I'd fall in love with Richmond, BC, but wound up almost hating it. At the Gourmet Century, I thought I'd come away with a glimpse of the Portland food scene as it intersects with the town's impressive cycling community, but I couldn't see straight enough to think about food at all. Yet on those trips, I traveled to places I'd never have thought to put on any sort of list—into my own memories, mostly—which, in the end, made me think I might have succeeded in staying *right here* in an emotional sense.

Although eventually I pined for an experience that allowed me to abandon the Pacific Northwest for a while, this book only reinforced my conviction that the physical *right here*—the region surrounding Seattle—is a magical spot. Overall, I was most impressed not by the food, in particular, but by how many wholly different landscapes can fit into such a small place—something I knew in the back of my mind, but that came rushing forward as I ventured from one place to the next, month after month. From the rolling dunes of southwest Washington's rainy coast to the craggy peaks of British Columbia's coastal mountains, the deep glacial grooves of the Okanagan desert to Yakima's high

plains and the deep greens near Portland, we live in an astound-
ingly diverse and beautiful place.

But my initial premise of staying in the great nearby overlooked the fact that we don't just travel farther away or abroad
to find food and beauty; we also travel to escape. We travel to
find the time to think thoughts about life that being moored
in our lives sometimes prevents. In that sense, the year gave
me a more concrete understanding of what it is about travel
abroad that feels so special: because adventures afar often
require different parts of our brains, due to language difficulties or mishaps or some combination of the two, experiencing
them often means we can't focus on everyday mundanities—
laundry, dishes, scheduling. It's no surprise that as our year
became difficult, I longed for some sort of escape. Travel
allows *me* to be the child. And although I live a life over which
I exercise a sometimes overbearing amount of control, the
childishness is something I learned that I need. Travel—and
specifically, traveling without my family—saves me from myself.

Strangely, the book essentially achieved what I wanted for
Graham, in terms of exposing him to more foods and giving
him a deeper relationship with the things that land on our
dining-room table. I am grateful that pushing him to taste new
things inevitably caused me to realize I should push him less,
but I am also not-so-secretly thrilled that, a year after starting
the book, he developed a much more open, more curious approach to food. He still avoids a large number of foods, but
his tastes are changing. They may be changing simply because
he is growing up. But they may also be changing because I
have become better about thinking of foods that are new to
Graham as foods I can share with him if he's interested, rather
than foods I want him to eat.

And really, it's never just the food we're learning about. It's
how food and life intersect—how learning about cider makes

you think of people you've loved but basically forgotten, or about how fishing might teach you more about a parent, to be sure, but also about your need to stare into space every once in a while. How doing whatever it takes to help your kid learn to walk is rather like helping your kid learn to eat: no matter how much it hurts or annoys you that your efforts might not be working, you simply have to wait until he's ready. Maybe what I should have known, when I vowed to spend a year *right here*, was simply that I would spend a year with myself. Maybe secretly, I knew that part would be the challenge.

When I was flying home from Paris, I sat in an economy seat with a screen embedded into the backrest sixteen inches in front of my nose. I watched absentmindedly as Delta Air Lines' advertisements scrolled by while we prepared for take-off, until one caught my eye.

"If your world is getting small, simply make it bigger," ventured the ad. *Indeed*, I thought.

Maybe that's just it. Maybe it doesn't matter whether we stay here, or go somewhere else. Maybe the crucial part is simply that we do something that makes our world bigger. To learn about razor clamming in Washington, or to learn that, on the northwest coast of France, recreational fishermen draw a similar species of shellfish out of hiding by sprinkling coarse sea salt across the sand. To order a new kind of coffee just to try it, or to go to Ethiopia and learn why the coffee beans grown there could possibly taste like blueberries. Or to stay right in Seattle, to do nothing for a while with your kid, so that later, the whole world can be his.

Index of Recipes

INDEX OF RECIPES

About the Author

FREELANCE food and travel writer Jess Thomson is the author of eight cookbooks, many written with Seattle-area restaurateurs, including *A Boat, a Whale and a Walrus: Recipes and Stories*, with Renee Erickson, and *My Rice Bowl: Deliciously Improbable Korean Recipes from an Unlikely American Chef*, with Rachel Yang. Her work has appeared in *Food & Wine*, the *New York Times*, *Cooking Light*, *Seattle* magazine, *Sunset* magazine, and *Edible Seattle*, and in multiple issues of the yearly *Best Food Writing* book collection. She received the 2012 M.F.K. Fisher Award for Excellence in Culinary Writing, and is the author of the food blog Hogwash (www.jessthomson.me). Jess lives in Seattle with her husband and son.